BLACK RACIALIZATION AND RESISTANCE AT AN ELITE UNIVERSITY

The presence and experiences of Black people at elite universities have been largely underrepresented or erased from institutional histories. In *Black Racialization and Resistance at an Elite University*, rosalind hampton documents narratives that span half a century and that reflect differences in class, gender, and national identifications among Black scholars. By mapping Black people's experiences of studying and teaching at McGill University, hampton reveals how the "whiteness" of the university both includes and exceeds the racial identities of students and professors. The study highlights the specific functions of Blackness and of anti-Blackness within society in general and within the institution of higher education in particular, demonstrating how structures and practices of the university reproduce interlocking systems of oppression that uphold racial capitalism, reproduce colonial relations, and promote settler nationalism. Critically engaging the work of Black learners, academics, organizers, and activists within this dynamic political context, this book underscores the importance of Black Studies across North America.

ROSALIND HAMPTON is an assistant professor in the Department of Social Justice Education at the University of Toronto.

ROSALIND HAMPTON

Black Racialization and Resistance at an Elite University

UNIVERSITY OF TORONTO PRESS

Toronto Buffalo London

© University of Toronto Press 2020
Toronto Buffalo London
utorontopress.com
Printed in Canada

ISBN 978-1-4875-0438-0 (cloth)   ISBN 978-1-4875-3005-1 (EPUB)
ISBN 978-1-4875-2486-9 (paper)   ISBN 978-1-4875-3004-4 (PDF)

Library and Archives Canada Cataloguing in Publication

Title: Black racialization and resistance at an elite university / rosalind hampton.
Names: hampton, rosalind, 1966– author.
Description: Includes bibliographical references and index.
Identifiers: Canadiana (print) 20200158848 | Canadiana (ebook) 20200158910 |
ISBN 9781487524869 (softcover) | ISBN 9781487504380 (hardcover) |
ISBN 9781487530051 (EPUB) | ISBN 9781487530044 (PDF)
Subjects: LCSH: College students, Black – Québec (Province) – Montréal. |
LCSH: College teachers, Black – Québec (Province) – Montréal. |
LCSH: McGill University – Students. | LCSH: McGill University – Faculty. |
LCSH: Blacks – Study and teaching (Higher) – Québec (Province) –
Montréal. | LCSH: Discrimination in higher education – Québec (Province) –
Montréal. | LCSH: Educational sociology – Québec (Province) –
Montréal. | LCSH: Race relations.
Classification: LCC LC212.43.C23 M6643 2020 | DDC
378.1/982996071427–dc23

This book has been published with the help of a grant from the Federation
for the Humanities and Social Sciences, through the Awards to Scholarly
Publications Program, using funds provided by the Social Sciences and
Humanities Research Council of Canada.

University of Toronto Press acknowledges the financial assistance to its
publishing program of the Canada Council for the Arts and the Ontario Arts
Council, an agency of the Government of Ontario.

**Canada Council   Conseil des Arts
for the Arts   du Canada**

**ONTARIO ARTS COUNCIL
CONSEIL DES ARTS DE L'ONTARIO**
an Ontario government agency
un organisme du gouvernement de l'Ontario

Funded by the   Financé par le
Government   gouvernement
of Canada   du Canada

Canadä

MIX
Paper from
responsible sources
FSC   FSC® C016245

Contents

Acknowledgments

I am thankful to University of Toronto Press for recognizing the importance of the issues discussed in this book, and especially to the editors at UTP who worked on the manuscript throughout the publishing process. The research presented in this book was supported by funding from the Fonds de recherche du Québec – Société et culture. The book has been published with the help of a grant from the Federation for the Humanities and Social Sciences, through the Awards to Scholarly Publications Program, using funds provided by the Social Sciences and Humanities Research Council of Canada.

The people I interviewed for this work generously shared experiences and insights that recalled painful, humorous, infuriating, and inspiring memories and events. I am deeply grateful to all of them for their enthusiastic participation and the candid conversations we had. Their narratives have been crucial to the analysis developed here; their voices remain central to this book and the story it tells about Black racialization and resistance in Canadian academia.

This book is also informed by my experiences over several decades as a community worker, educator, and activist in Montreal. I am deeply grateful to all of the many friends and comrades in that city with whom I have organized, theorized, played, created, taken to the streets, claimed spaces, linked arms, held hands, and yelled at the top of our lungs for a better world. I especially want to thank Cora, Sunci, Fernanda, Pattie, Mona, Robin, Ron, Hesser, Michelle, and Tameem for keeping me so full of love and light. This book was brought to fruition during a period of personal and career transitions throughout which I have been especially and enormously grateful to have such caring, brilliant, creative, funky, legit friends. I continue to be guided by the love and politics of my mother Judy, and am thankful to my father Robert Earl Hampton for his constant encouragement. My son Tyson's strength and creativity are unending sources of inspiration to me, as are the love and support of my sister Margot, who always keeps it real and gets me to laugh harder than is humanly possible.

My work is deeply indebted to many scholars, artists, and activists who have been doing Black Studies and critiquing social relations in and around Canadian universities for much longer than I have, and my gratitude extends to all of these people for their tireless work and refusal to be deterred. I thank Adelle Blackett, Aziz Choudry, Grace-Edward Galabuzi, Annette Henry, Carl James, Charmaine Nelson, Khalid Medani, and many members of the Black Canadian Studies Association who offered me critical feedback and encouragement as I pursued the research that informs this book. I especially want to acknowledge and thank my comrade-colleague and co-conspirator Michelle Hartman for her relentlessly generous mentorship, encouragement, and engagement with this and all of my academic work over the past several years. I am also indebted to Abby Lippman, who read and offered me invaluable feedback on early parts of this work, and knew before I did that one day it would become a book and I would become a professor. We miss you so, so much, Abby.

Finally, I wish to acknowledge the colleagues and graduate students who have welcomed me to the University of Toronto. My special thanks to Marcus Singleton and Cherie A. Daniel for reading this manuscript as I prepared it for publishing, and to all of the graduate students of Black Studies with whom I am teaching and learning and imagining that another university is possible.

BLACK RACIALIZATION AND RESISTANCE
AT AN ELITE UNIVERSITY

Prelude

"Why do you want to go to that white school and try to impress those white people?" a young person challenged me. I had just told him about my acceptance into a doctoral program at McGill University. I pushed back that according to his argument, we might just as easily ask why we live in this white province, or in this white country.

"Yeh, why *do* we live here?" the youth interjected.

"Well, just because the population of a place is predominantly white," I continued, "doesn't make it a white place only for white people!"

As a youth and family worker in Black working-class communities I'd had several similar conversations over time. Two years prior, when I had started my master's degree in art education at a different university, another Black youth had questioned: "Why do you want to go into art? Art is for white people, rosalind!" Despite widespread narratives celebrating Canadian multiculturalism, these millennial youth understand the society in which they live as racially demarcated space – white spaces and Black spaces, connoting white activities and Black activities, white and Black likelihoods and possibilities. Associated with this line of thinking is the idea that success in institutional contexts such as education and fine art requires a willingness to "act white."[1] The trap, of course, is that if "acting white" represents a betrayal of one's ethno-racial identity, community, and histories, failure to succeed within such institutions runs the risk of confirming racist stereotypes about the identities, intelligence, and potential of Black people.[2] Indeed, my own resistance to considering McGill as a "white school" was shaped by an educational career in which I was one of the few Black students in classes and "did well" and liked school nonetheless. I had grown up living in an ethnically and racially diverse poor and working-class neighbourhood and attended predominantly white and middle-class public schools. I resented the suggestion that enjoying and succeeding in school somehow contradicted my identity as a Black community member.

As far as I knew, I would be the first person on either side of my family to do a PhD, and I began the degree feeling nervous, confident, and excited. In one of my first classes of the program, we were assigned a reading by Black Canadian author Dionne Brand, in which the author explains her disengagement from a doctoral program. Brand describes how coping with racism and demands to assimilate in academia had made her feel increasingly, cumulatively "wounded in the brain."[3] She describes well-intentioned friends, family, and community cheering her on, not realizing that she would have to quit doctoral study as quite literally a matter of her own survival.

While appreciative of the rare assignment of work by a Black writer, I found Brand's essay and the brief discussion about it in class highly upsetting. Perhaps more concerning, the other students and the professor who had assigned the reading didn't seem particularly troubled by the implications of the text. It was as if soul-crushing racism in the academy was a given, along with the idea that the only viable options for racialized students were to assimilate (at great personal risk) or to leave.

The following week in this same class I chose the latter. I don't recall what if anything in particular was happening, but I was struck by the overwhelming feeling of having to get out. I barely managed to explain to the professor that I "needed a break" before tears began streaming down my face. I rushed out of the building and ran up the hill upon which the school is built and into the nearby woods. I sat on the ground by a stream, and listened to the water until I was able to catch my breath and collect myself. Then I went back.

The following week I quit my community pottery class, explaining to the instructor that I had just started a PhD and "didn't have time" to throw pottery anymore. I had been throwing pottery for two years and loved it, but suddenly felt impatient and unable to centre myself, or the clay piled upon the wheel. A repeated narrative of the doctoral program invoked a linear conception of time and a (loudly) ticking clock counting down the four years in which we were expected to complete the program. Students were told that in case of a personal crisis that might impede our progress we were to formally request to "stop the clock" so as not to run out of time. We were expected to progress: to produce, to be industrious, to be intelligent – as opposed to slow.[4] I was certain that being an academic would mean not having enough time, quantitatively, to engage in "non-academic" activities. Embedded within this belief were ideas about what time is worth as well as who and what are worth time; that is, qualitative assumptions about value and how it is defined, attributed, and measured.

Graduate students were also expected to apply for and secure funding, an immediate and high-stakes task unabashedly encouraging individualism, self-promotion, and competition. In considering me as a potential candidate for one the more prestigious of these awards, a senior professor referred to me as "Black, but gets along well with white people." Apparently based on my educational background and the professor's observations of my character, this assessment was intended as a compliment. It served as a clear assertion of the institutional value placed not just on my ability to get along with others, but on my perceived ability to get along with white people, even though I'm Black. The statement both acknowledged the white supremacy of the environment and called on me to cordially respect both the racial hierarchy and the norm of not confronting it. I think that was the day I acknowledged to myself that McGill is a "white school," even if I wasn't yet entirely sure what that meant. Part of this acknowledgment involved an overwhelming and racialized sense of class alienation. For the first time in my life I began to think critically about my working-class background and examine the meaning and implications of class beyond a strict economic sense, of capitalism as "not only an economic but also a social and political system."[5]

The culture of the university seemed to extend, uninterrupted, back to the early nineteenth century, a "traditional" time in which my Blackness was already predetermined and reified according to colonial logic and centuries of a dehumanizing and authoritative European gaze.[6] "Doing time" at the university seemed to require synchronizing my rhythm to that of the institution, but I couldn't get the moves. I was out of sync and felt behind, as though there would never be enough time for me to catch up with what seemed for everyone else to be the "natural" flow of the dominant university culture. I had never experienced such an emphasis on rapid, measurable production. Such a pace and orientation is contraindicated in my process-oriented art practices that require slow, reflective, whimsical experimentation with ideas and materials. It is in contradiction with community work that requires trusting relationships built over time. As neoliberal universities are run more and more "like businesses chasing money and customers," priority is increasingly assigned to the quantity of scholarship over its quality.[7] The demand to adjust to a normalized "work rhythm that is

rushed, riddled with anxiety and pressure to be ever-present" academically,[8] made sitting meditatively in front of a pottery wheel experiment-
ing with clay for hours suddenly seem like an expenditure of time that
should instead be allotted to academic production.[9]

Finding a Conversation

In the first semester of the doctoral program, we were introduced to
the idea of selecting an academic discourse community to join, through
identifying the scholars and body of scholarship within which we
hoped for our own work to be situated. In addition to research and
reading, this involved producing annotated bibliographies and literature reviews, as well as learning about peer review publishing and journal rankings. I continued to struggle – this level of academia seemed
entirely oriented towards competition, prestige, and hierarchy. I
learned the word "genuflect" when a professor explained that we were
to genuflect to established key theorists and researchers in our writing.

One night in a class on research methodologies we were asked to
work in pairs or small groups to create a film using a cell phone around
the theme "joining a conversation." I worked with Rima Athar to produce a short film we called, interchangeably, *Creating a Conversation* and
Finding a Conversation. As racialized women concerned about social justice, we had yet to locate an academic discourse community that we
wished to join. Our film ended up being dramatically different from
those of our colleagues, who produced pieces shot in well-lit indoor
spaces, featuring student and teacher characters addressing the theme
quite literally.

Creating/Finding a Conversation consisted of a series of short scenes
lasting just over two and a half minutes, with no (spoken) narration,
dialogue, or acting. We used an app that mimics old film (i.e., grainy,
flickering, with scratches, dust, and light leaks) and shot the piece from
a first-person perspective. It begins outside, at night, as the viewer-
protagonist approaches the building in which the Faculty of Education
is located. The only sound is that of the harsh wind that blew into the
microphone as we recorded. The door to the building is opened and
the viewer enters the lobby and looks around. The muffled voices of
other people in the building can be heard in the distance. The viewer
approaches a brick wall alongside a staircase, moves up the stairs,
slowly towards and eventually into complete darkness. The camera
movement is jagged as it approaches a door. Now in an enclosed stair-
well, the camera makes sharp movements – darting glances up and
down the stairs. There is no sound, except that of feet as the protagonist

quickly descends two steps, stops, and then looks back up. A brief glimpse from within a dark space into a brightly lit one; a disorienting angle makes it unclear whether the viewer is looking up or down. In total darkness, there is the sound of wind, followed by several seconds of loud banging, scratching, grinding noises. Then the sound of running water, then breathing: three slow, deep breaths. The closing shot is without sound and shows two hands and two bare feet in the grass.

Creating/Finding a Conversation is about disorientation, dislocation, fragmentation, fear, and grounding. Rather than carefully mapping out each scene, Rima and I set out to communicate a shared counter-story of graduate school and the ambivalent prospect of entering academic careers. We took turns holding the camera and decided what and how to shoot in the process. The completely dark scene towards the end was recorded in the woods by the stream that I had run to weeks earlier. The only time either of us appears in the film is in the closing scene, that features my left and Rima's right hands and feet. While the project was conceived, completed, and first screened all in the course of one three-hour class, making this film was a deeply meaningful experience that continues to resonate. The conversation that Rima and I found was ultimately our own, highlighting our unique collaborative vision as racialized women grounded in communities outside of the university.

"Becoming" an Activist

The largest union of "non-academic" workers at the university was on strike for the entire fall semester in which I began my doctoral program. The senior administration simultaneously downplayed the strike and attempted to criminalize the workers in both its public and internal discourses and through securing court injunctions controlling where and how workers could picket. Initiatives to support the striking workers on and off campus were the first "extracurricular" activities in which I became involved as a doctoral student, and where I started to meet other activist-minded students and faculty members.

On 10 November 2011, I participated in a massive student demonstration against proposed university tuition hikes in Québec. All afternoon I walked through downtown Montreal, arms linked with friends. For me, as for many people that day, it was the largest demonstration I had ever been part of. It forged for me an embodied connection to iconic images I had grown up with of the US civil rights movement in which my parents met. The demo ended outside of McGill, and protesters began flooding onto the downtown campus. It had grown dark and started raining, and the people I had been walking with had left. I stood alone, on the periphery at first, watching, eventually moving down into the crowd gathered outside of the senior administration building where several students had taken over the fifth floor.[10]

Everything was suddenly a blur: riot police, shields, batons, students, signs, banners, someone yelling into a megaphone. I was standing beside a young woman who appeared to be in her early twenties, younger than my son. Our arms were linked and we were squeezing tightly, bringing our bodies close together. The people were yelling "Solidarité!" The police were yelling "Bouge!" We stood still, and a big policeman forcefully pushed us to the ground with his shield, then reached forward and pepper sprayed us across our faces from no further than six inches away. I was blinded and became profoundly disoriented. I have no recollection of getting up and off of the campus. In the adjacent street, protesters were still yelling and police lines kept pushing people further away from the campus. Tear gas, yelling, screaming, rain. I finally turned from the scene and ran the two miles home, arriving muddy, wet, and stunned.[11]

The next afternoon I was back outside of the administration building with a group of students and professors, demanding answers from the senior administration about why riot police had been called onto campus. The press was there and we were asked for interviews. I was suddenly seen as "an activist," just in time for a province-wide student strike – the largest and longest in Canadian history.

I had found and joined an "activist" conversation, a discourse and action community within and against the university and its practices of labour exploitation, competitive individualism, oppressive top-down power hierarchy, and racist and patriarchal discrimination. Supplementing, complementing, and often challenging what I was doing in my formal program of study, the streets, administrative offices, and other sites of direct action were generative spaces of learning, and I found a strong sense of belonging in a small yet diverse group of students, professors, and activists. I found time for activism, found the timing of activism.

I began to develop a stronger class analysis through a range of involvement in the student movement on and off campus,[12] as well as through worker activism and labour union organizing at the university.[13] Unexpectedly, as the student movement gained momentum, I also found a new sense of belonging beyond the university, prompting me to engage critical questions about "citizenship" and the role of education in producing "good citizens." To quote a journal entry from late February 2012, I had "never before felt more like a 'citizen' of this province." I felt I had inherited a responsibility to fight for accessible education for all, to "defend the province" from neoliberalism, and to fight for its decolonization. These ideas drove the passion of the escalating mobilization, and reflected the influence of Québec nationalism that increasingly permeated the chants, rhetoric, and political discourses of the movement. Aspirations for the actual "decolonization" of Québec, however, were contradicted and undermined by the white settler colonial basis of that nationalism, posing a great challenge and source of tension with which racialized and Indigenous activists had to grapple. While many of us understood the neoliberalism driving the proposed tuition hikes as an extension of settler colonialism, it was clear that the *Printemps d'érable* was not an anticolonial or decolonizing movement per se. The student movement drew heavily on histories of class struggle in Québec, in which Québécois activists framed themselves as both colonized by the British and as the *nègres blanc*, leaving French colonialism and participation in the slave trade largely unaddressed.[14] Moreover, as it has been since the 1960s, the primary organizing frame of the student movement was combative syndicalism through direct democracy[15] with a notable influence and presence of anarcho-syndicalist and anarchist activists.[16] Consequently, persistent interventions from Indigenous, feminist, antiracist, and anticolonial activists were required to force more inclusive and progressive critiques and analyses.[17]

Despite these efforts of racialized and Indigenous students, within local racialized communities the movement was generally assumed to be white. In private emails, face-to-face debates, social media exchanges and published articles I argued for Black people's participation in the movement.[18] On more than one occasion it was suggested to me that I was being naive, uppity, and/or ignorant in aligning myself with "the students" (as if Black people were not students) and that the Québécois "them" has never cared about the Black (assumed not-Québécois) "us." By the end of the spring I would describe the greatest challenge of the preceding nine months not as the police violence, relentless pace of protest actions, surveillance or disciplinary hearings at the university – all of which I was subjected to. Rather, the greatest challenge was coping with what I felt were reductive and dismissive responses to the movement by some members of Montreal's Black community. Ultimately the question had shifted from why I would want to go to "that white school" to why I would associate myself with "that white student movement."[19] As the 2012 movement revived old Québécois organizing frames and tensions, it also exacerbated and renewed long-standing debates within Montreal Black communities about reformist and radical tactics, racial and Marxist analyses, and about exclusively Black political organizing and coalition building across racial and other differences.[20]

Such tensions are part and parcel of heterogeneous communities and reflective of the complexity and simultaneity of multiple aspects of identity and interlocking forms of oppression. While collective experiences of racialization and racism are very real in shaping the material conditions under which Black people live, no matter how powerfully it is lived "race" remains fluid, symbolic, and representational. Black people *should* be expected to hold a range of political and sociocultural positions, and indeed we do.[21]

Ultimately, racialized "problems of knowing,"[22] that is, disjunctures in what I knew about racism, class, and education – inspired the research upon which this book is based. The circumstances and events described above caused me to question the conditions of my earlier educational success, to think more critically about compliance and about what makes a student, a university, or an education "good" or "elite." Having been involved in community work and organizing in Montreal for decades prior to the 2012 student movement, I was struck by how universities can be such edifying sites of activism, and curious about activist communities' proximity to and visibility within universities. University-adjacent activists and activism attracted much more attention than the local communities I was used to organizing within. As Black and Indigenous feminists have long asserted, limited notions of "activism" erase the critical organizing and resistance of women and other members of racialized communities.[23] This important work often goes unrecognized by activists outside of these communities, thereby limiting the potential vision and capacity for disrupting dominant power dynamics within movements, as well as the potential for achieving broader social change.[24]

At the same time, activist experiences in and around the university broadened the scope of my concerns and analysis, and deepened my social-political engagement. Without leaving the city in which I had lived since I was five years old, in going to McGill I "left home" in the sense that Bernice Johnson Reagon describes as necessary in working for social change. Reagon describes the tendency to try to organize from within "little barred room[s]" that feel like home because they are organized around sameness and provide some retreat from broader social and political relations. While they exist, these can be nurturing spaces "where you sift out what people are saying about you and decide who you really are" and what you really want.[25] However, Reagon makes two critical points: first, we cannot survive by staying in our little room. It limits our reach as well as containing us and any threat we may pose to current social arrangements – "when those who call the shots get ready to clean house, they have easy access to you."[26]

Second, if we seek social and political change in the diverse societies in which we live, we have to know how to organize and struggle within these societies through building coalitions with others across multiple differences. Unlike work primarily with people who are like you and share your interests and perspectives, coalition work requires working across deep differences and consequently feeling uncomfortable, even unsafe. "Coalition work is not work done in your home. Coalition work has to be done in the streets. And it is some of the most dangerous work you can do."[27] Indeed, activism within the increasingly high-profile, coalitional Québec movement came with heavy conditions and consequences. Student activists were subjected to constant surveillance and political profiling by campus security teams as well as municipal and provincial police, and while governments manipulated legislation and used the court systems to criminalize protesters and repress the movement, university administrators manipulated and constructed new codes of conduct in attempts to discipline and control student and faculty activists.[28]

In sum, joining an activist community in and around the university was a messy experience of learning through engagement in social action.[29] Through the combined formal and informal learning I experienced on and off campus I gained a better understanding of myself and of Québec society and politics, and came to understand myself as a political actor within a broader sphere. These experiences raised my awareness of the production of knowledge as it relates to social and political power, and made me want to learn more about "the way relations of power and knowledge are organized in and through the university [that] makes it possible to live these relations without reflecting on them."[30] In the past, my educational experiences allowed me to keep one foot at "home" while going to and from school "getting" education. The combined experience of becoming an academic and being (perceived as) an activist was an entirely different, two-feet-in experience that led to an intense period of embodied learning. Inspired by and part of this ongoing journey, this book documents and draws on the experiences of twenty-one other Black people regarding their time at McGill, assembling and centring their experiential knowledge to offer an anti-colonial, critical race feminist analysis of the university as a dynamic site of the production of knowledge and power.

1

Introduction: The University as a Site of Struggle

I feel sometimes, when I'm at McGill, like you're *there*, and to come out of McGill takes a huge amount of effort. Especially once you've climbed up that bloody hill. If you're going down, you're not coming back up. So if you're up that hill, you're going to stay there a good long time. You're not coming back up if you go down. And once you're up that hill, there's nothing around you that's not McGill. When you're on that campus, it's all, y'know, *everything*. You can't buy food if it wasn't approved by McGill, you can't wipe your ass without it being McGill toilet paper, you can't step off and step back on. It's like a hard commitment to, like, be on or off. I feel like you drink the Kool-Aid or you don't. You really can't have a foot in both worlds.

In describing her perception as a Black student at the time of our interview, RC,[1] quoted above, recalls the historic significance of the hill upon which the McGill University campus is located. Conjuring a history of which RC was not aware at the time, the comments imply layers of meaning – particularly around social class – embedded in and still communicated by the location of the downtown campus in the area known as the Golden Square Mile. They recall how working-class and Black people "belonged" below the hill, offering a salient metaphor for the experiences of someone who has, however precariously, "made it up the hill," so to speak. Up the hill on the university campus can feel like "a place apart, a somewhat rarefied space" distinct from and yet part of the area that surrounds it.[2]

Indeed, from the mid-nineteenth to mid-twentieth centuries Montreal was considered to be like "two cities": one "above the hill," on the slope of the mountain, and the other "below the hill."[3] McGill University, located above the hill on the former estate of colonial merchant and slave owner James McGill, served as a key landmark in the development of the Golden Square Mile, home to the wealthiest families in Canada.[4] Embraced as an establishment of the anglophone elite,[5] the university would play a particularly significant role in the development of higher education in Canada and in the structural ordering of the settler nation overall. Meanwhile, the impoverished masses resided below the hill where, in the St. Antoine district, Montreal's first Black community developed alongside that of the poor and working-class Irish.

Against this historical backdrop, this book examines the experiences of Black people once we climb up that hill, referring both to this historic geographic demarcation of space in Montreal and to the implications of academic, social, and economic climbing. What are the conditions under which Black people, from Montreal as well as throughout the diaspora, have been admitted as students and hired as faculty at the university? How have these experiences been constitutive and reflective of dynamic and ongoing settler nationalisms? What do they teach us about resistance, community organizing, and academic activism? Drawing on critical ethnographic research that I conducted between 2012 and 2016, *Black Racialization and Resistance at an Elite University* responds to these questions. This work is driven by personal, academic, and professional commitments and is rooted in my lifelong relationships, experiences, and work in Black and working-class communities in Montreal. It is informed by my professional background in social service and community work, which over time established the basis for questioning how the dominant discourses and practices of institutions – government agencies, non-profit organizations, schools – shape experience and reproduce social and economic inequity.

McGill University provides the central setting of my critical ethnography, and this book is simultaneously about McGill and not about McGill. McGill is taken here as a particular site within the specific institutional complex of Canadian higher education. Examining racialized social relations from this site reveals its "points of connection with other sites and courses of action,"[6] thus generating better understandings of Canadian higher education and how it functions in society.

McGill provides a unique and generative environment from which to examine ruling relations in Canadian higher education. Established prior to Canadian Confederation, McGill is a founding institution of Canada and particularly of Canadian higher education. Its colonial origins – especially James McGill's having owned and traded slaves – are a glaring contradiction of national myths that deny Canadian histories of colonialism and slavery. McGill has been a site and symbol of unique tensions as a wealthy, anglophone institution situated within the context of the majority-francophone province of Québec and its dynamic history of class oppression and competing settler nationalisms. Finally, while McGill's student and faculty populations have always been predominantly white, Black people have attended and worked at the university for well over a century. As in Canada more broadly, this presence and the contributions of these people have largely been erased from institutional histories.

The research upon which this book is based contributes to correcting this erasure. It is centred on in-depth interviews with twenty-one self-identified Black people who studied and/or taught at McGill between the late 1950s and 2015. Participants were recruited through a written call for participation circulated in academic, student, and local Black community networks, as well as through word of mouth. Interviews with respondents were conducted in Montreal, Ottawa, and Toronto between 2014 and 2015. Participants include students, former students, course lecturers, and professors who studied and/or taught in the faculties of arts, education, law, and agriculture and environmental studies; individuals who have held elected positions in university governance and labour unions; and those who have served on a range of committees, working groups, associations, and organizing campaigns. Collectively, their experiences span half a century, coinciding with two major and ongoing transformations in Canadian universities: the expansion of higher education, creating more postsecondary institutions and greater access to a wider representation of the population in the 1960s, followed since the 1970s by rising corporatization, privatization, and the withdrawal of decision-making power from faculty, staff, and students.[7] In addition to contributing significantly to histories of Canadian higher education in general and McGill University in particular, the stories and insights of participants support and form the basis for the central arguments developed in this book. These are as follows:

1. The structures and practices of the university not only represent the settler colonial origins of higher education in Canada; they actively produce and reproduce settler colonial relations and promote settler nationalism.
2. These social relations are profoundly racialized and racializing; they have shaped the experiences of a diverse range of Black students and faculty over several decades in distinct ways.
3. Black people and our experiences across differences and time highlight and challenge the university's institutional investment in racialization and white hegemony. The "whiteness" of the university both includes *and exceeds* the racial identities of students and the professoriate, and works to reproduce interlocking racial, class, and gender oppressions that uphold racial capitalism.

The remainder of this chapter offers a historical overview of the contexts that frame my study. From the establishment of formal education under settler colonialism in what is now called Canada, I trace major highlights in the development of the Canadian university as a site of the production of white settler nationalism, as well as a site of anticolonial struggle and resistance. Situating Black Studies within the context of the contemporary neoliberal university, I conclude this chapter with an overview of the book as a project of anticolonial, critical race counter-storytelling.

Settler Colonialism and Education: A Brief Overview

Formal education in what would become Canada and the United States began in the seventeenth century, with the establishment of colleges and universities run by missionaries and geared primarily towards Indigenous populations. In New France, Jesuits founded the Collège des Jésuits in 1635 with the purpose of converting Indigenous peoples to Christianity.[8] This was followed by the Séminaire de Québec, founded in 1663 to prepare future priests and, as of 1668, to evangelize Indigenous youth and indoctrinate them into French culture.[9] British North American institutions in the Thirteen Colonies were also established during this era with similar purposes – for example, Harvard's Indian College (1636) and the College of William and Mary (1693) – to Christianize Indigenous youth; teach them Latin, English, and Greek; socialize them in English cultural norms and beliefs; and make them loyal to the British crown. In both British North America and New France, the belief was that such schooling would create a generation of Indigenous young men who would go on to propagate the Christian European beliefs and values that they had learned in school within their own communities.[10] A "rudimentary Christian education" was also provided for slaves,[11] and this seems to have included at least some of the Black slaves whom the colonizers brought with them and imported.[12] Olivier LeJeune, for example, largely thought to have been the first Black slave sold in New France, attended the Collège des Jésuits.[13] Overall, the role of formal education in the seventeenth- and eighteenth-century colonies was understood to be the religious conversion of colonized populations and the training of priests and nuns.[14] Otherwise, for the white settler population, children's education was understood as something that took place at home in the family, rather than in schools.[15]

As the settler population grew following the military conquest of New France by the British in the mid-eighteenth century, the role of education expanded and gained prominence. The British authorities created the Royal Institution for the Advancement of Learning in 1801 to establish state schools to teach Protestantism, the English language, and British culture to the white settler youth of the growing colony. However, the Rebellions delayed significant educational institutional development until after the united Province of Canada was formed in 1841.[16] By the end of the nineteenth century all provinces except Québec had a ministry of education and compulsory education laws.

In Québec, where French-speaking Catholics formed a majority of the population, the Catholic Church secured the role of "principal defender of French Canadian culture and values,"[17] within a broader context of national Anglo-dominance. As part and parcel of this role, the church held control over education in Québec until well into the twentieth century, and the province had no compulsory education laws until 1943. French Catholic schools operated at a disadvantage compared to those of the Protestant system, as the latter were better supported and had more resources.[18]

Central ideas and concerns regarding the education of Indigenous and Black populations also shifted during the nineteenth century. Indigenous peoples were perceived as having lost their value to the settler colonial society as they were no longer needed as military allies and no longer played as vital a role in the fur trade. Dominant perceptions of them thus shifted from "the warrior image" to that of "an expensive social nuisance."[19] Colonial officials subsequently sought both to contain Indigenous populations through the establishment of reserves and to assimilate them through an aggressive and intrusive program of religious and vocational education. By 1860 "the 'nation-to-nation' relationship" between Indigenous peoples and the settler colonial authorities was effectively abandoned.[20] At this same time, the Black population was growing by the thousands, as the 1850 Fugitive Slave Act in the United States drove former Black slaves into the Province of Canada. As Black communities began to form and Chinese labourers were recruited to complete the Canadian Pacific Railway, concerns within the settler population about "keeping Canada white" increased, as did practices of racial exclusion and segregation. I discuss this history in more detail in chapter 3.

When the Canadian government was established in 1867, the Constitution Act granted the provinces control of settler education systems, while the federal government claimed jurisdiction over Indigenous peoples through the Indian Act. Lamenting the failure thus far to achieve assimilation of the Indigenous population, a series of reports built a case for what would by the end of the century become Canada's Indian residential school system.[21] Colonial authorities determined that it was necessary to remove Indigenous children from their parents' immediate influences and (re)socialize them in government-funded industrial boarding schools for religious and agricultural training.[22] Within these schools thousands of Indigenous children would die and tens of thousands would endure horrifying experiences of physical, sexual, emotional, and psychological abuse. The formal federal program was instituted in the 1880s, and the last of these schools was not closed until 1996.[23]

By the turn of the twentieth century, practices of excluding and segregating Black people were increasingly accommodated by Canadian legislation.[24] White parents did not want their children educated with Black children, hence school segregation – *de jure* in Ontario and Nova Scotia and *de facto* in many places elsewhere – existed from the mid-nineteenth to mid-twentieth century.[25] Black communities – particularly Black women – took control of educating Black children through opening their own schools for those denied access to public education, as well as through organizing academic, vocational, artistic, cultural, and spiritual education programs in Black community centres and churches.[26]

The Canadian University

With the establishment of separate schools for Indigenous education, the primary role of "new world" colleges and universities became to educate the sons of the colonial elite and unify the British colonies.[27] In addition to promoting European classical knowledge, the university served as a site for the development of racial ideology that aimed to justify slavery and colonization without contradicting European Enlightenment ideals about freedom and equality.[28] Especially after the publication of Charles Darwin's influential works – *Origin of Species* in 1859 and *The Descent of Man* in 1871 – scholars sought to resolve tensions between religious beliefs and values and the science of evolution while generating the ideological foundations for building and shaping new nations. The promotion and production of "knowledge" that asserted the genetic superiority of white people and denied the humanity of Indigenous and African peoples was thus a key aim of the university as it sought to produce "noble, intelligent, unselfish men" to serve the social good of the nation.[29]

Over the course of the nineteenth century several universities were founded across Canada and, as in the United States, Scottish merchants and clergymen were especially active in establishing these institutions.[30] Colonial administrator George Ramsay (Lord Dalhousie) founded Dalhousie University in Halifax in 1818, modelling the school after the University of Edinburgh. McGill University was established in Montreal in 1821 on the former estate of colonial merchant James McGill, and by late century was popularly touted as the "Harvard of Canada."[31] McGill played a particularly significant role in the further development of higher education as part of the westward expansion of the settler colonial nation. The University of Toronto was subsequently founded as King's College in 1827 by Bishop John Strachan, close friend and associate of James McGill, one of four trustees of McGill's will and among the founders of the university that bears his name.[32] The Church of England controlled King's College until 1850, when it became a secular institution and was given the name it bears today. Queen's University was established in 1841 by the Presbyterian Church of Scotland and modelled, as was McGill, on the universities of Edinburgh and Glasgow. By 1871, there were seventeen universities and colleges in the Dominion of Canada, across which 1,561 students were enrolled – roughly 0.4 per cent of the overall population at the time.[33] In 1908, the University of Alberta opened under founding president and former McGill professor of mathematics and physics Henry Marshall Tory, and the McGill University College of British Columbia was established under the chancellorship of Francis Carter-Cotton. The latter was set up under the governance of the Royal Institution for the Advancement of Learning[34] and awarded McGill University degrees until becoming the University of British Columbia in 1915.[35] Highlighting the roles of the universities in the expanding Canadian Dominion, Carter-Cotton stressed his gratitude in a letter to McGill principal Sir William Peterson written in the early twentieth century:

> The benefit our Province has derived from your connection with it, it would be impossible to estimate. Many young people have received a University education for whom otherwise it would have remained an unaccomplished dream. An interest in higher education has been fostered, not only in the young, but in our people generally, and our sense of unity with other parts of the Dominion and with the Empire as a whole, and of the possession of common ideals of citizenship and culture has been deepened.[36]

Along with founding institutions in Australia, New Zealand, and South Africa, the settler colonial universities of Canada functioned as part of an expansive, transnational British imperial network, symbolizing and propagating European civilization and Western knowledge while helping to shape and define the emerging societies in which they were located. The settler universities were connected to but distinct from colonial universities established by the British in India and Africa, with racialized and gendered institutional values and practices that promoted connections between settler scholars and those in Britain.[37] While Americans were generally marginalized along with Africans and Indians in the British academic networks, given its geographic proximity to the United States "Canada came to function as something of a 'hinge' between the British and American academic worlds."[38]

In the lead-up to the First World War, the role of Canadian universities began to shift again in order to adjust to rapid industrialization and the development of capitalist society. "The inauguration of the Canadian Officers' Training Corps at McGill in 1912 symbolized a more direct military role for universities" in the "growth of militarism and self-conscious imperial sentiment."[39] Educational institutions played crucial roles in "teaching the war" and "preparing students to take their place in it."[40] Universities served as sites of military research, recruitment, and training, and academics published articles and essays geared towards public school teachers and their role in promoting patriotism in elementary and secondary school classrooms.[41] As the war increased the need for and importance of scientific research, the National Research Council was founded in 1916 and began offering national scholarships for graduate student research, most of which were awarded to students at McGill and University of Toronto for the next twenty-five years.[42] This new era in higher education was also characterized by increased access to the university by the middle classes as well as the development of academic specialization and professionalism, including new professional programs such as social work, nursing, and education.

Hence the role of the Canadian university of the first half of the twentieth century was to promote patriotism and the values of the country's European "founding nations," and to provide middle-class youth the necessary education to maintain or improve their social status and contribute to the well-being of the nation.[43] During and following the Second World War, perceived (and in some case demonstrated) connections between science, communism, and espionage positioned Canadian universities as critical sites within the "emerging national security state."[44] The founder and president of the Humanities Research Council of Canada from 1943–47, Watson Kirkconnell, was fervently anticommunist, believing that Canadian scholars had a duty to combat totalitarian education and that he "had a special mission to clean communism out of Canadian campuses."[45] Many Canadian academics were accused of and investigated for being communist sympathizers and/or traitors to the Crown, most notably at Queen's, University of Toronto, and especially at McGill. Following investigations of several scientists at McGill in the late 1940s, the university gained an "unearned" reputation as a "hotbed of Communism," even though then-principal Cyril James was "an impassioned public advocate of Cold War preparedness."[46] It was a very serious charge, especially in Québec where Marxism was understood as a threat to Catholicism worldwide and anticommunism rivalled that of McCarthyism in the United States.[47] Media reports of communist traitors at McGill must have only exacerbated the perception of the university's role in the oppression of the province's francophone majority.[48]

Whose University? The 1960s

By the 1960s, Canadian universities had entered another period of extensive growth. Following the war, the federal government provided support for veterans to attend university and increased funding to universities. In this way, universities were expected to become accessible to a broader, more diverse portion of society and to be governed in ways that involved the participation of professors, staff, and students.[49] In Québec, education was a central issue of the Quiet Revolution from the late 1950s to late 1960s as an emerging francophone middle class mobilized and demanded the state take greater responsibility for education and other social services. Full control over education shifted from the Church to the government following the establishment of the provincial ministry of education in 1964.[50] Most adults in Québec did not have more than a sixth-grade education, and postsecondary school attendance was especially low for French Canadians. Major reform aimed to redefine education as a secular, state-run system crucial to the social, economic, and political development of Québec. Beginning in 1967, a system of tuition-free (French and English) collèges d'enseignement general et professionnel (CEGEPs) was created to prepare students for university or the work force. Subsequently, beginning in 1968 the public, French-language Université du Québec system established several campuses throughout the province, expanding access to university education for greater numbers of francophone students.[51]

As in many other societies where oppressed people rebelled in the 1960s and early 1970s, Québec universities were critical sites of anti-colonial and antiracist organizing. A new generation of Québécois nationalists increasingly understood themselves as a colonized people under the colonial-capitalist domination of the English and argued for national independence and socialism for Québec. As a particularly provocative symbol of enduring, white Anglo-Canadian power in Québec in contrast to an inadequate French school system (at all levels), McGill University was a significant target of such activism.[52] During this time the universities also faced increasing anticolonial and antiracist resistance from Black students and activists, particularly at Sir George Williams University (which later became Concordia) and at McGill. As I examine more closely in chapter 3, two overlapping events in the 1968–69 school year stand out in this era of Black activism.[53] First, an international Congress of Black Writers was organized by students and held at McGill in the fall of 1968. The congress was understood within the context of Black Power and Pan-Africanist movements of the era, and featured speeches by several high-profile Black scholars and activists. At the time a persistent campaign by Black students at Sir George Williams University (SGWU) was also underway, demanding that the administration openly and fairly address allegations that Black students were being subjected to racially discriminatory grading practices by a white lecturer.[54] After months of pursuing justice through the formal channels of the university, the students escalated their tactics and took over the university's computer centre in February 1969. Up to two hundred students held the space for nearly two weeks until riot police intervened to clear them from the building. The eviction ended with a fire, millions of dollars of damage to university property, and the arrest of ninety-seven students (more than half of whom were white). Deeply impacting universities and galvanizing Black communities in Montreal, across the country, and beyond national borders, these events would have repercussions felt for decades and generations to come, and continue to inspire Black students and activists today.

The events of the Sir George Williams affair and its aftermath focused local, national, and international attention on institutional racism and Black resistance in Montreal and other parts of Canada, prompting national and international government agencies to conduct major investigations of activists that in some cases resulted in prison sentences and deportations. Black student activists courageously maintained pressure on the universities in the months and years that followed the Sir George Williams Affair, communicating and collaborating with students and activists in other Canadian universities and Black communities, demanding the decolonization of education and establishment of university Black Studies programs. In the following chapters I examine this work by successive cohorts of Black student activists at McGill, and university administrators' strategic management of and resistance to such pressure for institutional change.

Black Educational Activism and Black (Canadian) Studies

When I first came here [to McGill], as I said, there were no Canadian Blacks. Well, that's not true – there were *a few*. I remember meeting two. And became fairly friendly with them. But they were the only Canadian Blacks I knew … [and they] came from upper-middle-class families and in some ways were less typical of the Black Canadian community. When I was an undergraduate the thing that kind of brought it to fore was the DaCosta Hall program. McGill basically gave free tuition to kids who made it through that first program … It changed the colour component here … All of a sudden you had forty or fifty [Black Canadian students] every year, young people coming in, and going back to their own communities, and their younger brothers and sisters could figure "well, my older brother's at McGill so I guess that's where I'm gonna' go." That's the difference. And I think the Concordia [SGWU] affair, played a strong role. (GR)

As a response to Black student activism and within a broader context of growth and change in Black communities of the 1960s, Black educators and community members organized new programs to promote Black educational achievement in general, and access to higher education specifically. The Quebec Board of Black Educators (QBBE) was founded in Montreal in 1969 and established the DaCosta Hall summer school program in 1970 to provide Black senior high school students with academic support and mentorship to this end.[55] Originally called "Across the Halls," the program was initially organized by Black students at McGill, to offer local Black high school graduates the opportunity to complete courses they required to gain admission to McGill. The university had admitted there were only fifteen African Canadian students enrolled at all levels of study for the 1969–70 school year,[56] and made a one-time contribution of twelve thousand dollars to the project. McGill, SGWU, and Dawson College (CEGEP) guaranteed admission to graduates of that first cohort as long as they had graduated from high school.[57] McGill agreed to accept twenty of the ninety students in the summer program, and in fall 1970 fourteen students from the Across the Halls program were accepted and registered at McGill. Six others had been accepted but were unable to register for and attend courses at McGill "due to an inability to pay fees."[58] This last point is significant, highlighting that even when tuition is waived, various mandatory fees associated with higher education can maintain financial barriers.

Similar programs were set up in Toronto and Halifax during this time, and Black student activists played key roles in pressuring universities and gaining institutional support. Transitional Year Programs (TYP) at the University of Toronto and Dalhousie University were established in 1970 to support Black and Indigenous students in accessing university education.[59] Although the educators and students involved with the TYPs have had to remain vigilant and mobilize support through periods of intense struggle to keep the programs in place,[60] both continue at the time of this writing.

The Dalhousie and University of Toronto TYP programs have supported thousands of students in entering and succeeding at university. However, the ongoing need for their existence speaks to continued widespread social-economic inequity and to the slow pace of institutional change within Canadian higher education.[61] Much work remains to be done to make the university experience an accessible, engaging, and intellectually relevant and nourishing one for working-class, Black, and Indigenous students once they are admitted. Some argue that TYPs challenge the status quo of universities by their very existence – for example, in the students they attract to the university, their critical pedagogical approach, their emphasis on mutual support and collective well-being, their community orientation – and as such can be critical instruments of change.[62] However, as University of Toronto TYP co-founder and educator Keren Brathwaite has argued, ultimately universities have a responsibility to "move beyond the add-ons of TYPs, Steps to University, Bridging, and other special programs (important as these are) to a more holistic, encompassing approach."[63] The need for such institutional change beyond admissions is made clear in DaCosta Hall graduate Clifton Ruggles's reflections on his time at McGill in the 1970s:

> As the professors made references to people I had never heard of, it was as if they were speaking in a foreign tongue. I stood there transfixed, afraid to open my mouth. It was like being in an insane asylum; nothing made sense. It was as if the terrain had suddenly shifted precariously and I had lost my bearings and reference points. I had been stripped of whatever voice I had. As I sat there trying to decode this unfamiliar gibberish I hesitated to contribute my ideas because I felt I would not be understood. I had this wonderful opportunity to go to university and I did not want to blow it; I did not want to embarrass myself for fear it would reflect badly on my race. When I did speak, the other students stared at me blankly. I felt that they did not hear my words, they only saw my Blackness. It seemed they could not comprehend the significance of my presence there. As a result of these experiences in white academia I became mute and invisible.[64]

As Ruggles's reflection powerfully attests, genuine access to the university for Black Canadians is a matter of much more than formal admission.[65]

This is something that Black students and activists have long been aware of. One of the students I interviewed from this era, GR, describes this struggle as one that most of the students experienced once they got to McGill. He says that while "some of [the DaCosta Hall graduates at McGill] did extremely well, and one of the people who graduated from the first group – [now professor of law] Esmeralda Thornhill – is still somebody here that people look up to," many were not prepared for McGill; "if I had to guess I'd say probably six or seven out of the first group were able to really [successfully] make the transition." GR said that he and other Black Caribbean students at McGill tried "in a non-threatening way" to mentor the incoming local Black students, to listen and "be there for them." Such informal peer mentorship as well as popular programs of Black study formed an essential aspect not only of campus movements of the era – including those at McGill and SGWU – but of Black power and liberation movements overall.[66]As in the Black student movements that were sweeping across the United States, Black Canadians were simultaneously re-educating themselves and demanding institutional change, beginning with the hiring of more Black professors and the establishment of formal Black Studies programs. A wave of Black student strikes and direct actions at majority white universities in the United States since 1968 had begun to force the institutionalization of Black Studies.[67]

Given what was at stake at the time, McGill's funding of the Across the Halls/DaCosta summer program can be understood as a case of interest convergence: an attempt by the university, in the words of one activist, "to pacify [the previous] year's Black Studies group without installing a Black Studies program."[68] As I discuss throughout this book, the erasure of the histories, experiences, and cultural and intellectual work of Black people in university curricula can marginalize and alienate Black students. Such exclusions make Black students feel devalued, normalize white hegemony, and obscure alternatives to European knowledge systems. Black Studies provides intellectual space for recontextualizing such experiences, placing them under a critical analytical lens that reveals how they mirror and reinforce social marginalization and exclusion in the broader society.

I join other Black scholars who understand the refusal to establish Black Studies programs in Canadian universities as reflective of a broader, persistent devaluing of and refusal to recognize the intellectual work of Black people.[69] More specifically, institutional resistance to recognizing Black Canadian Studies reflects long-term investments in the systematic construction of Canada as a white nation wherein Black people are imagined as visitors or immigrants having always recently arrived from elsewhere.[70] Within this national imaginary, "Black Canadian" is a negated and contested identity, despite the fact that as of 2016, the Black population of Canada was 1,198,540, of which more than 44 per cent (531,070 people) were born in Canada and roughly 9 per cent were third generation or more.[71]

Through decades of persistent work by Black teachers, students, artists, community workers, and activists, Black Studies in Canada may slowly be establishing its own space in academia. The James Robinson Johnston Chair in Black Canadian Studies was established at Dalhousie University in 1991 and finally, in 2016, an interdisciplinary Black and African Diaspora Studies minor was established at Dalhousie.[72] In recent years African Diaspora Studies have expanded at York University, Queen's University, and University of Alberta;[73] more recently, at York University long-term efforts by students and faculty have come to fruition with the 2018 launch of a Black Canadian Studies Certificate in Humanities. In 2018, a position in Black Studies in Education was established in the Department of Social Justice Education at the Ontario Institute for the Study of Education (University of Toronto). The Black Canadian Studies Association was founded in 2009 and hosted national conferences in 2013, 2015, and 2017 before joining the national Congress of the Humanities and Social Sciences in 2018.

To engage in Black Studies within the tradition of Black radical thought, as I aim to here, is to actively pursue ways of knowing and being that challenge settler colonial and racial capitalist ideology, and to create possibilities for building more equitable societies. In this sense the very notion of Black Canadian Studies disrupts assumptions about the meaning of "Canadian" and forces us to reconsider our identities as they relate to national belonging, Indigenous peoples, and the Canadian state.[74] At the same time, the disruptive potential of the field should not be taken for granted; it has been and remains necessary for Black scholars and communities to actively defend and maintain the radical political vision of Black Studies. Since its inception, Black Studies in the academy has been the topic of much debate. Is it to be a project through which Black people gain recognition by and inclusion within the liberal university and society? Can the implementation and integration of formal Black Studies programs in universities be a vehicle for radical change in education and society overall?[75] These questions and concerns are of great importance to Black scholars in Canada, as neoliberal policies and practices reignite critical debates about what and who the categories "Canadian," "Black," and "Black Canadian Studies" represent, how these categories function, and the role of the university in their (re)production or refusal.

Neoliberalism and the University

Universities are still largely governed and supported by members of the business elite and represent particular capitalist, corporate, and political interests.[76] Today these interests are largely framed by neoliberalism, a set of ideas and social-economic policies geared towards capitalist expansion through increasing commodification and privatization. Overall, what some refer to as "the neoliberal university" is characterized by rapid increases in tuition fees, increasing corporate presence on university campuses and increasing corporate control of research agendas, increased surveillance and repression of activists and scholars, decreasing job security, and increasing demands on teaching and administrative staff.[77] Since the 1980s universities have been adjusting curricula and research priorities to attract funding through corporate partnerships.[78] Support for the "hard sciences" and technology continues to increase in an era of growing value placed on militarization and entrepreneurship, while the study of societies and social problems is increasingly dismissed as a concern of the past.[79]

Building on extensive histories of colonial and imperialist relations between industrialized and underdeveloped nations, neoliberal capitalism is an ongoing, global, and globalizing project, and its impact on postsecondary education is a transnational issue.[80] Rather than thinking of universities as mere victims of separate, external economic pressures, it is important to understand them as representative institutions of a historically constructed "transnational politics of higher education," which is and always has been driven by "competing interests, asymmetrical power relations and political contestation at local, national and regional levels."[81] It is within this context that the Canadian government seeks "truth and reconciliation" with Indigenous peoples and in which Indigenous Studies are consequently receiving increased funding and other forms of institutional support. Therefore, many question the sincerity and motives of a newly claimed willingness of Canadians and Canadian institutions to "recognize" and engage Indigenous peoples.[82]

We must ensure that histories of African enslavement and the presence and experiences of Black people are also considered part of the national conversation regarding "truth and reconciliation" in Canada.[83] As Rinaldo Walcott reminds us, we must ask "what is being reconciled, with whom and to what [ends]?"[84] From an anticolonial perspective, the role of the Black scholar in Western academia is not a matter of identity politics or the promotion of an essentialized Black subject or experience, but of building on an anticolonial Black political, cultural, and intellectual project and "challeng[ing] Eurocentric mimicry and the seduction to become white in the imperialist Western academy and global trajectories."[85] Black and Indigenous scholars continue to argue for Indigenous epistemologies that recognize the interconnectedness of the individual, community, natural, and spiritual worlds as a means of grounding the political and maintaining hope, courage, and a sense of one's wholeness and humanity in the face of overwhelming oppressions.[86] The goal, as Sandy Grande writes, is to "imagine political/pedagogical strategies that go beyond simply resisting settler relations of power and work instead to redefine the epistemological underpinnings through which the colonial world order is conceived" by engaging and developing Indigenous knowledges that can facilitate social and political change.[87]

What might "truth and reconciliation" look like for Black people in Canada? What and who do "Canada/Canadian," "Black," and "Black Canadian" represent? How do Black racialization and assertions of Black Canadianness function within the settler nation? What is the role of the university in their (re)production or refusal? If it remains a goal to formalize programs of Black Studies in Canadian universities, how might we do so in ways that protect it from becoming a product and servant of neoliberalism? How can we retain and build its radical politics? What is the role of the Black scholar in the neoliberal university and how, if at all, is this role changing in the twenty-first century? This book is oriented towards such crucial meta-questions. I offer a collective critical race counter-story about Black people's experiences at McGill in order to help us think critically about their implications for radically different futures. Using methods of institutional ethnography and political activist ethnography, I examine how the university, in accordance with the ideologies of the political regime of which it is a part, uses various textual forms and practices to produce objectified knowledge (ideology) that regulates people's activities and shapes their experiences.[88]

Racialized social relations can seem to mysteriously impact and organize our lives. As Wahneema Lubiano describes:

Some mystifications can kill or maim us. "Like being mugged by a metaphor" is a way to describe what it means to be at the mercy of racist, sexist, heterosexist, and global capitalist constructions of the meaning of skin color on a daily basis. Whether or not I am a card-carrying believer in distinctions of racial biology, I am nonetheless attacked by the hegemonic social formation's notions of racial being and the way those notions position me in the world. Like a mugging, this attack involves an exchange of assets: some aspect of the social order is enriched domestically and internationally by virtue of material inequities stabilized and narrativized by race oppression and I lose symbolically and monetarily. Further, I am physically traumatized and psychologically assaulted by an operation that is mystified. It goes on in the dark, so to speak – in the dark of a power that never admits to its own existence.[89]

This book proceeds from the assumption that social life is not chaotic; rather, it is organized through interacting social relations that coordinate people's day-to-day activities.[90] Critically examining what we know, how we know it, and how that knowledge shapes our everyday lives is aimed at demystifying racialized power relations and developing more effective forms of Black educational activism. In talking back to several dominant institutional and national narratives, this work highlights histories of and future possibilities for knowing and being otherwise, in ways that do not uphold hegemonic whiteness and a capitalist, colonial social order but instead reveal possibilities for replacing it. Institutional ethnographers do not seek to examine an entire institution, but rather "explore particular corners or strands within a specific institutional complex in ways that make visible their points of connection with other sites and courses of action."[91] In this study, the institution under examination is that of the university in Canada, while the "particular corner" of my investigation is McGill. Black students' and professors' lived experiences of the university and how they narrate them serve to establish and maintain the perspective from which the social relations of this institutional order are studied.

Critical Race Counter-Storytelling

This book offers a critical race counter-story informed by the individual narratives it brings together and shaped by anticolonial politics. It is not intended to suggest a master narrative of Black experience – claims made about Black students and Black professors are not to be taken to refer to *all* Black students and professors. Mapping power relations from a particular standpoint is not meant to suggest that there are no other valid standpoints. This book is not objective or neutral; rather, it is grounded in the experiences of the people whose narratives I engage and is shaped by the critical theories, methods, and activist traditions that inform my analysis.

Critical race counter-storytelling works from the premise that knowledge "is never neutral, which means it is always a story of some kind, produced by a situated knower."[92] It involves the intentional and strategic use of stories to challenge the assumptions and logic of "racial domination at the epistemic, spiritual and material dimensions of dehumanization."[93] As Denise Taliaferro Baszile argues, Black abolitionists "understood radical change required first and foremost a rhetorical revolution,"[94] and Black counter-storytelling has been an astute political project grounded in a demand for self-representation and the assertion of counter-discourses, challenging not only racist representations of Black people but the very "rationality of Rational man."[95] Understood in this context, the narratives of the people I interviewed are valued for the experiences and analyses they represent, in all the ways they may contradict, challenge, or align with one another. It is through listening not just to how participants choose to respond to my questions, but also to what they seek to share regardless of my questions, that some of the most interesting and unexpected insights have emerged. Documenting these narratives is an important project in and of itself, especially given dominant Euro-Canadian histories of the university in which the presence and activities of Black students and professors have generally not been highlighted.

As a work of critical race theorizing in the Black radical tradition, this work has a collectivist orientation that emphasizes "the importance of social networks, symbols of identity, and transnational ties" in maintaining collective cultural grounding.[96] Therefore, in recognizing the importance of moving beyond the notion of "race" and refusing to attribute agency to "race" and "racism" as sole determinants of experience, I simultaneously recognize the salience of collective experiences of racialization, antiracist resistance, and "the quest for freedom as community."[97] These shared experiences and sensibilities were particularly apparent in my conversations with participants; their narrative accounts demonstrate the influences of the intergenerational cultural wealth nurtured within Black communities. Examples of this wealth, as Tara J. Yosso and other critical race educators observe, include language and communication skills nurtured by traditions of storytelling, oral history, and the sharing of parables and proverbs in addition to artistic forms of communication. It also includes a sense of *familia* (or extended family) that expands beyond immediate family and nurtures "a sense of community history, memory and cultural intuition."[98]

Many of the participants, including those I had not met prior to the study, communicated with a sense of familiarity suggesting an assumed shared experience of both Blackness and academia. In the interviews, some speak creatively, making use of metaphors, similes, Black vernacular, and various cultural references to convey meaning. Some are careful to limit their comments to direct responses to the questions I asked them, while others take the opportunity to lose themselves in their recollections – as expressed by one interviewee who interrupts herself mid-response and exclaims, "Lord Jesus, I don't even remember your question [*laughs*]!" Several people who spoke to me control their voices to achieve particular effects – almost yelling at times, laughing raucously, whispering in moments (especially when speaking about white supremacy), manipulating their tone for emphasis and using a range of sounds to communicate meaning. At times interviewees acknowledge their awareness of being audio recorded, suggesting that it was causing them to self-censor or choose their words carefully: "There are certain things that I couldn't really get into in the way I wanted to, because I don't want it recorded, you know? But I think I've made my points." Others seem to speak freely while trusting me to protect their identity (which I have), occasionally making comments such as "maybe you'll have to edit this part out or people will know who I am [*laughs*]." More than one interviewee expressed concern for my well-being in relation to the personal and professional risk they perceived me to be taking by openly conducting research that challenges dominant narratives and institutional power. These concerns were expressed in caring ways, reflecting a sense of *familia,* of Black people looking out for one another's interests as Black people. They also express an awareness of the subversive power of their own stories. While no one publication can fully examine these stories in all of their complexity, creativity, and nuance, they form the core of this book and contribute much towards building community and institutional memory, especially for current and future cohorts of Black learners and teachers.

This book is divided into two parts of three chapters each. Chapters 2 and 3 continue to provide a historical overview of the founding and development of higher education in general and of McGill University specifically, situating the university within broader social-political contexts from the colonial era until the 1960s. I critically engage dominant historical narratives, drawing on a selection of texts published by and about the university.

I treat the independent student newspaper *The McGill Daily* as an alternative institutional archive providing records that supplement and at times challenge and contradict the university's official narratives. The *Daily* has a strong history of activist journalism,[99] and it has proven to be an invaluable resource documenting decades of student activism and concerns, and institutional politics over time including the presence and activism of Black students.

The second part of this book draws more heavily on my interviews, and is organized according to the three overlapping key themes raised by Black peoples' experiences at McGill University since the 1960s. Chapter 4, "The Idealized Elite University," examines idealized notions of the elite university that shape what students and faculty expect at McGill. Once they arrive at the university, these expectations often conflict with lived experiences of racial othering and exclusion. Chapter 5, "Being and Becoming Black," examines various experiences of Black racialization at the university, and how Black students and faculty cope with and confront conditions of racialization and anti-Black racism. Finally, in chapter 6, "Academic Service and Resistance," I critically examine the potential and limitations of working for anticolonial, anti-racist change from within the structures of the neoliberal university. The book concludes with some closing reflections from the research participants, followed by my own.

2

Colonial Legacies and Canadian Ivy

Just the legacy of the place y'know, if you just learn a little bit, just learning that James McGill was a slave owner, right, and he had both Black and Indigenous slaves, and this is the name of the place that we're in; there's some sort of inherent contradiction in that, that we're coming here. So just kind of like, whether you know it or not almost, your identity as a Black person or a person of colour is under threat. Just right off the bat. (KB)

[The university is] corrupt, they're criminals, and they have to leave. We never surrendered our lands, never. McGill is squatting on our land.
    – Kahentinetha Horn of the Bear Clan, Mohawk Nation[1]

McGill University is located on traditional Kanien'kehá:ka land. As woman titleholder Kahentinetha Horn explained in September 2015 after serving the university a Notice of Seizure,[2] the land was taken through the colonial invasion of Kanien'kehá:ka territories and has since been occupied in contravention of the law of the land and Great Law of Peace of the Haudenosaunee. Horn asserts, "We have never seen a document from McGill that they actually got our permission to build that university on our land and that we ever relinquished any title to our land."[3] While in this chapter I examine the university's histories as negotiated and recorded by settlers, it is important to remember that the land upon which these stories take place is that of Indigenous peoples and was never ceded.

Through colonial dispossession the land became recognized by settlers as the property of James McGill, who in his will bequeathed his eighteen-hectare Burnside Estate and ten thousand pounds to the Royal Institution for the Advancement of Learning in order to establish a college in his name. James McGill died in 1813, and in 1821 McGill University was established after receiving royal charter from King George IV.

In 1829, the Montreal Medical Institution was accepted as the Faculty of Medicine of McGill College, and following a series of delays largely caused by litigation concerning McGill's will, the McGill College Faculty of Arts opened for teaching in 1843.

In this chapter, I discuss McGill University's origin stories and histories, situating it within a network of white settler colonial families and institutions that have played significant roles in shaping the economies, politics, and cultures of Montreal, Québec, and Canada. I consider the university and its celebrated founder historically, within the context of New France and British North America. In doing so, I draw on institutional documents, newspaper articles, and a range of literature published about and by the university, particularly that written by the official historian of McGill, Stanley Brice Frost.[4] The university employed Frost for half a century as a professor, administrator, founding director of the History of McGill Project, and McGill's official historian.[5] He was described by students as an "authoritarian," a "true blue old reactionary who doesn't hide in liberal clothing" who was vehemently "opposed to frenchification of McGill in any form,"[6] suggesting both the personal investments and the institutional interests that shaped the histories he composed. On behalf of the university, Frost played a key role in the construction of the contemporary identity of James McGill and the dominant history of the university.

Meeting James McGill

As the fall 2011 semester got underway, the principal's welcome message on the university website introduced a new cohort of students to James McGill, calling attention to "just how much our past shapes our present":

> When James McGill left Scotland to build a new life on the edge of the Quebec wilderness, he came equipped with his University of Glasgow education. He brought with him the values of the Scottish Enlightenment: an openness to different views, a commitment to hard work, and a belief that knowledge betters the world. Communicating in French, English and some aboriginal languages, McGill flourished where others floundered. His values not only led to the creation of McGill University, but continue to profoundly shape us today.[7]

The four-paragraph statement mentioned James McGill in every paragraph. It went on to posit students as inheritors of this colonial legacy, suggesting the potential to become like James McGill through entering onto his former estate:

Just as James McGill himself did, people come to Montreal with ambition and optimism. They come, from all over the world, to embrace potential where others balk at obstacles. I invite you to join them. Bring your dreams to McGill. Come stroll our downtown campus, set against the same mountain slope that inspired James McGill so many years ago.

The former principal's statement has since been removed from the university's website, but this sort of celebration of James McGill is typical of McGill's institutional discourse. It is available in several other places on the university's website, is mobilized in speeches and reports by administrators representing the university, and is reinforced by display practices on the downtown campus featuring various portraits and tributes to the university's "founding father." Reinforcing the notion of a European colonial inheritance passed on to students and faculty, alumni of the university are referred to as "McGillians," carrying forward a McGill (simultaneously man and institution) legacy into and across the contemporary world.

A prominent example of the display practices I am referring to is a tapestry that hangs near the entrance to the McLennan Library.[8] The left side of the tapestry offers a larger-than-life representation of James McGill, his gaze directing the reading of his legacy. A ship, signifying his journey from Scotland to Québec, and three stacked images on the right illustrate events highlighted in written text: "JAMES MCGILL; BORN 1744 GLASGOW; BEGAN FURTRADING 1767; FOUGHT IN WAR OF 1812; MARRIED MADAME DESRIVIERES 1776; BOUGHT BURNSIDE FARM 46 ACRES 1778; DIED 1813." The young McGill clutches his will in one hand, and with his other clutches to his breast the university founded after his death.

The top image on the right features a scene reminiscent of voyageurs and *coureurs des bois* (wood runners), unlicensed fur traders in New France who bypassed the French authorities and went into the woods to trade directly with the Indigenous peoples. The second frame. representing the war of 1812, shows what appear to be two British soldiers in red-and-white uniforms and an Indigenous man with brown skin, a strip of dark hair down the middle of his head. He wears sandals on his feet while the central soldier wears closed black shoes. The image is somewhat ambivalent about the relationship between the two men. The soldier's rifle is aimed at the head of the other man and the latter carries a tomahawk, suggesting he is ally as well as captive. The bottom frame depicts Burnside farm, completing a celebratory narrative of adventure, discovery, conquest, and cultivation that, like the principal's message, scripts students, faculty, and staff of the university into a colonial inheritance.

Far from simply being a harmless nod to history, the embedding of the persona of James McGill within the master-narratives of the university provides constant (sub)textual messages about who is and who is not meant to belong within the "McGill community." Understanding the tapestry as an active institutional text (rather than merely as a fixed object depicting *the* objective history of the university) allows us to consider how it appears to function descriptively (recalling particular selected highlights of James McGill's life), while also performing prescriptively, identifying "categories of persons and events that are not specified in terms of individuals."[9] Notably, McGill's "marriage to Madame Desrivières" (born Marie-Charlotte Guillimin) is mentioned in the word text but is not depicted. Within the European modernist conception of the human, the white bourgeois colonial man is the ideal subject of a universal mankind, while the European bourgeois woman is imagined "as someone who reproduced race and capital through her sexual purity, passivity, and being homebound in the service of the white, European, bourgeois man."[10] Within this very limited and limiting notion of the human, "Madame Desrivières" – subsequently known as "Madame McGill" – need not be seen in order to fulfil her supporting role in the story. In actuality Marie-Charlotte Guillimin was a member of the French elite by birth, a status elevated and secured through her first marriage at sixteen years old to wealthy colonial merchant Joseph-Amable Desrivières. McGill's marriage to her elevated his social status,[11] and in historical narrative helps to construct him as the embodiment of the overall settler colonial project and accompanying myth of two (European) founding races and nations. McGill's marriage to Desrivières thus extends his social capital and reinforces his identity as not only founding father of the university but "landed paterfamilias" of the settler colony.[12]

As Annie Coombes argues, white settler identities are made distinct from one another – Canadian, for example, as culturally distinct from New Zealander, South African, or Australian – through their perceptions and appropriations of the various Indigenous peoples and practices they encountered in the so-called New World.[13] The narrative of the tapestry reflects how the Canadian white settler self and nation are bound up with and rely on identification with both the European "old world" and with signifiers of Indigenousness unique to this part of Turtle Island and appropriated as Canadian. In sum, the tapestry enunciates and reconstructs a celebrated category of (white, European) conquering colonial patriarch, which relies on an ambivalent, incidental subcategory of Indigenous peoples. But where were Black people in this historical, founding narrative? The answer, of course, is that Black people were slaves, imported, exported, traded, and owned by James McGill and his fellow merchants.

Slavery and the Transatlantic Slave Economy

James McGill spent time in the American colonies after leaving Scotland and before he moved to Montreal upon joining the fur trade, and would have been well prepared to navigate trade relations between Europe, Québec, and Indigenous peoples. Frost explains that during his time in the Carolinas, McGill became familiar with the business of "capital and manufactured goods flowing from Britain, raw materials and produce flowing back from the colonies."[14] The British became "the absolute masters of the fur trade,"[15] aided significantly by their access to rum – produced out of molasses, first on the (British) island of Barbados and later in New England – that they traded with and used to exploit the Indigenous peoples with whom they did business.[16] Upon his arrival in Montreal, James McGill quickly established himself as a member of an elite group of "merchant princes" of Montreal, many of them Scottish born.[17]

The group of elite merchants to which James McGill belonged formed the leading class of slave owners in what is now Québec, during both the French and English regimes. "Merchants had ready cash, they traded with Amerindians, or they maintained commercial relations (sometimes secretly) with the Thirteen Colonies: they were thus the best-placed people to acquire slaves."[18] James McGill personally owned at least four slaves, two Panis (Indigenous) and two Black, between the late eighteenth and early nineteenth centuries.[19] His close long-term friend and business associate John Askin was the owner of twenty-three slaves, the most of all the English merchants.[20] Of the 1,574 slave owners identified by Trudel in his study of two hundred years of slavery in colonial Canada, Askin's slave holdings were exceeded only by the French Jesuits, who owned forty-six slaves, the Séminaire de Québec that owned thirty-one, and former governor general of New France Charles Beauharnois, who owned twenty-seven slaves.[21] J.I. Cooper claims that "throughout James McGill's career few persons were of greater significance than John Askin," with whom McGill's firms did extensive business over decades.[22] The two men were part of an extensive trade network between Montreal and Michigan, particularly around Detroit and Michilimackinac, where Askin lived. Askin's daughter Madeleine – the youngest of his children, born to an Indigenous slave – also lived with James McGill and his wife in Montreal for several years.[23]

In his biography of James McGill, Frost introduces McGill's involvement in slave trading as a matter of business transactions, noting that "as a merchant, McGill was obviously ready to accept 'any commission for a commission.'" He recounts:

> In 1787, [McGill] was reimbursed by the Department of Indian Affairs for various expenditures he had made in the government's interests, including a payment to a Jacques Lefrenier for the cost of four slaves, presumably Indians, whom Lefrenier had purchased to hand over to other Indians as replacements for those lost by the tribe in a battle, while fighting on the British side in the late war.[24]

Frost adds that the transaction represented the fulfilment of "a promise made by a local British commander." Negotiating national mythologies of Canadian exceptionalism that deny and diminish histories of slavery and the historical presence of Black people in Canada, he adds:

> This item from McGill's accounts reminds us that slavery, although not a prominent institution in Canada, nevertheless was not formally illegal in the province, and *existed widely among the Indians*. In the southern United States and in the West Indies, of course, enslavement of Africans and the use of indentured labour of men and women shipped from England were both recognized formally.[25]

When Frost does situate Black slaves in Canada and implicate McGill in the practice of slavery more directly, he does so in negotiation with this mythology. He acknowledges McGill's 1788 purchase of a "negress," while at the same time minimizing the conditions of slavery and absolving McGill as someone merely reflective of the era in which he lived:

> With regard to the institution of slavery, McGill must have been very familiar with it during his Indian trading years, and if he spent some years in the Carolinas, he lived in a society where slavery was very much part of the social fabric. When we hear that in 1788 he purchased from Jean Cavilhe at a cost of fifty-six pounds a negress named Sarah, aged about twenty-five, to be a servant in his household, it must be remembered that McGill was conforming to the mores of his time. He was generously ready to administer the city's care of foundlings and those adjudged insane, and he would, as we shall see, personally care for the widow and the orphan, but he was not a social reformer. No doubt Sarah was well treated in the McGill household, but the fact remains that she was purchased and owned as a slave. James McGill was a man of the eighteenth century, not of the twentieth.[26]

Frost's account is emblematic of narratives that minimize the severity of slavery in what today is Canada, trivialize and downplay the lived experiences of slaves, and further dehumanize Black and Indigenous peoples. Stories of the "niceness" of Canadian slavery ignore that enslaved people were exploited daily, risked their lives to run away, committed suicide, were raped and whipped and cut and burned, and were bought and sold, imprisoned, imported, and deported at the whims and to serve the interests of the people who owned them.[27]

Mobilizing this assumed good treatment of Canadian slaves, Frank Mackey, author of *Done with Slavery: The Black Fact in Montreal, 1760–1840*, is concerned with a phenomenon he refers to as "pseudo slavery," whereby slaves "who had come to feel like part of their master's family refused to leave" once they were no longer legally enslaved.[28] Mackey identifies one of James McGill's slaves, Jacques, in this way: "His attachment to prominent merchant and Executive Councillor James McGill and his family was such that he remained with them for twenty-five years after his master's death." Mackey adds that an "apocryphal story" – which he does not cite – identifies this same Jacques as possibly having been the last slave in the province, belonging to McGill's stepson François Desrivières as late as 1820. He also acknowledges that Marie-Charlotte McGill (Desrivières' mother) identified Jacques as "Jack, mon Domestique" in her will, leaving instructions for her son to "take 'Jack' under his wing and keep him in his service until his death."[29] Mackey concludes this passage by noting that at the time of Jacques's death in 1838 "he was identified ambiguously as 'negro of the late Honorable James McGill,' but no one would suggest that he was a slave at that late date."[30] Mackey's failure to consider slavery beyond its legal definition is striking. As a matter of law Black "freedom" has always been a matter of "relative freedom within unfreedom,"[31] particularly the "freedom" to be a worker.

Indeed, the Act for the Abolition of Slavery Throughout the British Colonies that officially ended slavery in Canada in 1834 ordered that slaves older than six years *"become and be* apprenticed Labourers" and continue to work for their previous owners until 1840.[32] Slaves were bound to this arrangement unless they were able to buy their way out of the apprenticeship earlier, essentially purchasing themselves.[33] In return for their work, apprenticed labourers were to be provided by their employers with "food, clothing, lodging, medicine, medical attendance, and such other maintenance and allowances," consistent with what the labourer would have received as a slave. The act is directed at the owner-employers and their rights: they remained entitled to the labourers' services with the right to transfer possession of said labourers "by bargain and sale, contract, deed, conveyance, will, or descent" as long as such transactions did not result in the separation of labourers from their immediate family members.[34] Furthermore, those who were "entitled to the services of slaves" who were "set free" by the act were entitled to be paid for their losses,[35] that is, essentially bought out in a shifting market economy. These legal conditions under which former slaves were "freed" do not even begin to speak to the complex impacts and reverberations of slavery on the enslaved and their descendants.

The reduction of James McGill's participation in slavery to a matter of his personal holdings of slaves and how they may or may not have been treated in his household directs attention away from the transatlantic slave trade and slave economy in which he was a critical participant and from which he benefited immensely. It also ignores potential slave holdings and trading activities of his firms. For example, we know that the North West Company that McGill co-founded and in which he held shares until 1784 owned slaves.[36] Returning to Frost's description of McGill's transaction with Jacques Lefrenier regarding four "presumably Indian" slaves, further research challenges Frost's account. Likely referring to the same transaction, Trudel acknowledges the purchase by Jacques Lafrenière in 1787 of "four *blacks* on behalf of the 'Département des Sauvages' or 'Indian Department,'" noting that "these slaves were destined to serve Amerindian masters."[37] From J.I. Cooper we further learn that "McGill was one of the most trusted advisers and suppliers of the Indian Department."[38] Moreover, the Indian Department relied on McGill for "assistance in securing specialized supplies" such as tobacco, and "to provide Negro slaves to replace slaves that the Indians had lost."[39] Rather than an example of how slavery "existed widely among the Indians" as Frost claims, then, the Lafrenière example provides one record of a common practice of the fur traders. This points to the greater significance of McGill's and other merchants' uses of slaves and slave labour as they competed with and built upon one another's networks and businesses, increased their wealth, expanded the reach of the British Empire, and developed the economic, social, and political foundations of several major Canadian institutions.

Into the nineteenth century, James McGill and his business partners traded in a variety of merchandise acquired and produced through the transatlantic slave economy such as rum, tobacco, molasses, and cotton.[40] As was typical of colonial merchants of the time, McGill also functioned as a banker, using reserves of capital to make loans and accept mortgages.[41] Such loans and mortgages enabled the purchasing of (among other "things") slaves by "prospective buyers with neither the cash nor goods to barter."[42] This permitted the extension of slave

ownership to all levels of Québec society as "a form of public extrava-
gance which conferred prestige on to members of high society but also
to all levels of society indulging in it."[43]

Deeply loyal to the British crown, McGill also served as a colonel
in the Montreal militia and held powerful political positions in what
in 1791 became Lower Canada, serving as justice of the peace and as
a member of the legislative assembly. Given the ways in which their
fortunes were dependent on the slave economy, it is perhaps hardly
surprising that McGill and his associates used their power to oppose
attempts to introduce abolition legislation at the end of the eighteenth
century. In April 1793 the House of Assembly killed a bill proposing
abolition, with "a large majority of members" favouring that the institution of slavery be maintained.[44] McGill was among twelve highly influential men in the fifty-member House of Assembly of Lower Canada
who "were, or would become slave owners." Hence slavery in Canada
was abolished slowly, with great concern for the "ownership rights"
and satisfaction of the slave owners.[45]

The University and Its Sponsors

McGill College, as the school was then known, was established at the
beginning of the nineteenth century, but it would not have survived
were it not for the settler colonial networks and power that James
McGill had helped to build. He had arguably been the most notable
of the merchants and professionals who owned estates on the side of
Mount Royal. These men were known as "gentlemen farmers" whose
expansive properties served "as summer residences, where they could
enjoy the fine views and fresh air and harvest crops without any pre-
tence of making a living of it."[46] Following McGill's generation, the
college on his former estate and the image of the "gentleman farmer"
continued to play a crucial role in attracting the wealthy anglophone
class into the area that would become known as the Golden Square
Mile during the transition to industrial capitalism.[47]

McGill College first reached out to Montreal's private citizens for
support in 1856, and as Frost describes, "the responses were ready and
generous ... [as] English-speaking Montreal began to take a proprietary
pride in developing the institution. McGill became very much 'our university.'"[48] To be clear, Frost's "our" refers to British (especially Scottish)
anglophone businessmen and their families, from whose philanthropy
and service as chancellors and other members of the board of governors
the university benefited enormously. Before addressing these benefactors, however, I hasten to note that in the mid-nineteenth century the

university was granted a forty-thousand-dollar loan from the Province of Canada, eight thousand dollars of which was "borrowed" from the Six Nations Trust Fund held by the colonial government.[49] The fund had been established through the sale of land,[50] and was "to be accounted for and invested by the Indian Department and a Crown-appointed trustee for the benefit of Six Nations."[51] McGill University was one of several national institutions that received "loans" from Six Nations accounts without permission or repayment; a 2006 exposé published by *Windspeaker* identifies unauthorized loans totalling tens of thousands of dollars taken from Six Nations funds for which there are no records of repayment.[52]

The presence and development of the McGill property was critical to the creation of the Golden Square Mile in the later 1850s and 1860s.[53] In addition to how the university's landscaping enhanced the surrounding community, the institution helped to secure the area as almost exclusively anglophone owned and predominantly Protestant. These landowners typically owned estates that stretched from the summit of the mountain all the way down to the escarpment[54] that separated the haves from have-nots, or "the city above the hill" from "the city below the hill."[55] Below the hill was where the masses lived, for the most part in poverty. It was home to the Irish working class (particularly the area now known as Griffintown) and was where, in the St. Antoine District (now Little Burgundy), Montreal's first Black community developed.[56] The language of "two cities" is important; it underscores the interlocking relations of race, class, and gender that characterized this geographic division. The only members of the working class that ventured into the Golden Square Mile were the servants of the Anglo-Protestant elite, particularly women domestic workers.[57] As Ames tellingly described it at the end of the nineteenth century:

> Most of the residents of the upper city know little – and at times seem to care less – regarding their fellow men in the city below. To many of the former the condition of the latter is as little known as that of natives in Central Africa.[58]

During the late nineteenth century, McGill principal John William Dawson secured several key members of the "above the hill" community as major benefactors of the university. Thereafter, much of the land, buildings, and collections and millions of the dollars that built up the university came from families such as the Molsons and Redpaths, as well as Sir Donald A. Smith (Lord Strathcona) and Sir William Macdonald. These families and other members of the anglophone elite would carry the institution into the middle of the twentieth century, beginning with William Molson, at the time a McGill governor, who funded the restoration of the Arts Building and construction of its west wing and corridors.[59]

Both the Redpath and Macdonald fortunes, accumulated through the sugar and tobacco industries respectively, were directly based on the Southern slave plantation economies. As sole owner of Macdonald Tobacco Company, Macdonald also benefited from exploitative labour conditions in Québec. His factory employed roughly a thousand urban, Catholic, French-speaking workers (including children under the legal work age of the time) for whom Macdonald had little concern.[60] When "asked if he had considered schemes to share profits with his workers, Macdonald replied: 'I have really been very desirous to do it, but cannot see how it is going to be brought about with any degree of safety to the capitalist.'"[61] McGill University was the primary recipient of Macdonald's philanthropy; in all, "Macdonald's gifts and bequests to McGill exceeded $13,000,000."[62]

The Redpaths were not the only sugar barons who were major supporters of the university. Most notably, John Wilson McConnell was vice president and a majority shareholder of St. Lawrence Sugar refinery, as well as owner and publisher of the *Montreal Star*. Beginning in 1911, McConnell was "an extremely effective fundraiser for McGill" and was "the greatest individual benefactor to McGill from 1920 onwards."[63]

McGill Lineage

From the very conditions of its establishment, McGill University can be understood as having been an institutional signifier of British imperial victory over the French and a site of the competing white settler nationalisms that continue to characterize Québécois-Canadian politics.

James McGill did not have any biological children, and the endowment for a university named after him reflected his concern about ensuring the continuity of the McGill family name.[64] The conditions of McGill's bequest required the Royal Institution for the Advancement of Learning to establish the college within ten years of his death, and failure to do so within this time would result in the money and property being given to his stepson, François Desrivières. Desrivières, who had been one of McGill's business partners, contested the bequest for the college, claiming the ten thousand pounds was rightfully his, and refused to vacate the property for several years.[65] In the extensive litigation that ensued, Desrivières became "a symbol of French Catholic opposition" to the powerful Anglo-Protestant establishment at the time.

When eventually he lost the legal battle with the Royal Institution for the Advancement of Learning, Desrivières was left in financial ruin.[66]

The extended period of litigation surrounding the execution of James McGill's will and the establishment of the university meant that the school did not begin to hold classes until thirty years after McGill's death. The first two principals of the university – George Jehoshaphat Mountain from 1824 to 1835 and John Bethune from 1835 to 1846 – were Anglican clergymen associated with the Church of England. In 1852 the trustees of the Royal Institute became the board of governors of McGill University, facilitating a shift in control of the university from Anglican clergymen to "merchants and professional men."[67] After the Royal Institution became a corporation, the statutes of the university from 1864 to 1934 dictated that "all members of the Board of Governors of McGill College must be lay members of one or the other of the Protestant denominations in the Province of Lower Canada."[68] These changes set the conditions for an era of significant foundation building, growth, and expansion that would solidify the university's (self-)perception as the "greatest educational achievement of Scotchmen in the American hemisphere" by the end of the century.[69]

For the sixty-four years from 1855 until 1919, McGill University had two principals: Sir John William Dawson (1855–93) and Sir William Peterson (1895–1919). Both Dawson and Peterson were of Scottish origin and both had studied at Edinburgh University in Scotland. Dawson has been described as "the man who made McGill" during his nearly four decades as principal of the university and as the founder and first principal of McGill's Normal School (later the Faculty of Education) for teacher training.[70] As "the colonial principal of a colonial university,"[71] Dawson's views on education were highly influenced by his close friend and mentor Egerton Ryerson, chief superintendent of education in Upper Canada, whose suggestions regarding a separate school system for Indigenous children directly informed the development of Canada's residential school system.[72]

During Dawson's time as principal, James McGill's remains were returned to what had been his Burnside estate. Following his death in 1813 McGill had been buried in the nearby Protestant cemetery; however, the City of Montreal had decided to turn the cemetery into a public square and encouraged family members of the deceased buried there to relocate their family members' remains to Mount Royal Cemetery. The university had the skull and remaining bones of James McGill's body exhumed and relocated to the university campus along with the monument that had marked his grave. The Anglican bishop of Montreal consecrated the patch of land outside of the Arts Building where McGill was laid to rest once more.[73] Soon after the burial, "official McGill songs emerged to express the pride alumni felt for their founder":

> James McGill, James, McGill,
> Peacefully he slumbers there,
> Blissful, though we're on the tear.
> James McGill, James McGill,
> He's our father, oh yes, rather,
> James McGill![74]

Thus, by the twentieth century James McGill's wishes had been realized and the university was well established. Following Dawson's tenure as principal, Peterson's strong imperialist loyalties ensured that the university continued to expand and entrench itself "as a microcosm of which Montreal, Canada and the Empire were the progressively larger manifestations."[75] Peterson guided McGill University into the twentieth century, ensuring its place within "an imperial academic community that straddled the distances of empire," and understood academia in the United Kingdom and the settlement colonies as one extended, though by no means homogeneous, British sphere.[76] Peterson represented McGill at the 1903 Allied Colonial Universities' Conference in London, the goal of which was to institutionalize what was seen as "already existing imperial ties and to 'make [them] effective for practical purposes.'"[77] By then, the settler colonial universities were understood as "a community of shared culture, shared race, shared values and shared interest,"[78] an extension of the British Empire and of the racialized, gendered, and class cultures of British academia. These shared ideals and interests continue to be promoted throughout the institutional texts of the university and the way in which they are mobilized as policy and practice to uphold relations of settler colonialism and racial capitalism. "Racial capitalism" describes the "development, organization, and expansion of capitalist society" through structural racial inequity. As Jodi Melamed succinctly puts it, "capital can only be capital when it is accumulating, and it can only accumulate by producing and moving through relations of severe inequality among human groups."[79] In other words, all capitalism is racial, in that racism naturalizes and secures the differentiation of human value and disposability of some lives – for example Black lives, Indigenous lives – that capitalism requires. Universities are directly implicated in producing, maintaining, and reproducing these relations.

3

Trying to Keep Canada White and the Power to Write History

As one critic has suggested, nations themselves *are* narrations. The power to narrate, or to block other narratives from forming and emerging, is very important to culture and imperialism, and constitutes one of the main connections between them.[1]

From the beginning of the settler nation, the assumed whiteness of Canada was consciously constructed and embedded in a national culture fuelled by narratives of British imperial greatness and heroic, white male, rugged individualism.[2] John A. Macdonald, Canada's first prime minister (1867–73), made it clear that racialized people – particularly Blacks and Asians – were not welcome in Canada,[3] citing their incompatibility with European civilizations and his commitment to protecting and maintaining "the Aryan character of the future of British America."[4] For some, such as lawyer and anthropologist Robert G. Haliburton, the new Dominion consisted of a unique union of "men of the North" who were descended from the "Northern races," which in addition to the Saxon included the Celtic, Teutonic, Scandinavian, and Norman French.[5] Imperialists such as Stephen Leacock and Andrew Macphail, however, were committed to maintaining the assumed "purity" of the Anglo-Saxon "race" and passionately opposed to all manner of "race mixing," including that between Anglo-Saxon and east-central Europeans.[6] In both positions, it was a given that Canadians were of European and Christian ancestry, and the lingering presence of Indigenous peoples and increasing presence of Jewish, Black, and Asian people were seen as problems.

Throughout the first decades of the twentieth century up until the Second World War, academics were among the greatest proponents of racial nationalism, anti-Semitism, and anti-immigration politics.[7]

Leacock and Macphail were both professors at McGill, Leacock in economics and political science (1900–1936) and Macphail (who had also completed his undergraduate and medical school there) as the first professor of medical history (1907–37). The two men were close friends, staunchly conservative imperialists, outspoken writers, and high-profile public speakers known for their anti-immigrant, anti-feminist, and anti-American politics.[8] They were among the leading proponents of a Canadian nationalism defined by assumptions of Anglo-Saxon racial purity and moral superiority, opposed to "race mixing" even among Europeans. The ideal citizen was the Christian white male, while Canada's "northern" geography and climate were thought to make it the "natural" new homeland of the "dominant race."[9] This widely held belief was used to naturalize and justify British imperialism.[10] Leacock was among the powerful voices in the country who argued that the "southern races" were unsuited for the Canadian climate and should not be permitted to immigrate,[11] delicately balancing the need for exploitable labour with the desire to keep Canada a "white man's country."[12]

As concerns regarding the flow of non-British immigrants into Canada increased, the discretionary authority of immigration officials was expanded in 1906 to deny entry to those considered "non-assimilable" into British culture,[13] particularly immigrants of Asian and African descent. Moral panic around maintaining the "purity" of the British character of Canada fuelled and was fuelled by racist, heteropatriarchal ideas about Jewish, Black, and Asian sexuality and the fear of miscegenation, highlighting the deep interconnectedness of relations of race, gender, sexuality, culture, class, and spirituality in nation building.[14] Subsequently, the Immigration Act of 1910 included a clause refusing entry to applicants of "any race deemed unsuited to the climate or requirements of Canada,"[15] as well as persons deemed mentally or physically "defective" and "prostitutes and women and girls coming to Canada for immoral purposes."[16] So concerned were officials that Canada not have to face its own "negro problem" due to Blacks immigrating from the United States that in 1911 an Order in Council was passed specifically prohibiting Black people from entering the country, identifying them as "unsuited to the climate and requirements of Canada."[17]

During the 1920s and 1930s, a range of right-wing nationalist and white supremacist organizations formed throughout the country, and anti-Semitism and racism were widespread among anglophone and francophone, Protestant and Catholic alike.[18] In Québec a French Canadian nationalist movement had formed under the mentorship of Lionel Groulx, a priest, historian, and professor at the Université de Montréal from 1915 to 1949.[19] Groulx promoted the colonial achievements of the French "race" and *la survivance* of French language, culture, tradition, and faith,[20] becoming the "spokesman for a profoundly conservative nationalism" that would influence generations of French Canadian intellectuals to come.[21] Concerned with tradition and with maintaining the assumed biological and moral "purity" of the French "race," Groulx was virulently against interracial mixing as well as the capitalist economic pursuits of the British and Americans. In constructing narratives of French Canadian racial purity and tradition, Groulx and other prominent historians such as François-Xavier Garneau omitted reference to slavery in New France and essentially wrote Black presence out of Québec national history altogether.[22] Then as now, the primary basis of uniting the far right was a belief in and commitment to "keeping Canada white."[23]

McGill and the Modernization of Québec

From 1931 to 1961, although Montreal's anglophone elite continued to dominate Québec economically, migration from the rural areas of the province doubled the city's French population, increasing the number of unilingual French speakers and decreasing the rate of bilingualism.[24] Particularly with Maurice Duplessis as premier of Québec from 1936 to 1939 and 1944 to 1959, English-speaking businessmen enjoyed a "pattern of elite accommodation" with francophone politicians that entailed a "certain deference toward English and an acceptance of Montreal as a bilingual city in which French was a subordinate language."[25] McGill University was one of the most visible symbols of ongoing Anglo-Protestant economic and political power, and J.W. McConnell – McGill governor from 1928 to 1958 – enjoyed a "particularly close" relationship with Duplessis.[26] By the late 1950s, however, a new French middle class had emerged from within Université Laval, Université de Montréal, and Montreal's cultural industries. From the new urban French middle class came "the québécisation of the French-Canadian national identity"[27] and a movement to "reconquer" Montreal; "Francophones could never be 'maîtres chez nous'" if Montreal, the urban centre of French-speaking Québec, remained dominated by the anglophone-Protestant elite.[28]

At the start of the 1960s, arrangements of anglophone-francophone elite accommodation came under threat by the displacement of the traditional francophone elite and a burgeoning secular movement promoting the cultural and economic interests of the broader French Québécois population. In this emerging context of social, cultural, economic, and political upheaval and transition that threatened Anglo-Protestant dominance, McGill University's board of governors shifted their dominant narrative to one that promoted bilingualism. They asserted, "in fact, the Western world is one, troubled but simultaneously enriched by linguistic differences. Our universities have a common heritage, to which they owe a common allegiance."[29] In making their case, the board drew on the writings of McGill professor of English and celebrated Canadian novelist Hugh MacLennan. Particularly helpful in this regard was a collection published by MacLennan in 1960 based on the argument that McGill University had been too quiet about "her" past, particularly about the "great men who were associated with her. She hardly takes any credit for them."[30]

MacLennan taught in the English department at McGill from 1951 to 1980, and joins Stephen Leacock as one of twelve "pioneers" celebrated on the McGill website. MacLennan, born in Nova Scotia of Scottish ancestry, is noted for helping "to develop a literature that was distinctively Canadian" and "to define a country in the imagination of its citizens."[31] He thought of himself as "a partial outsider" to McGill,[32] but the university seems to have captured his imagination and filled him with Scottish-Canadian pride:

> If Quebec is the enduring French Fact in America, this university, first in the Commonwealth to be granted a charter outside of the home islands, is the most valuable enduring product of the Scottish Fact embedded in the core of Quebec since Wolfe's Highlanders stormed the citadel.[33]

For MacLennan, the "original Canadians – French, Scots and United Empire Loyalists" – had heroically come together to build the economy and civic institutions of Montreal; however, "if it had not been for the astounding energy of a small group of great men," including James McGill, "the Canadian nation would never have existed."[34] His timely book about the university marked the beginning of a contemporary institutional project of constructing and documenting McGill's formal institutional history, notably around the identity of James McGill.

The "Brief to The Royal Commission on Education of the Province of Quebec, submitted under the authority of the McGill Board of Governors, with the approval of Senate, November 29th, 1961" demonstrates MacLennan's direct contribution to institutional discourses and political strategizing. The brief draws on MacLennan's claim that largely due to having to cope with the tensions produced by the English and French "races" living in the same city, "what Montrealers know best about one another they never say in public."[35] Mobilizing "the romantic mytho-historical narrative of Canada" to which MacLennan's writing had significantly contributed,[36] the board describes the French and English as the "two greatest cultural inheritances in the West, ... two cultures who precisely complement one another and who exhibit a common origin transcending the English Channel."[37] The brief describes McGill and Université de Montréal as generally isolated from one another and asserts the need for a "far greater degree of contact between the two groups of universities."[38] The board asserts that the need for this increased contact is underscored by both "the Communist Revolution that still bedevils the world, and threatens our Western Christian society" and a responsibility to "help the underdeveloped countries," particularly through providing them with access to Western education:

> It is no good pouring money into a country that lacks the institutions, the educated class, and even the plain personal honesty necessary to spend it well. The paramount need is for education, for a class of men within each country willing and able to drag their fellow nationals into the modern age.[39]

The tone of the document exemplifies an approach to and perspective on "underdeveloped countries" characterized by notions of Western superiority, benevolence, charity, and a white man's burden to help Others, elsewhere, to become "civilized." I address the persistence of this approach to the African continent at the university further in the chapters that follow.

Anticolonial Resistance and Black Power

As noted in chapter 1, the 1960s were an era of social-political uprising in Québec as they were elsewhere in Canada and across the world.[40] McGill was deeply implicated in and a target of the new Québec nationalist movement and was affected by changes to the postsecondary education system.[41] By 1968, the university was a volatile political environment with a Radical Student Alliance of several leftist groups creating regular and escalating disruptions on campus.[42] Black students at McGill and SGWU were also organizing and mobilizing during this time around anticolonial, antiracist, Marxist analyses of Canadian politics at home and abroad. By the time some of them organized a Congress of Black Writers at McGill in October 1968, their work had gained the attention of senior administrators of the universities, and rightly so – as the front page of the 27 September issue of *The McGill Daily* announced, "Black Power is coming!"

Among the invited speakers were four high-profile young Black American activists of the day: Stokely Carmichael, Eldridge Cleaver, H. Rap Brown, and Leroi Jones. Hardly downplaying the militancy of these men, the cover story in the *Daily* describes the problem of getting Carmichael, Jones, Brown, and Cleaver into the country given that all four were "under prosecution and persecution" by various US state agencies.[43] Cleaver was in the midst of a highly publicized battle with the University of California-Berkeley and then Governor Ronald Reagan over his right to teach there, a case that was followed closely in the *Daily*. In the end, Carmichael would be the only one of the four to speak at the congress at McGill, explaining the absence of the other invitees in his keynote speech: "one thing the Americans don't want," he said, "is the black man making international ties."[44] Indeed, such international ties were being made, and were most certainly a concern of both the United States and Canadian governments. The student organizers as well as the congress itself were closely surveilled by government agents.[45] As one of the original organizers of the congress, BT relates in our interview that in the weeks and months leading up to the conference there were increasing concerns about the presence of government agents and accusations about who was "a puppet for the CIA." He explains:

> You've *always* got to look out for infiltration. The morning I went to introduce Stokely, one of those guys [whose role and motives had been called into question] looked at me and says: "You're not introducing anyone." And I said, "Who are you, Superman?" There's the guy and I went straight in. And I introduced Stokely. There was a lot of dissent. We don't know who infiltrated that group. *A lot of people* infiltrated that conference.

On the Monday following the weekend of the congress, a picture of Carmichael with Black Canadian activist Rocky Jones shielding him from photographers appeared on the front page of the *Daily* with the headline "Stokely Preaches Violent Revolution."[46] Despite the sensationalism, however, for many it was James Forman of the Student Nonviolent Coordinating Committee and Pan Africanist C.L.R. James who left the most lasting impression, having "put the question of race in a wider context, that of a broad socialist revolution."[47] As BT recalls with excitement almost fifty years later:

> It was very heated, it was very, very [powerful] in the sense that I remember coming out of there when C.L.R. James spoke and I see all

these young white girls *crying*, man, saying, "we didn't know this, we didn't know anything about this! This was a traumatic experience because I can't believe what I just heard!" Because C.L.R. James was a guy, when he starts to speak he could be speaking for four hours, no notes, and you didn't hear anything repeated. He was *prolific*! He wrote things like the *Black Jacobins* where he way goes back in history and tells you Napoleon was – read the books, you know where Napoleon was defeated? In Santo Domingo. That's where he lost so many people. But you won't see that in no book no white person wrote. They say he was defeated at some other place. It's true – our whole history, everything that we learned is corruption of our history.

BT's recollection captures the importance of C.L.R. James's speech and of the congress overall, especially but not exclusively to Black students who attended. While the dominant framing of the congress had placed it within the American Black Power movement of the day, BT and other organizers understood the event as part of a tradition of Black intellectuals and artists from across the diaspora coming together to share ideas. He explains, "We had three main conferences that took place before the Black Writers Congress [of 1968]: one was in Europe in the fifties, there was a second one, and ours was the third one." BT's use of "we" to refer to the first Congress of Black Writers and Artists held in Paris in 1956 and the second held in Rome in 1959 reflects his sense of belonging to a diasporic Black/African community that was making history. He arrived at our interview with several pieces of memorabilia from the era, including his copy of *Let the Niggers Burn*,[48] to make sure I was familiar with the book that he and fellow Black students had written and published about this historic moment punctuated by the congress and the uprising at SGWU that would follow months later.

The radical Black politics and tone of the congress further inspired and informed the analysis of students waiting for the SGWU administration to act in response to their allegations of incompetence and racist practices on the part of one of their instructors.[49] Students at McGill – and no doubt senior administrators and professors as well – followed the unfolding events at SGWU closely, and Black students continued to organize across the two universities as what began as a complaint about one teacher grew into a campaign exposing and confronting the systemic racism of the institution. The situation came to a head on 29 January 1969 when over two hundred students took over the SGWU computer centre and later the faculty club.

For the duration of the thirteen-day standoff between student activists (including several McGill students) and the SGWU administration that ensued, rallies in support of the students were organized on McGill campus and McGill students marched from their downtown campus to SGWU in solidarity. The McGill West Indian Students' Society brought and passed motions at the Students' Society at McGill condemning the behaviour of the SGWU administration and requesting that $660 from the Students' Society be given to the Debating Union to initiate an "informal Black Studies program."[50] Student associations at the Université Laval and Université de Montréal also issued official statements of support for the SGWU students.[51] Halifax native Rocky Jones, who had spoken at the Congress of Black Writers and had close ties to the Black Power movement in the United States, spoke at a rally in the hallway outside of the SGWU computer centre a week into the action, calling for national and international support for the students and pledging "to drum up outside support for the occupation including '200 busloads of people' if necessary."[52]

For two weeks the *Daily* featured front-page stories about what was happening at Sir George. While direct links were not always explicitly made between the struggles taking place at SGWU and those of radical white student activists at McGill, in several cases the reporting suggests or reveals how university administrations were themselves organizing and collaborating with one another, police, government agents, and at times with conservative student groups to suppress leftist student activism. The takeover[53] of the computer centre at SGWU finally ended when riot police entered the building to evict the students on 11 February. During the eviction a fire was set, the computer centre was destroyed, and ninety-seven students (forty-two of whom were Black) were arrested. The *Daily* continued to print updates on the subsequent trials of activists who faced criminal charges, several of whom were enrolled at McGill, as well as letters from various students and community members expressing their thoughts about what had happened. Referring to the events of 11 February as a "tragedy,"[54] the coverage was considerably more cautious in tone than in previous weeks, a point not lost on a Black student named Marguerite J. Alfred. Alfred wrote back to the paper, reminding everyone that "this 'tragedy' occurred because a weak and incompetent Administration panicked and mishandled" the situation and that the events had "lifted the façade – the myth – of Canadian justice and racial harmony."[55]

For Black students across cultural and class backgrounds and levels of study, the events at Sir George affirmed lived experiences of racism in Québec schools and situated them within a transnational movement of Black educational activism. For GR and other international students at McGill, the events facilitated the building of relationships within

Montreal's Black community and created a sense of responsibility to mentor a younger generation of local students. GR recalls that there had been "no connection" between Black students and the local community: "We didn't know people in the Black community, they didn't know us." The events at Sir George changed that:

I think what the Sir George Williams Affair did, those of us who were in academia then sort of discovered that there was a [local] Black community here; people actually went into the schools and invited kids to come and meet us. And that's how I ended up meeting these kids at Trinidad House; they'd come straight from school at the end of the day. And they were curious because they wanted to see what was going on, and then they found out about the music. They'd had some idea about it but didn't know much about it, but to them, they suddenly began to talk to you: "What are you doing?" "Where do you come from?" "What are you studying?" ... And the other point is that the guys who were charged in the Sir George Williams Affair couldn't work, they had no income, and what happened is that a lot of people in the Black community, the older Black community, these women would get together and cook masses of food and have a kind of a rent party almost. And raise funds for these guys, to support them. That's how they were supported. So it brought the community together in a really, really strong way. And I think it changed all of us. It changed us. And it changed the community.

For the majority of McGill's student body, however, the confrontation with riot police and property destruction at SGWU – not to mention the RCMP's taking control of the SGWU building and one of the Concordia student newspapers – seems to have crossed a line. The Students' Society passed a motion "deploring the excessive violence on the part of the students who participated in the occupation" and urging "students to attempt to use the existing constitutional channels in seeking to bring about changes in the university."[56] Nevertheless, McGill would not be spared its own escalation involving riot police and multiple arrests within just a few weeks. On 28 March activist Stanley Gray – by then fired from his lecturing position at the university – and Québec nationalist Raymond Lemieux led ten thousand protesters including students and labour union activists in Opération McGill français, marching on McGill's downtown campus and demanding that the university become a pro-worker, francophone Québécois institution.[57]

During this time, McGill University established an African Studies program, said to be the first such program in Canada. McGill's historian describes the program as the result of "a confluence of academic interests from anthropology, history, political science, and other social science disciplines."[58] In documenting the university's history he mentions the establishment of the program only briefly, stating, "Studies in the culture of African nations, which were in general without strong representation in Montreal and lacked effective governments to promote their interests, developed more slowly" at McGill. He adds:

> It is somewhat ironic that a similar Canadian Studies program was not established until 1972, but the answer might lie with those who contended that such a program was superfluous because the relevant departments were already fulfilling the function without the need for further academic bureaucracy.[59]

Frost's comments suggest his disdain for what he described as "the preponderance of non–Anglo-Saxon teachers, researchers and students in the lecture rooms and laboratories of McGill of the 1960s" as the university struggled to adjust to a new social-political reality in Québec.[60]

In the fall semester following the uprising at Sir Georges, several professors and students from McGill participated in an international conference of the African Studies Association (ASA), held at the Queen Elizabeth Hotel in downtown Montreal. The conference took place 15–18 October 1969 and was repeatedly disrupted by the Black Caucus, a group of students and faculty from US and Canadian universities, including several students who had been involved in the Congress of Black Writers and SGWU Affair. On the second day of the conference, members of the caucus interrupted the plenary session, asserting that the conference was being run by Western interests and shaped by "pro-colonialist and neo-colonialist ideological bias."[61] Referring to the aftermath of the events at SGWU, the protesters argued that the conference did not relate to "the serious problems" confronting Black students and the Montreal Black community in general.[62] Members of the caucus returned on the third day and disrupted multiple sessions, demanding the conference be suspended until the board of governors met to discuss their demands: that the all-white ASA board of trustees be reconstituted with equal representation of Africans, that changes be made in the ASA to facilitate greater participation of African scholars, and that the ASA provide financial support to the SGWU students facing criminal charges, whom the activists described as "political prisoners of a colonialist government."[63] The position and demands of caucus members relied on their use of "African" in referring to all Black people: hence the ASA's responsibility to address and be accountable to issues and members of the African diaspora. This conception of the relation between "Black" and "African," which I discuss further below, was not readily accepted by all, and some of the conference attendees challenged the activists to explain this assertion.[64] According to one report, the activists were confronted in this regard by the ambassador of Senegal and were asked by some African students whether they had ever been to Africa.[65] The Black Caucus ultimately shifted the content and tone of the conference, exposing sharp divisions within the ASA. The fellows of the ASA, described in one report as "the upper layers of a white-dominated academic elite," voted against equal Black and white (African and European) representation on the board, while agreeing to provide support to the SGWU activists.[66]

The following week, two McGill graduate student members of the Black Caucus, Rosie Douglas and Carl Parris, published a full-page article in the *Daily* defending "disruption as a means of self-determination for Black people." They defended their position against the ASA, arguing that "the development of new methods of control" required particular attention to "those neo-colonialist agencies (ASA) financed by imperial interests, whose goal has always been and still is the continued colonization and dehumanization of African people."[67] Asserting that "there is no longer a middle ground," they called on Black people to stand against "organized violence" be it from "the State department or the ASA" and called on white allies to tend to rooting out racism within their own communities.[68]

While the article does not explicitly address their use of the term "Africans" to refer to all Black people, Douglas and Parris's analysis suggests that they understood Black peoples as colonized Africans turned first into slaves and then into a Black underclass. For Black people in the diaspora, embracing an "African" identity – often in the absence of specific knowledge of one's personal African ancestral origins – has been a means of rejecting Eurocentrism and resisting white supremacy. Black liberation politics since the nineteenth century has variously promoted Black/African cultural pride, a racially defined sense of nationhood, Black social and economic solidarity, Black armed self-defence, and the return of Black people to the African continent. While various Africentric activists and movements have been critiqued for promoting racial essentialism and romanticized notions of Africa,[69] they have also provided critical counter-narratives to colonial propaganda presenting the continent as the antithesis of civilization and progress and Black people as less-than-human and unintelligent. Moreover, the continual erasure from memory of the colonization of African countries and dispossession of African people from land reinforces the notion of Black people as the property of Europe and its settler nations and undermines solidarities in anticolonial struggle.[70] The students pressured the ASA to recognize the Black diaspora in this way, while at the same time they continued to promote Black Studies as a critical social-political project distinct from area studies.

In a February 1970 article in the *Daily*, Black student activist Dennis Forsythe described "a movement to institute a Black Studies Program at McGill" that had been underway for "some months,"[71] reasserting some of the same arguments made by the Black Caucus months earlier. Forsythe asserted that "whites are still committed to the principle of whites speaking for blacks" and that ongoing resistance to Black Studies at McGill reflected the desire to maintain the "convenient cover-up" of being able to claim ignorance about Black peoples and histories. Forsythe identified himself as one of several student members of a "subcommittee of the Academic subcommittee" set up by the university's vice principal "to look into the matter of Black Studies."[72] Carl Parris was also a member of the subcommittee, and wrote a follow-up article two weeks later expressing frustration that the process was already taking too long.[73] By 5 March, the chairman of the subcommittee and dean of the Faculty of Arts and Science made it clear that a Black Studies program was not a priority at McGill, clarifying that "setting up the committee does not mean we give the program priority." The dean asserted that the subcommittee had been set up upon the request of a group of staff and students, and one of its roles was to consider whether Black Studies or a Canadian Affairs program that would include study of "Indian, Eskimo and Métis Affairs" should have priority. The dean felt that a Black Studies program was "not justified at the moment" and vaguely referred to the newly created African Studies program in noting "parts of African Studies are included in the concept of Black Studies."[74]

As in Stanley Frost's historical writing, here the dean asserts a "natural" hierarchy of belonging in Canada and a prioritizing of "Canadian Studies" that, it is implied, is not about Africans/Black people. While Frost would find it "ironic" that the Canadian Studies program was to be established at a later date than African Studies, the dean's comments suggest how the administration used the African Studies program to resist demands for the formal study of Blackness and African diaspora peoples in Canada. The formation of African Studies in the aftermath of the SGWU Affair allowed McGill administrators to posit it as a response to the demands of Black students while preserving dominant narratives of Canada as "white" and Black people and anticolonial struggle as foreign. The student activists calling for Black Studies understood Canada as a settler colonial project, an extension of the British Empire, implicated in the local, national, and international oppression of Black, Indigenous, and Third World peoples. A Black Studies program would necessarily reveal histories and legacies of setter colonialism and slavery in Canada, challenging dominant myths of Canadian whiteness and benevolence. In September 1970, student-activists formed the Black Students Association in response to "being fucked around left, right and centre at McGill" by institutional bureaucracy and racism.[75] Demonstrating their awareness of the broader movements of which they were a part, the students vowed to work with Black student groups across Canada. As I examine in chapters 5 and 6, the Black Students Association and the Black Student Network that followed it would carry on the struggle for Black Studies at the university for decades to come.

Some members of the English-speaking white professoriate and administration at McGill were quite open in expressing the resentment they felt towards the leftist political movements of the sixties and seventies, and their impact on higher education.[76] For example, Hugh MacLennan expressed his contempt for the uprisings in a 1972 television interview with the CBC. In his opinion, "no matter how disreputable" Montreal had been in the past, it had always been "a very amiable place" until "the last two or three years." MacLennan lamented that as a professor at McGill, he found himself "swimming in the broth of students" who didn't appreciate and indeed were "absolutely hostile" towards the capitalist society that they were set to inherit. The British colonial nostalgia that MacLennan communicates in the interview is quite remarkable, perhaps no better captured than when he ventures to address the issue of racism:

> This question of racism, I think we'd agree, in some aspects it can be merely humorous, but when it gets like what we've seen in this century it's about as bad as you can get anywhere. I mean, you don't have to go into it; look at Hitler. But that is different again from what we overlook in American history, which was chattel slavery. Based on colour, slavery was – this is going to shock anybody who's listening, but if anybody asks me what was the greatest institutional invention ever made to advance civilization I would have to say slavery.[77]

MacLennan's comments do more than reflect his sense of white supremacy and entitlement. They also speak to his awareness that the assumptions regarding this privileged status were under threat.

A former student I interviewed, JN, recalls an incident in an English literature class taught by MacLennan in the early 1970s that suggests both how MacLennan's racial ideas were communicated in the classroom, and how he was being challenged by an informed and newly empowered Black student population:

> I still remember, [MacLennan] was talking about one of his many – I mean the man had a tendency to wax lyrical and drop names in the most ferocious way! And he talked about being at some kind of dinner gathering which included Julius Nyerere I believe, and a number who we'd see as prominent African government leaders who had led liberation struggles. So I'm sitting at the back of the room and you can appreciate that I'm thrilled to hear this, until his next words were "and I found them so civilized!" I *remember* what he said! I was *beside myself* with temper! I picked up all my things and I walked out of the classroom. Then I realized, this is not gonna' go. This is *not* gonna' go. And I went and I told him.

Laughing, JN describes wondering "who the freakin' hell" MacLennan thought he was, "referring to some of the greatest leaders from the African continent as *civilized*," and mentions this as one of those moments at McGill when her "head was on fire." But she also adds more solemnly that the incident made her feel "terribly diminished":

> It wasn't just the statement; it was my disappointment. I was in that class with *Hugh MacLennan* because he'd written *Two Solitudes* and I was interested in it. So I'd gone in, because I had this respect for the man. I'd gone in because I felt so privileged to be in this English Lit program that had these amazing people, only to realize that in saying this he didn't understand anything about me as a Black person. And I knew I wasn't in an African or a Caribbean literature course. But I expected fundamental respect and it wasn't forthcoming.

"That … Statue"

Apparently heeding MacLennan's critique that the university had been too modest and quiet about its origins, McGill University paid much greater attention to documenting and promoting institutional history starting in the mid-1970s. The History of McGill Project was established in 1975, and Frost was appointed its founding director. Frost co-founded the James McGill Society that same year, a group dedicated to fostering interest in and appreciation for the university's histories and personalities. He authored at least six books and several articles documenting the university's history, with particular attention to celebrating the "great men" (to use MacLennan's term) who were its founder, principals, and primary benefactors. In 1995, Frost published the biography

James McGill of Montreal, which arguably remains the dominant source of information about James McGill's life. The biography was part of a campaign that revived James McGill – or at least the spectre of the man – and re-established a sense of his presence at the university, two hundred years following his death.

The following year, on 6 June 1996, an article published in Montreal's *Gazette* drew on Frost's biography to describe McGill as "a shrewd, fiercely ambitious Scot," "tough and unremitting," as it announced the unveiling that day of the statue of James McGill that now stands on the lower field of the university's campus:

> You might catch a glimpse today of James McGill leaving Burnside, his summer estate just under Mount Royal. A ghost? No, he's alive – not living – but alive as in spirited, palpable. He is in purposeful motion, as he was in life, right hand aggressively outstretched, firmly grasping a walking stick. A blustery Montreal wind forces his open coat high behind him.
>
> His left hand gracefully touches his tricorne hat. He might be keeping it on his head. Or he might be in the act of doffing it to a friend, because on his face is an expression of greeting. The famous corkscrew lips reveal the beginnings of a smile. The eyes have a subtle twinkle.
>
> He is a solid man, standing – idealistically larger than life – at about 6 feet. His long waistcoat reveals some immoderation where it pulls gently down over a rounded belly. His soft, knotted neckerchief is that of a gentleman.[78]

The McGill Associates, a group of non-alumni business people in Montreal and long-term supporters of the university, had commissioned the statue as a gift to the McGill Twenty-First Century Fund. The *Gazette* article describes the sculptor of the statue as a British "amiable redhead of offhand wit and ambushing intelligence." The statue is personified within the article, from its title, "James McGill Strides by the Roddick Gates Today," to its concluding sentence, "He'll be unveiled today between 5 and 7 p.m. by the Roddick Gates, forever to stride among the students whose school was his great legacy."[79]

The unveiling of the statue took place on lower campus during a combined reception for convocation and McGill's 175th anniversary garden party. "The theme for the day was intended to recreate the spirit of James McGill's era," according to an article documenting the event published in the official newspaper of the university, the *McGill Reporter*:

> Dignitaries were dressed in costumes from the 1820s, arriving on campus in horse-drawn carriages and led by members of the Grenadier Guards

and pipers from the Black Watch. The theme for the day was intended to recreate the spirit of James McGill's era. The weather was beautiful and the atmosphere was lighthearted as thousands of staff, graduates and alumni, along with their friends and families, roamed the campus taking in the cricket match, the croquet competitions, and entertainment both traditional and contemporary in the forms of juggling and jazz.[80]

Photographs accompanying the article show Principal Bernard Shapiro and Chancellor Gretta Chambers arriving at the event in horse-drawn carriage, in full costume with broad smiles. Another image features "Education professor Phyllis Shapiro and Kate Williams, director of the University Relations Office" looking down at the camera from the steps of the Faculty Club – former home of "wealthy German sugar tycoon" Baron Alfred Baumgarten[81] – holding lacy umbrellas and wearing floor-length powder-blue gowns and hats. Stanley Frost is quoted as referring to the sculpture's installation as a "splendid resurrection" of James McGill.[82]

With the campus providing a "natural" set and stage for this colonial costume party, the event created the sense of transporting the university back in time – or rather, resurrecting and re-establishing the past in the present – with no apparent regard for the presence and perspectives of Indigenous or Black students and faculty. No matter how many times I have looked at the images of this colonial garden party over the past several years, I never cease to be amazed by how joyous those pictured appear. This was in 1996. As I discuss further in following chapters, Black students were making themselves and their concerns highly visible at the time, and a renewed Black student-led campaign for a Black/Africana Studies program at the university had been ongoing for at least five consecutive years. So how did the university expect Black students and faculty to position themselves in relation to this all-out institutional celebration of a time in which they were legally considered chattel? Were Black graduates and their families expected to attend the event? Had there been any Black dignitaries at the university, what costumes would *they* have been expected to wear? Were these questions ever even considered by senior administrators?

While none of the students I interviewed from this era referred to the garden party, some did describe profound responses to the ongoing celebration of James McGill and especially to the statue that continues to maintain a visual presence of the man on lower campus. Over the decades since its installation, the statue has served its purpose of constructing a palpable sense of James McGill's immortal presence. The most frequently and passionately expressed comments about the physical environment of the campus by the people I interviewed are about the statue of James McGill and being aware that McGill was a slave owner. Both professors and students say they "don't *look* at the statue" or do not enter campus by the main gates of the university in an attempt to avoid it. I came to understand this refusal to see the statue as representing a refusal to engage in its performance as a monument naturalizing the conditions, histories, and ideology associated with McGill and his legacy.

Both MR and SB explain that they try not to enter campus from the front gates in order to avoid conjuring the traditional view of the path leading to McGill's Burnside house,[83] and especially in order to avoid seeing the statue of McGill. MR explains: "There's that fucking statue there, I *hate* that statue! I remember when I was an undergrad I was like 'what if we just broke it when no one was watching?'"

> ROSALIND: The statue of James McGill?
> MR: Yeh, I hate that thing. I hate it. It's disgusting.
> ROSALIND: What do you hate about it?
> MR: Like, this [*curse*] was like *owning* – he was all up in the slave trade.
> It's just this celebration of this history of like, "we owned slaves (but no we didn't 'cause this is Canada, but actually we did and it's really well documented) and this wealth has been bequeathed and has been exclusively preserved for white people including not even certain white people, for generations, but oh, it's different now, because we're diverse" – and it's just this narrative that makes no sense and it's like so screwed up and yeh, and it's [the statue] just a symbol of that.

SB also describes her avoidance of that part of campus, identifying a "conflict" she had as an undergraduate, "dealing with McGill, James McGill, as the founder of the school but being a slave owner." She explains,

> I used to go up to the statue – I know this is weird, but I used to say, "huh! I guess your slaves really turned it around!" Because I felt like, yeh, I just felt it was weird. I had these weird things in my head when I was younger ...
> The thing with James McGill, I think I chalked it down to irony. I just didn't bother. But I did say some bad things to the statue, I did. I was kind of like "You're a loser, look what happened!" ... But there's something really strange. Like I never come through those gates. I have an issue ... Coming through the front gates, like, I don't like seeing him.
> ... It's just, it's weird. It's a weird kind of – I have to be honest, I think about it every time I see the statue. But I guess I chalk it down to irony, and shake my head and think, "Yeh, I guess you didn't do well."

SB's feelings about the statue, her impulse to talk to it and refer to the statue as "him," all highlight the ways the statue stands in for James McGill the man, two hundred years following his death. While the monument marking the location of the man's remains outside of the Arts Building serves a commemorative function, the personified statue invites interaction, and interactions with it serve to reinforce its personification. It attracts visitors and graduates who pose with it for photographs, reinforcing the understanding of McGill as institutional "father" hosting an extended family of "McGillians" on "his" property. The statue thus reinforces the idea of a historical trajectory seamlessly connecting past and present, which serves to naturalize racialized social hierarchy and settler colonial notions of national belonging.

Statues are neither the historical figures nor the histories they signify and represent; hence the installation or removal of a statue is not tantamount to the installation or removal of history itself. Rather, statues are political symbols that function in particular ways at particular times, generating emotional impact beyond their material existence.[84] What is at stake, then, according to Sabine Marschall, "is not necessarily the substance or content of a public monument (i.e. identification with or objection to the specific historical figure or commemorated event) but the overall quality (i.e. the added value, the general set of values and meanings) associated with it."[85] In other words, while not everyone sees and experiences the statue of James McGill in the same way, its installation on the university's lower campus promotes uncritical veneration through everyday encounters that memorialize the man and the colonial relations he represents.[86] The statue thus reinforces the sense of the university's downtown campus as a (white, colonial, elite) space separate from the rest of the city, adding to the historical mystique of what is popularly referred to as "the McGill bubble."[87]

Conclusion: On a Critical Engagement with History

The brief historical overview provided above reveals how a critical engagement with history and how it is constructed can force dominant assumptions about the university and about the nation of Canada into question. In addition to exposing fundamental illusions and falsehoods embedded in Canadian national myths – such as the absence of colonialism and slavery – understanding the conditions under which universities were founded in Canada reveals their intended roles in society and provides a baseline for understanding how they have and have not changed, and are and are not changing now. More than the treatment of history solely as series of events that happened in the past, this requires a historiographical project that examines the role of institutions in the construction of history itself. Attending to the historiography of McGill University highlights the contemporary construction of a partial – that is, both incomplete and not-impartial – origin story. Eric Hobsbawm's notion of "invented tradition" is helpful here in analysing the institutional function of the "legacy of James McGill." Hobsbawm defines invented tradition as

> a set of practices, normally governed by overtly or tacitly accepted rules and of a ritual or symbolic nature, which seek to inculcate certain values and norms of behaviour by repetition, which automatically implies continuity with the past. In fact, where possible, they normally attempt to establish continuity with a suitable historic past.[88]

Invented traditions function as though they represent the continuity of a historic past, but this continuity is "largely factitious."[89] Such traditions draw from and mobilize the past to misrepresent the ever-changing modern world as fixed and static. They are most likely to be constructed when "a rapid transformation of society weakens or destroys the social patterns for which 'old' traditions had been designed."[90] Thus, particularly dynamic periods of social-political pressure on the university coincide with institutional constructions and re-assertions of "tradition."

When those who govern the university construct and mobilize the past and notions of tradition in its institutional texts and discourses, they (re)establish parameters of membership and belonging, legitimize the institution's status and authority, and promote particular (e.g., British/ Anglo-Canadian, middle class) "beliefs, value systems and conventions of behavior."[91] In legitimating the social order of which it is a part, the university's investment in its founding myths exposes it as a national instrument of racialized class hegemony. In other words, while the colonial foundations of the institution may be of the distant past and as such beyond the control of university administrators today, the unabashed celebration of these foundations and memorializing of "great men" associated with them, the contemporary construction of invented traditions, and persistent anchoring in the "old ways" represent active, organized ongoing processes of exclusion and institutional resistance to change.

The "perception of historical continuity is particularly important to [maintaining] the power of the elite in the context of a capitalist society,"[92] because such a perception suggests that not only is the social order just the way things are, it represents the way things always have

been. In addition to inventing traditions and anchoring them in particular historical narratives, the production of this continuity requires
the erasure of histories that might interrupt through contradictions and
challenges. Such erasures are intended to eliminate Indigenous knowledges that suggest and can inform alternatives to capitalism and European humanism.[93] They are part of what Gary Kinsman and Patrizia
Gentile so aptly term "the 'social organization of forgetting,' which is
based on the annihilation of our social and historical memories."[94] In
other words, it is not accidental that the presence and contributions of
Black people (and especially their resistance) are minimized and erased
in Canada – these histories must be forgotten in order to maintain
Canadian mythologies of whiteness.

The colonial histories of McGill continue to echo into the present,
not by accident but rather through the ongoing construction and maintenance of ruling relations that uphold settler colonialism and racial
capitalism. Indeed, following the *Printemps d'érable* of 2012, McGill celebrated its "Scottish antecedents" by awarding honorary degrees to
the principals and vice chancellors of the University of Glasgow and
University of Edinburgh, and had a new monument installed on the
downtown campus. Outside of the James Administration Building in
James Square – renamed "Community Square" by activists and the
site of many protests that academic year – three benches made of Scottish granite were installed. According to the accompanying plaque,
the benches "commemorate the longstanding bonds that link McGill
University with the University of Edinburgh and the University of
Glasgow." They are meant to symbolize the "three universities, each
made of three pieces of the same stone, all three similar, like siblings,
but each unique in form and expression,"[95] with replicas made of Québec granite planned for installation at McGill's Macdonald campus.[96]

As the preceding chapters indicate, McGill University and prominent individuals associated with it feature significantly in ongoing histories of appropriation, settlement, exploitation, and development of
Indigenous lands in the name of the Canadian state. Universities and
academics play crucial roles in constructing and reproducing dominant national and international conceptions of Canada and of Canadians that obscure and further these continuing histories. National
and institutional identities thus function co-constitutively. Canada is
widely recognized as a multicultural and welcoming country with
affordable postsecondary tuition rates and highly rated universities. It
is promoted to international students as a "modern, progressive country with friendly, open-minded citizens, and … famous for its large,
dynamic cities and its picturesque, untouched landscapes."[97] Canada

has recently been identified as the most preferred study-abroad destination among students worldwide,[98] and McGill, University of Toronto, and University of British Columbia consistently place among the top fifty in the Quacquarelli Symonds World University rankings.[99] In the chapters that follow, I bring these dominant national and institutional narratives into critical conversation with the experiences and insights of Black faculty and students.

4

The Idealized Elite University

My expectations for university were quite idealistic: I thought of university as sort of a hallowed place where you were going to have all these wonderful discussions – it was the idealized university. (GR)

McGill is well known as an elite, international university, consistently ranking first or second in Canada and among the top in the world.[1] While the primary reason professors report being drawn to the university is the availability of a job in their field, almost all of the students I interviewed had chosen McGill because of its excellent reputation. Students had been advised by family members, peers, and faculty members at other institutions that if they had the chance to attend McGill they should take it. As DN was told: "If you get into McGill then go – for sure!" KB said that everyone he consulted, "from teachers to parents to any family member," strongly encouraged him to "apply to the presumed best university in Canada," based on the belief that the "elite university experience would give a certain amount of prestige." Both international students and those from Canada referred specifically to global rankings and the renowned reputation of the university internationally. Indeed, one student appeared to feel trapped by the university's reputation even as they called it into question: "I just feel like, I don't know, I'm one of those people who despite what I know about the world I still adhere to this meritocracy bullshit, so in my head I'm like I have to go to the best schools."

Especially among members of local Black communities, myths of meritocracy intersect with race and class to make McGill seem generally out of reach. As one former student shares: "There was, I remember growing up, in CEGEP and stuff, this perspective, particularly in ... the anglophone Black community, a sense that McGill was inaccessible and that we all go to Concordia. There was nothing that aggravated me more than hearing that." This "common knowledge" of McGill constructs Black students who do attend the university as great exceptions. Another student, BR, describes an interaction that further exemplifies this:

> I play basketball on Saturdays with some predominantly Black guys. So, the first time I got there, this guy said, "Where are you from?" I said I'm from [Caribbean Island] and I'm here studying at McGill. And the guy was like, "*McGill?*" He was like really, really shocked, that I was from McGill, in graduate studies, and actually playing basketball. Because I think where I play basketball is close to George Vanier metro in Little Burgundy, so it's a more, I've heard it described as a deprived area …
>
> So, he said he was really surprised at me, even though I was Black, y'know what I mean, that I was there playing basketball with them, and I was studying at McGill. And I told him, "Well, I mean, I'm from the Islands, and I'm just here to study, I don't live here. I mean I'm just here trying to get out with some friends." He said, "Well, I mean McGill. I mean McGill is a …" [*gestures as though at a loss for words*].
>
> So I think, and it reminds me of [University of] Bristol [in the United Kingdom] as well, 'cause I think there's the issue of McGill, in terms of universities, in terms of anglophone universities in Montreal. There's McGill at the top, and there's Concordia somewhere below. And that is the impression I get. Because I said I'm studying at McGill and he said, "Oh, wow, I'm just at Concordia trying to get my degree." And I was like – it reminded me of Bristol.

Another student, who had lived in Little Burgundy, explains coming to terms with the disappointing realization that despite her unique affiliation with the elite school, being a "proud McGillian" did little to mitigate the way she continued to be racially profiled by police in her neighbourhood:

> STUDENT: I was very proud to wear my McGill [faculty] jacket and I lived in [Little] Burgundy, but I often would get stopped when I wore that jacket, and I used to think to myself –
> ROSALIND: Sorry, stopped?
> STUDENT: Stopped by police. I used to think it was really strange. Because I thought that now that I went to McGill, the police would leave me alone. We often got stopped in Burgundy because they could. That's just the way it was … I always thought that when I wore my McGill jacket I felt like I had this cape, and that they wouldn't talk to me because

I'm a McGill student and what do you mean Black people can't go to McGill, right? So I used to get highly offended by being stopped by the police when I was wearing these McGill items. I was that very proud McGillian; I used to wear my sweater, my McGill sweats, and I used to get extremely offended when I got stopped … But then I came to the realization that when it comes to police brutality it doesn't really matter what country you're from or what island – it's the colour of your skin. It didn't matter what station I was in life, if they wanted to stop me they were going to stop me. [This realization] didn't decrease my power in McGill it just increased [my awareness of] the reality that I was always going to be in the battle of being a Black person. No matter what I was doing in my life, they were still going to look down on me.

This student was among several participants whose parents had been teachers or had placed tremendous value on formal educational attainment. She shares that when her mother had been pregnant with her,

my parents would walk around the campus together and they would talk about how I was going to go here. So, it was always kind of drilled in my head that McGill was my destiny, because my parents used to walk around here pregnant and my mom used to work at the bookstore.

Reflecting how level of parental education is a key indicator of university educational achievement,[2] several students had parents who attended university, and two of the interviewees' fathers had attended McGill. One explains, "there was McGill in the air since I was a kid," while the other describes growing up aware of "an unsaid expectation that we'd all end up going to McGill."

McGill's long-standing international reputation associates it with notions of what GR, quoted at the opening of this chapter, refers to as the "idealized university." This idealized university has been shaped by dominant ideas about knowledge production and enlightenment, and popular depictions of old British institutions and the Ivy League in the United States. These ideals are thus both racialized and associated with class privilege and upward mobility. As VR describes:

McGill is the bastion of white power-type-looking institution … I know it sounds disturbing, but I kind of enjoyed that kind of, the old-looking university … Y'know, you see the movies, with the professors and the podiums, and the halls, and I think that I thought that was the university experience and I actually am glad I had an experience with a historical university.

Several people I interviewed similarly describe the downtown campus as "traditional" and "historic" and commented on the "old buildings" and "very British, perhaps Victorian architecture" that reminded them of the United Kingdom. One student mentions that he thinks that because his mother was British and he was very familiar with "British culture," he "felt at home, in a way, architecturally" on McGill's downtown campus. Another student feels that the Britishness of the environment communicates a particular tone and set of expectations:

> It's one of the things I've noticed about McGill, we have an old-school style. I don't even know, I don't know the different architecture styles but I just know it's very old-school. It's very British, it's not even American. It's very British and it sets the tone; it very much sets the tone. But I think that's what McGill's tradition is about, it's about setting the tone, and it's kind of like when you come into McGill, [it's] setting the tone of what they expect from us in a weird way. (SB)

Some participants state that the architecture of buildings on campus makes them feel uncomfortable: "I'm certainly more uncomfortable in those [older buildings], that's for sure. I'd never say that I can be totally myself in those spaces." Buildings that participants most often describe as uncomfortable to be in are former Golden Mile mansions associated with exclusivity: Chancellor Day Hall (location of the Faculty of Law), Thomson House,[3] and especially the Faculty Club, located in the elaborate former mansion of sugar magnate Baron Alfred Baumgarten. As GR recalls:

> The Faculty Club was a weird place anyway, it was always a weird place. And I only went there on invitation because you have to remember, I don't know if you're aware that the Faculty Club had only started removing all its restrictions on women not that long before. Twenty years before, a woman couldn't eat in the dining room of the Faculty Club, as amazing as it seems.

Another student describes their conflicting feelings about the prominence of the Redpath family name on campus (i.e., Redpath Museum, Redpath Library), knowing that family's wealth was built through the sugar industry and plantations in the Caribbean:

> It's like on the one hand it almost feels, sometimes it makes me more paranoid, like I'm kind of walking around like, looking at these huge buildings and I want to know ... who's this, what this name represents,

or what history this is implicated in. And it kind of, like it sometimes feels like it's engaging a sort of paranoia or sort of schizophrenia, right? But on the other hand, it's really more a kind of empowering feeling to have that knowledge.

Many of us experience the campus setting and this discord as haunting, an embodied and sensuous experience that draws us into a "transformative recognition" of what is "living and breathing in the place hidden from view: people, places, histories, knowledge, memories, ways of life, ideas" that are no longer being adequately contained or repressed.[4] This kind of haunting, as Avery Gordon theorizes, represents an opening of time through which the past becomes visible, pointing us towards something-to-be-done.[5] It is an experience that at times generates flight, and at other times, we fight. Similar to the student quoted above, a professor expresses a sense of empowerment in knowing and undermining histories of white supremacy represented by and reflected in the campus environment:

> I think some people are like: "Let's not go to the Faculty Club, that place is a racist baron sugar guy's house." I'm like: "Let's go occupy the friggin' Faculty Club!" Like why aren't we making that *our* space? There's two ways to go about it right? ... You know what I'm saying. I have a right to take up space in this [place], on this campus, built by this racist slave owner. I bet he didn't think *I'd* be teaching here when he gave that money! [*laughs*] You hear what I'm saying?

Class and Class-Mindedness

Over nearly two hundred years, McGill has been associated with some of the most economically wealthy and powerful families in Canada, while increasingly expanding its transnational reputation and influence. Class plays a pivotal role in defining its "eliteness" and determining assumptions and expectations of McGill, and a student's social class background and economic status contribute significantly to shaping their experiences at the university.

GR describes the students at McGill in the 1960s as having come from "middle- and upper-middle-class families," noting that "most working class kids – white or Black – didn't end up at McGill. So ... you would very rarely meet someone here whose father worked in a factory. If you went to a French university you'd be more likely to find that." His comments call attention to "middle class" as something that is not strictly dependent on income. As he explains:

When I talk about middle class among Blacks I'm not – because that's always kind of a loaded term – your father may be a worker on the railway, but *the aspirations* were middle-class. Y'know, the Caribbean lifestyle was very much a kind of a, in some ways, a middle-class *lifestyle*.

Even though the income might not be middle income, the values you had – the importance of education, the importance of keeping your reputation – these things were always very strong in those families, those were things they brought with them from the Caribbean and [that] stayed with them.

GR believes that these values have often allowed Caribbean people in North America to navigate institutional spaces and to achieve greater social class mobility than Black people born in the United States and Canada. This understanding of class and socio-cultural differences among Black people is well documented in the literature, highlighting Caribbean middle-class values that stress the importance of education, hard work, discipline, and respectability.[6] Black lower and middle economic classes can be understood as further divided into social class identities along behavioural differences and cultural values, with "the degree of acceptance of white middle-class ideology" perceived as a significant determinant of being "middle-class minded."[7]

Given the co-constitutive socio-economic and racial class stratification in Canada,[8] it is not surprising that Black Canadian students at McGill seem to be less likely to come from affluent backgrounds than other Canadian and Black international students. One student describes the economic class expectations and financial demands of university as "soul crushing" and says:

I think that the most emotional aspect of school has been not having any money, and feeling like you're going backwards, and seeing how these environments affect your health – it's just so personal.

Canadians tend to underestimate the extent of class inequality in this country. Canada is among the most economically inequitable industrialized nations, characterized by ever-increasingly severe income and especially wealth inequality. In 2012, for example, "the 86 wealthiest Canadian-resident individuals (and families) held the same amount of wealth as the poorest 11.4 million Canadians combined."[9] Subjected to an organized, racialized class hierarchy that Grace-Edward Galabuzi refers to as Canada's "economic apartheid," Black Canadians face severely disproportionate rates of unemployment, underemployment, and poverty.[10] "The average total income of racialized Canadians was

74 per cent of non-racialized Canadians in 2015," representing a one per cent growth in Canada's racialized income gap in the past decade.[11] University-educated, Canadian-born visible minorities face an overall 12.6 per cent racial wage gap compared to white Canadians, highest in Québec at 19.7 per cent and higher still for Black women in Québec at 20 per cent.[12]

It follows that Black Canadian students at McGill are more likely than white Canadians and international students to be challenged by financial issues and by a sense of what can be described as "class shock" in the elite university environment. They describe having to hold jobs throughout their degree and/or to earn scholarships to pay tuition and fees. For some, this creates a sense of urgency to finish their degree program, and prevents them from becoming involved in extra-curricular or activist activities. One student explains, in relation to antiracist organizing as an undergrad: "I had four years, my parents didn't have the money, I worked my *ass off* for scholarships, and so I really didn't have time to deal with McGill and their stupidness in that sense."

Part of the allure of the idealized elite university is the potential of increasing one's social-economic status. While students "didn't expect to come here and be balling from funding money," as one puts it, they do expect to be able to access a full university experience. Hence, they are disturbed by how economic status tends to be taken for granted and to limit their experience. As RL explains:

> Money's really something. Economic reasons are really something that factor in at McGill. I feel like you kind of miss out when you're not that affluent. You miss out on a lot of opportunities, like I have a friend who right now went to do an internship with the United Nations in New York. And this is a full-time internship for the whole summer. But it's with the UN and to go there, you have to have enough money to live by your own [means] because it's not paid.

Another student, LR, who was also a course lecturer, notes how social-economic expectations are communicated to students by status symbols like Mac computers, adding that when she teaches she brings another brand of laptop so "students in the class know, you don't have a Mac, it's damn okay. You can come with your little PC." She points to the wilful blindness of the institution to the needs of less affluent students:

> The university does not understand, or pretends not to understand, that there's a financial strain on people who do not have access to jobs on campus, or there's assumptions that you come with a lot of money – which

is not true – and there are a lot of people who are suffering financially, and I'm also one of them … There is this assumption that everyone who comes here is rich, or has a lot of money, and if you have to say you don't have a lot of money somehow that's a problem. And I think that has to change.

Class differences in relation to their Black peers were most shocking of all to Black Canadian students, challenging both their lived experiences of interlocking race-class oppression and preconceived notions of life on the African continent. As one such student observes, "Even the Africans who study here, the international students, a lot of them come from really rich backgrounds … Especially if you buy into this media [narrative] that Africans are poor people, that's really something that strikes you as a new impression."

Meeting international students from African countries not only challenged dominant stereotypes but revealed that assumptions about Africans and Black racial solidarity do not necessarily hold in the face of class difference. Some of the Black students from Canada are uncomfortable around affluent African students and describe how this experience of significant class difference among Black people was new to them. As one student shares:

> I remember one time I was talking to this woman and we were talking about identities and all these things and she was – it was very bizarre because on the one hand she was quoting Frantz Fanon, … and then she goes on to say, "I'm from Sudan, y'know, we speak *this* kind of Arabic, versus the people from Algeria who, they're just the poor ones, we don't really respect their way of speaking." And I was just like – at first, I thought she was joking, right? Especially since she was quoting *Frantz Fanon* y'know, who's like so connected to Algeria, right? And then, but then I realize she's *not* joking; she has this very, very class-privileged view of people from Algeria!

Another Canadian student expresses resentment towards affluent African students, whom she describes as "so ready to hustle for [the university]" and to use the "language of diversity … to their advantage." Describing to me how interlocking relations of race and class have shaped the material conditions and affected the mental and physical health of her family and community, this student distinguishes herself as "somebody who's actually experienced structural disadvantage" as opposed to peers for whom the extent "that racism factors into their life is the extent that it impairs their job search." She describes the behaviour of affluent African students in her department, who are willing to "hustle" and avoid confrontation, as alienating and undermining Black students like herself who seek to challenge the university's racialized and classist norms and expectations.

International students also recognize the role that class privilege plays in shaping their experiences. For example, LG acknowledges it would have been far more difficult for her to navigate the university had she come from a "poor background" and not had access to experiences similar to those of her white peers:

> People consider a McGill [faculty name] student, you know, to be elitist, and I can see where that comes from because most people are more privileged and what have you. So indeed like, I think that if I came from a poor background and didn't have these experiences that are very similar – like ohhhh, we can talk about trips we've all done, or like volunteer opportunities, oh, we've all gone to South Africa for three months – indeed I think there was a ground of commonality which was, which is class … I think indeed I probably wouldn't have been able to be so involved and feel so like I belonged if it wasn't for at least one ground of commonality, which was class. It's absolutely true.

LG says that in her home country there is a clearly demarcated divide between "rich and poor" and "if you're part of the rich it means you can sit with governors and go to their birthdays." As a consequence of being raised on the "rich" side of this divide, she explains:

> I've felt like I don't struggle [at McGill and as an intern] and I'm not threatened by these wealthy men who like feel like they're the biggest gift to the world, and are so cocky. I'm able to sit, look at them eye to eye, [and] talk. Maybe because y'know, my dad is a banker, and I'm not afraid of these kinds of [settings and people].

The financial means necessary for African students to attend McGill as international students tends to create a confluence between Africanness and class privilege, a phenomenon that will likely continue, as Québec tuition fees for international students are more than six times those for local students and are most frequently and dramatically increased.[13] This should not, however, be taken to suggest that African students are necessarily from affluent backgrounds or that their experiences are necessarily less alienating than those of Canadian students. Juliana Makuchi Nfah-Abbenyi highlights this point in writing about her experiences as a Cameroonian woman attending McGill in the late 1980s and early 1990s. She describes having arrived with strong familial and cultural grounding, a strong educational background including university, and the advantage of being fluent in both English and French. Despite these strengths and "though armed with the knowledge that McGill is the bastion of Anglo-Saxon scholarship," she explains, "when I walk through the gates and halls of McGill, nothing prepares me for the reality of its *whiteness*."[14]

The McGill Bubble: A "Sea of Whiteness"

I never felt at home, it was like in and out, in and out; if I didn't have to be on campus, I wouldn't be on campus. And I don't know if that had to do with the history of the campus, or the lack of racialized people I would see, but there was nothing there for me. If I didn't need to get a book, I'm not going. If I don't need to be in class, I'm not going. I would rather just sit at home, and listen to my music and wile out. Yeh. (CH)

Black students have studied at McGill since as early as the mid-nineteenth century, and research by and about members of Montreal's Black communities is scattered with references to the prominence of McGill and to notable Black students and "Black firsts" who attended the university.[15] As that important work demonstrates, McGill is part of our collective storytelling even as we are largely erased from McGill's. The university's avoidance of references to race reinforces a normative whiteness communicated and buttressed through visual display practices.[16] As students observe:

I think there are a lot of portraits on the wall, and I don't see a lot of role models who would be of my particular ethnicity there, that's for sure. So that is definitely very noticeable. (DN)

I don't think there's a push to highlight [the presence and contributions of] other ethnicities. I think it seems like a very – It seems like a very white Canadian campus. There's significant numbers of Black, Asian and other students of colour here; I'm not sure the university does a whole lot to represent their influence on the university. Maybe they do and I haven't seen it. But the campus just appears, you know, like a very white space, maybe, I could be wrong. (BR)

The integration of women into the university is well acknowledged,[17] but no similar institutional recognitions are offered regarding the first Black (or racialized) students at the university. Even the most notable of Black alumni receive little attention, with the arguable exception of Charles Drew (1904–50), a medical school student and a track and field star at McGill in the late 1920s and early 1930s, who later became famous for his contributions in the field of blood preservation. Other notable early Black graduates of the university include Québec-born William Wright (1827–1908), the "first accredited 'coloured' medical doctor in British North America,"[18] who graduated from McGill in 1848 and taught at the university for thirty years thereafter. Canadian entomologist Ernest Melville Duporte (1891–1981) came to McGill's Macdonald College in 1911 on a scholarship from Nevis in the British West Indies and stayed at McGill for seventy years, earning his master's and PhD and in the early 1920s becoming the first Black Canadian to teach at the university. Duporte was one of thirteen original members of the Thirteenth District of Omega Psi Phi, a predominantly African American fraternity founded at Howard University in 1911. Two members who had come to Montreal that fall from Howard founded the first international chapter of the fraternity, the Sigma chapter, in December 1923 at McGill. Among the thirteen members in 1924 was also Reverend Charles H. Este, who attended the Congregational College that was then affiliated with McGill. Rev. Este came to Montreal from Antigua in 1913, and through his lifelong community leadership and activism became one of the most well-known and beloved figures of Black history in Montreal.[19] These and other Black people should be included in institutional written and visual histories; however, as one student critically asserts in her interview, the point here is to address "a broader history, not just focusing on the first Black whatever." This student, LR, was commenting on photographs displayed in the Faculty Club, noting that most "people who go in there are white people and they are not forced to confront anything else when they go in there, it's just like their world, y'know?" LR argues that as a Caribbean woman she wants to see "the relationship between the Caribbean and the Faculty Club," specifically representation of the Caribbean slave labour and sugar industry that made the mansion's former owner Baumgarten wealthy. This would allow her to locate herself in relation to the institution, to "see, oh yeah, so part of *my* history may be related." This is a critically different intervention than the celebration of "Black firsts" as a means of promoting "a white supremacist discourse of individual Black exceptionality."[20] It is the critical difference between reinforcing the competitive individualism of capitalist relations and challenging the myths that seek to justify such relations. To recognize the dialectical relationship between Black *peoples* and the university throughout its history is to denaturalize the university's whiteness and problematize an entitled white hegemony.

The absence of contemporary race-based data collection on the part of McGill and other Canadian universities means that there continues to be no formal institutional awareness, let alone acknowledgment of the presence and size of Black student populations over time. This lack of quantitative, disaggregated information about racialized groups impedes those groups from making demands on institutions. As Professor Enakshi Dua stated in a 2017 interview for an investigation by CBC News, "We need to collect data to have an understanding of how accessible our universities are and where there are barriers and hurdles." CBC News found that sixty-three of the seventy-six Canadian universities they asked were unable to provide racial demographics on their student populations.[21] While McGill refused to respond to CBC's request for information, the university has stated in the past that data concerning the racial and ethnic identity of students are not collected as part of the university's admissions statistics.[22] In 2009, however, undergraduate student demographic data was collected through an online "Diversity Survey," which indicated that 71.3 per cent of the students surveyed ($n = 1,421$) identified themselves as white. The next largest group was 10.1 per cent of students ($n = 201$) who identified as Chinese, while 2.7 per cent of participating students ($n = 54$) identified themselves as Black. Just 0.8 per cent of students surveyed identified as Indigenous.[23] The survey found that among racialized students, 26 per cent reported race-based discrimination by students, and 18 per cent reported race-based discrimination by employees.[24] Discrimination based on language, ability, gender, country of origin, religion, and sexual orientation was also recorded. The university concluded that these results "confirm the basic assumption that McGill's student body is extremely diverse,"[25] and that the university is "a welcoming and tolerant environment."[26] Typical of Canadian multiculturalism, implicit in such a statement are racialized assumptions about who is tolerant and who is being tolerated; who is where they belong and whose presence is being stomached.

Several people I interviewed say they were very accustomed to navigating predominantly white institutions prior to McGill and still found the racialization particularly striking at the university, reinforcing notions of a "McGill bubble" distinct from the place (and arguably the time) within which it is located. References to the "bubble" commonly refer primarily to class and language – the distinct (wealthy, Anglo) McGill society within the distinctly French Québec with a long history of class struggle. However, for the vast majority of the people I interviewed, regardless of when they attended or worked at the university, the most defining feature of the environment within the bubble was the "whiteness" of McGill. Several used the phrase "sea of white," a powerful metaphor communicating the sense of being alone amidst an all-encompassing and overwhelming homogeneity.

And in that room, in that lunch hour, basically it's a sea of white students. It's a bunch of white students, I'm usually the only one, or there's only one or two non-white students at the time. (RL)

My first introduction to that field was frosh. And the kids just all over there, and it's just a sea of whiteness and liquor. And I don't have a problem with drinking, not at all, but the extent to which everything just happened, where it was just – it just wasn't a place for me ... I guess to just come to that setting where I didn't see me. I just wanted to see me on that field, and I didn't. (CH)

As a professor I'm going to – and this is going to sound really bitter, but y'know why I avoid [the main entrance to the university], can you guess? I avoid it because it really, I just don't want to see so many white people as I walk into the campus. And I think when you go into that pathway, I don't look at the statue, because I've probably sublimated it, but I think that I just – just between you and me [*laughs*] – I just don't really, it makes me, I just don't enjoy the notion that I'm employed in a place where it's just a sea of white people. And also, it's not only the students, because they're younger; but also to see so many faculty, all of whom are white. And every time I go through that gate I have to endure that, and so it's, I just really – what I do is I always go through different avenues to go to my office. But the sea of white we talk about, to see that and to feel that your life is going to be really determined on a daily basis by this absence of diversity, not only the students but to see, you see a lot of faculty going up and down, it really unnerves me and I don't like it. (MT)

The racial demographics of the student population and professoriate of the university thus combine with the erasure of the historical presence, roles, and contributions of Black people in the past to reinforce and contribute to a culture of whiteness. This whiteness functions through the conception of race as a visible marker of identity – we look for evidence of the presence of those who "look like us" to tell us we belong – and is extended and operationalized through a network of power relations.

Several interviewees use the common reference to "the bubble" to evoke the interlocking factors of race, class, and language that create the distinct McGill environment: "the Anglo bubble aspect of [the university]," as one student describes it, "the English fortress in the centre of the city." Pointing again to the role of social class and economic privilege and highlighting a race-class analysis of the university environment, KB describes the undergraduate social experience at McGill as "an interesting game." He recalls,

> I was aware of this from very early on, aware that I did not want to be assimilated into the McGill bubble ...
>
> I knew, even from coming to visit, that the sort of crowd that I was encountering there, and I guess it's a, y'know, in general a very white, affluent crowd, I knew right [from that visit] I would not be comfortable coming into the bubble. Because there *is* a bubble, even though McGill's integrated into Montreal as a whole, there is a bubble, y'know. You have the McGill ghetto, you have the whole residence experience, and besides being way out of my budget, y'know, I could not afford to [live in] residence, but it was also [a matter of] what kind of environment is that gonna' be for me? ... This idea of just being able to live all year round without a job, and just to be paid for by the parents and to kinda', I don't know [*laughs*] ... I shouldn't necessarily make fun, but it's this whole idea of how people accentuate their first-world problems. As an example: the "McGill ghetto," right? It's a fairly affluent neighbourhood to begin with [*laughs*] and the McGill students *love* to call it "the ghetto," because it's a cool word, y'know, and they like to be able to pretend they're poor, y'know: "ahh yeah, I'm living in the ghetto" – it's like, *what* are you talking about?

Similarly, a professor explains: "It's just a bit of this white fantasy land. You know, I'm kind of walking around thinking *where* are the Black people, where are the people who are not white? Where the hell are they? ... It's scary." This person also mentions the so-called McGill ghetto: "I hate the fact that it's called the 'ghetto' over there – McGill ghetto? When I first heard that I was like *'What?'* ... But again that kind of goes to this idea of that fantasy land that people live in."

It is important to note that while the vast majority of interviewees comment on how the university campus environment differs from the culture of Montreal overall, the nature and extent of this difference has changed over time. Montreal's population has become more racially diverse, and social-political norms regarding explicit racism and anglophone hegemony have shifted since the mid-twentieth century. Talking about the late 1950s and early 1960s, BT explains that "in the old days ... the most conspicuous thing about being Black was when you went to rent." While he personally did not experience problems renting apartments in the area surrounding the university, he said it was widely known that Black people regularly faced racist discrimination when attempting to rent rooms and in the so-called McGill ghetto, as they did elsewhere in the city. "Yeh, and not only that," he adds, "they go to the landlord, the apartment is taken, this, this, this, and this and then they'd send their girlfriend who might be white and suddenly it's alright.[27] That sort of thing, I don't know if it still goes on." GR confirms that during that era Black students faced racial discrimination when renting apartments, even as he says that he "never had a lot of problems or negative experiences of being Black in Montreal":

> I never did. I had one or two examples in my entire time here – of trying to get an apartment and being turned down and then sending a white friend and finding out the apartment is still available. But that was it, probably two or three.

In this climate, both BT and GR recall that being affiliated with the university sometimes served as a valuable credential against the anti-Black racism of the broader society. Relating this broader context to the whiteness on campus, GR explains:

> I think that the physical space of the university was quite welcoming. I think, however, it's that if you're Black on campus you didn't see yourself reflected in that space. But then you didn't see yourself reflected in any space outside of the campus either. We were just invisible, in a lot of ways … [The campus] was not a reflection of you, but then that was no different than anywhere else you went. But in some ways, you probably felt more empowered on campus than off campus, because the circle of tolerance was bigger on campus, at the same time fully understanding that there were limitations to even that.

Overall, GR found that in the 1960s the "liberal values" of the university generally mitigated racism such that in his experience, any "under the surface" racist views "were well controlled" and "most senior people at the university were far too sophisticated for that."

Indeed, liberal notions of meritocracy and academic excellence informed many people's assumptions about the university. Most people I spoke to had been aware prior to coming to McGill that it was "less racially diverse" (than Concordia University, for example), and had not allowed this to dissuade them. As a student shares:

> My friend who also got accepted to McGill told me that there are very little amounts of Black people who go to the school so you better be ready. But

that didn't deter me, I said, "Y'know what? I want to go to McGill!" and so when I got admitted I was ecstatic, I was over the moon and I knew I was going there. 100 per cent.

In this way, the idealized university was imagined to be an institution where knowledge is embraced and produced, beyond such crude matters as racism. Some students had even left other universities to come to McGill hoping to find a more fulfilling – and often less racist or less racially alienating – experience. One student in this situation was RL, who had transferred from his previous university anticipating an environment at McGill where critical discussions of "race and multiculturalism" would be more welcomed:

> But I soon noticed that it wasn't all I expected. I felt like the Other. I felt like the Other because I was Black, and that was really different from what my friends had told me. But then I realized that most of my friends who actually said these good things about McGill were not even Black themselves, they were white students. So their experiences, yes, I guess they were genuine experiences, but they didn't really apply to me and my case.

A professor from outside of Canada recalls how struck they were by the role of "being the only faculty person of colour" in departmental meetings, and especially by the overall avoidance of discussions about race. They note how claims of racial neutrality are used to deter difficult conversations about Black student representation:

> I guess that one of the things that struck me was the lack of discussion about race here in Canada. And I remember one of the first meetings, maybe in the first six months, looking at stats and looking at the student population and thinking "Where are all the Black students?" And thinking "Why doesn't anyone else think that this is an issue?" ... There just wasn't the same dialogue around it. It was kind of like, "well, you know, Canadians aren't racist so there's no real need to discuss it." And I thought that's bizarre.

Enduring myths about the meritocracy of Canadian universities posit that success is based solely on ability, talent, and hard work, ignoring long histories of racialized systemic inequity, oppression, and social hierarchy.[28] These myths are part of the liberal ideology that characterizes Canadian multiculturalism and are used to mask structural inequity and try to justify elite social status.[29] As critical race theorists have long argued, merit is a "subjective value rather than an objective fact";[30]

it masks historical practices of inclusion and exclusion in relation to social opportunities. Meritocratic discourse erases the historical and ongoing construction of inequity by promoting the idea that power and privileges are allocated in society based on effort, ability, and achievement. This allows those who benefit from current structural arrangements to redirect and transform social critiques of the power relations that work to their benefit into judgments of individuals and groups as deficient, not good enough, not working hard enough.

Assumptions about multiculturalism in Canadian education are contradicted by Black students' cumulative experiences of schooling characterized by white hegemony. A PhD student, Cora-Lee Conway, wrote a poem addressing this experience during her first year at McGill. She explains that the poem came to her as she was trying to work on a course paper, and found herself preoccupied with how her PhD program was turning out to be yet another educational experience characterized by a "lack of Blackness." She recalls:

> Obviously, the big thing was just the lack of Blackness at the university: Black students in the graduate program, Black faculty, Black administrators, Black faces on the walls. I mean, it's not like York [University] was any better. Y'know, walking through the hallways. And y'know, that's been my academic experience probably for my entire life ... Because it was just y'know, not having any representation of who you are, is really – it's a tricky thing to be in spaces where you don't see yourself ... That poem I wrote, and I got it published somewhere; it's always the way I feel.[31]

The poem, titled "White Hallways," captures many of the concerns as well as the sense of purpose and agency that participants in this study expressed.

White Hallways

white hallways,
and white floors.
white ceilings,
and white doors.
white clocks with black hands tellin' white time,
blackboards affixed to chalk white lines,
white teachers to tell white history,
Where are the teachers that look like me?
black janitor to clean white mess
black mothers to hear black girls' distress
They say I'm not pretty, they say I'm not clean,
They tell me I'm not smart, I know they're being mean
white girls with long hair
white privilege does not care
black girls in white schools
"educated" to make smart a fool
color bound, twice removed
disavowed and unapproved
talking back is not condoned
silence deep like treasures owned
but kinships across time and space
insist that resistance is not to be replaced
at the site upon which you are truly embraced
race erased to make new place for that sweet face
laced like trebled notes over that low bass
spoken slow
you make no haste
deliberate and bold
there is no mistake
you take
white hallways
to burst through
white doors
crash through
white ceilings
glide over
white floors
black girls move like rag-time
rightfully inclined to redefine the line
take your spotlight, rise and shine.[32]

The Professoriate

I always have this kind of defensive – now that you're asking me I'm thinking why didn't I think about it more closely – I think my safety valve ... has always been that consciously, I'm from – I'm *in* [country of origin]. My identity is [nationality of origin]. That is a source of comfort and sustenance, and it is also a source of defence. And so when I get up there, ... even from the beginning I think I always have this kind of issue. Because I'm by myself. I don't see anyone [Black] around me. So when there are three hundred students and they're predominantly white, I just really tell myself that I am from this country that I really care about and that's what really matters to me, no matter what happens in this class. That's where I get my dignity and reinforcement and to this day I think that is a source of real defence.

Faculty members and students alike talk about the scarcity of Black professors at the university and how it affects their experiences. Most were highly aware of who the few Black professors in their faculty were, if there were any. One professor explained that there had been a few Black faculty hired in the 1970s and 1980s, but that since then the university has been "going backwards" in term of the recruitment and retention of Black academics. As another simply states, "I would like it to be so that it's not an anomaly, so I'm not the only one."

Indeed, as they do elsewhere, Black professors do remain something of an anomaly in Canadian universities. As of 2016, racialized students account for more than 40 per cent of the undergraduate population, while racialized professors represent only 21 per cent of university faculty. Black professors represent just 2 per cent of the university professoriate – an increase of just .2 per cent over the past decade – and face an average earnings gap of -11.7 per cent in relation to their white male colleagues.[33]

Being part of such a small minority significantly shapes the experiences of the Black faculty members I spoke to. All of the professors and lecturers I interviewed talk about having to vigilantly anticipate and strategize around the impacts of interpersonal and institutional racism. As I discuss below, several feel that Black professors are required to do more work than their non-Black colleagues in order to obtain and maintain job security. They emphasize that these efforts go largely unacknowledged: "this is the kind of thing where having your *t*'s crossed and *i*'s dotted doesn't mean anything for a Black person," as one professor put it. They describe being situated (to quote one professor) at "the bottom of the fucking bottom" of a racialized professional hierarchy, and disadvantaged by a culture in which white social and professional networks overlap and reproduce white privilege. As one professor explains:

> Part of it is, for me, me not being close friends with the chair at the time was because I'm a Black [person], and I don't necessarily want to socialize with [the chair] and I don't get invited ... to certain things and I wouldn't invite [the chair] to certain things, because I don't necessarily look to my white colleagues to be my friends.

White social-professional networks are thus seen to limit Black professors' chances of being appointed to senior positions through blurring the actual requirements and potential for advancement.

> In my specific department it's really, really bad, and I would argue that they have – my white colleagues have – strategically come up with requirements for full professor especially that have nothing to do with what's on the books. So quietly amongst themselves they can tell each other after sitting on DTCs, department tenure committees, that they have silently agreed that you have to be a chair or a graduate program director to have done enough administration to go up for full professor. The university regulations say nothing about that.

Discussing how racism and white hegemony have impeded or prevented their promotion, another professor lowers their voice to a whisper to emphasize the profound need to get a Black professor – or at least a racially literate ally – admitted into the ranks of the senior administration. The professor states that the chairs of departments "are usually appointed from on high" and "know exactly what they're doing" and are "expected to do" in relation to racialized gate keeping. "The thing is," another explains,

> people don't want to give up their power. And as ugly as it may seem it's [that] people don't give it up easily or readily. That's, I think, what makes it so difficult: that people benefit from this, the structure here, and so nobody wants to give it up – individually *or* institutionally.

Professors feel, as do graduate students, that the only way to gain professional recognition is through building very strong academic profiles full of accolades and high "credentials from the white establishment" that make it difficult for them to be denied advancement. One professor uses the metaphor of "whittling" to describe how the value they bring to the university is reduced:

> I had a strong dossier, but I felt I had to – well, you know it's that old thing that I have to do better, I have to have more because people are going to be looking, to whittle – I know you can't audio record arm movements, but whittling [*laughs*].

With the value of their work often illegible to their colleagues and superiors, professors have subsequently been accused of "being exclusivist" when they attempt to create academic events and activities that centre Black histories, politics, or scholarship. What one professor describes as their "overachieving" in this regard raised suspicions with the chair of their department. Following an event that the professor had organized, the chair received letters from outside the university praising the professor as "a wonderful addition to McGill" who should be tenured. The professor explains:

> And [the chair] immediately saw that as something that I must have orchestrated ... So, she kept probing me for "What was so great? What was so special about your [event]?" kind of thing. "Why do you think you're so great?" ...
>
> So that was really shocking for me because in my naïveté I didn't realize that people gun for you when you outperform them. And that should make a lot of sense, right? Because the whole history of Blackness, through the process of slavery, is that the Black person has to know their place. And their place is forever below the white person ... But I don't know how you adjust for that, except by lowering your standards, which is something I'm not willing to do.

Professors I spoke to were the only Black scholars in their departments, and as a result experience what one identifies as the "intellectual and emotional costs" of "alienation and isolation." As they variously explain, being and remaining energized as an intellectual is "all about engagement" and dialogue with others, "so that distance in an academic community is really difficult. It has genuine intellectual costs, because you have to really kind of generate your own engagement with yourself." As one explains:

> I emailed [another Black professor] I had in mind as well because we're both equally alienated. I'm just as alienated as she is; I just talk more than

she does. And I was thinking, I know we're also burdened about this issue, and I know what she's going through too in that sense. But it's not a complaint; it's more like you feel guilty all the time. You just feel guilty all the time. [My friend] tells me, "Don't lose your politics and don't be afraid." And there is nervousness, because you're by yourself, and I know what that is. It's not a burden of "Oh, why am I in this position?" It's "I know what I should be doing more," and you know you want to help these students more, but you also want to, [*pause*] y'know, [*whispering*] try to take care of yourself.

Professors work to balance the need to prioritize self-care with their concern for their students. Without exception, the professors and lecturers I interviewed express care for their students and concern especially for the well-being of Black students as they navigate the culture and demands of the university environment. They talk about the importance of opportunities to support the academic work of Black students as well as to support them in developing racial literacy, critical analysis, and corresponding action within not only the university but the broader society as well. Several also acknowledge how much they value and are energized by opportunities to work with Black students, and are critical of racist and classist decisions in student admissions. For example, one professor shares their experience of debating colleagues about a student candidate originally from a country in central-east Africa:

> We got into this conversation about affirmative action and it was really gross, in that there was just this equating affirmative action with hiring or admitting students who are "not as good as," just because they come from a particular group. And I was thinking "Oh my gosh," I felt like, "Is this, I don't know, 1950?" I was really, I was *really* upset. And they were talking academics, and the standards of McGill, and ... she was basically insinuating that it would *cheapen* the university experience for others ...
>
> So, when I was talking about wanting to recruit more Black students, people, it wasn't like they said, "Why?" But it's like, "Oh, we can understand wanting to recruit more Indigenous students, but we have that mandate," and blah blah blah – it's just not on their radar. I don't understand.

As several comments suggest, under-representation of Black professors and Black students functions in a vicious circle, reproducing the whiteness of the university. The scarcity of Black professors can undermine the personal and professional well-being of those who are there, while sending a message to other Black and critical race scholars who seek intellectual community that they may be better off to seek work elsewhere. Consequently, Black students who come to the university are left without Black mentorship, and students who wish to pursue critical race scholarship have difficulty finding adequate guidance and supervision. For example, CH, expecting the university to offer "a plethora of knowledge," was disappointed to find she had "to scramble" to put together a meaningful academic experience. She is among several students who associate a lack of course offerings and curricula centring African/Black intellectual thought with the severe under-representation of Black professors.

On Mentorship and Academic "Expertise"

If I had at least one non-white professor at McGill then I would at least be able to see someone who looked like myself that I can actually relate to as far as being different. (RL)

What does it mean when the generation that produces knowledge is so unrepresentative of the generation that consumes it? ... One of the things I've always argued when I think of Blacks' relationship with the university is that we spend a lot of money providing and giving students scholarships to universities and colleges ...; but we never think about what that person is going to consume once they get there. We just think it's nice for them to go to university, but if the university is constantly only reproducing European ideas and the people doing the research are doing the same – *what* are we sending the young people to university *for*? What can we expect of them in helping to further knowledge that is needed and relevant to our community?[34]

The professors I spoke with all express awareness of the impacts of anti-Black racism on their students at the university (and in academia in general), and are aware of the valuable role that they can and do play as mentors for these students. As one professor says, "seeing someone like you: this is what Black mentoring is all about because ... for every white student there are a million mentors, and it happens automatically." Students echo and confirm this point, as CH explains:

Sometimes you just need someone to talk to about how you're feeling as a Black student navigating the space. And unfortunately, sometimes you can only do that with an individual who understands your plight, because they share the same, being in the position they are as a Black professor ... McGill, contrary to belief, still has a practice of the old boys' club that inaugurates young white men into that club, if you will. So young white men for example have [plenty] of professors that they can go to and talk to and joke with and laugh with.

All of the professors I interviewed talk about helping Black students navigate the institution as Black people in a predominantly white institution and system. They explain that while mentoring and working with Black students in addition to the students they are assigned creates extra work for them, this work is important and most often fulfilling. Some professors, particularly the women, face significant challenges with white students at the university who show disrespect towards them and challenge their authority, while others describe white students as supportive and aware of the benefits of racial diversity in their educational experiences. As one professor says:

My feeling is always – very, very confidently – that the presence of Black students in a class is really, really beneficial to all the students. And I think that the younger white students in large numbers believe that in their heart. They want to [be in a racially diverse environment] for either deep intellectual reasons, or just [as] a younger generation that wants to feel part of the world and prepared for the world. And so I get a lot of support from the younger white students, absolutely. There's no question about it.

Students express great appreciation for the few Black professors they do have, as well as empathy in acknowledging that those professors must also navigate institutional whiteness.

Several students comment on how few professors have this embodied knowledge of racialization (that is, knowledge of what it feels like to be racialized as a lived experience) and how few can teach about and from Black historical, cultural, and social-political perspectives. Most students describe identifying Black professors in their area of study and seeking out contact with and support from them. KB had been able to take a research seminar with a Black professor and recalled that doing so inspired him to engage in the course and to work at an academic level that he didn't know he was capable of. "I'd never really seen myself doing that or even kind of imagined what that would be like," this student recalls, explaining how powerful an experience it was to receive instruction from a Black professor whom he felt he could "relate to on different levels." My exchange with another student, LB, exemplifies that students are aware of how the under-representation of professors is both tied to and reinforces colonial ideas about Black people and our intelligence:

ROSALIND: Have you had any Black professors at all at McGill?

LB: I haven't, no. Which is kind of disappointing.

ROSALIND: Do you think it's important to have Black professors?

LB: Yes. I think it's *very* important. I think it's important because it shows students, Black students and also non-Black students, that Black people are intelligent and can have positions of power and authority. And I think they're role models. I think they're role models for Black students, but I also think they're role models for diversity in general. It also shows that McGill is committed to diversity. It shows that McGill makes an effort to find, I don't know, to find a diverse group of people that represent the students and that represent intelligence, and that represent what McGill stands for. Because I think what McGill stands for can be represented by people of many different colours. And I think that by having a mostly Caucasian professorship and people in authoritative positions, it doesn't really reflect Canadians.

ROSALIND: What does McGill stand for?

LB: Hmmm. Well I guess when I think of what McGill *should* stand for it's an intellectual, academic community. Y'know, like leadership … I think there are a lot of stereotypes in society. I remember talking to a former friend, and he genuinely believed that Black people are not as smart as white people. I was super offended. And yeh, we're not friends anymore. But I just think that stereotype is perpetuated every time you don't see Black people in positions of power and authority. Yeh. So for that reason I think it's really important.

Some students are less concerned about representation in relation to professors' racial identities per se than they are about how few professors have knowledge of African and Black diaspora histories, politics, theories, and epistemologies. It is in this sense that LG describes Black professors as "human resources" that are lacking at the university, and attributes much of her academic success to her ability to seek out Black professors for informal mentorship and support. For example, when she found the master's thesis supervisor she was assigned was not available to her or particularly knowledgeable about Africa, she sought support for her work from a Black African professor in the department. She met regularly with this professor, who kept her up to date on African politics, introduced her to additional mentors, reviewed her writing, and critiqued and challenged her thinking: "There was a connection there and he took me under his wings." BR recounts a similar experience of developing a strong working relationship with a professor from the Caribbean:

He's originally from [nation] in the Caribbean, and so he became more of a mentor to me. I had a closer relationship to him than I did to my supervisor. Maybe being from the Islands, maybe we, I guess we hit it off immediately; being from the Islands I guess we could relate to each other. So, I think we had a good rapport. He'd always give me very good and sound advice. And I guess in more ways than one he was more influential to me than my supervisor was or is.

As LG explains, "the more someone looks like you, sounds like you, or has the same experience as you, the more comfortable you feel approaching them ... So I saw this professor who looked like me, who had similar interests, and I got in touch."

Some students describe having underestimated the kind of correlation between lived, embodied experience and academic knowledge noted by the students quoted above. When asked to reflect on what it means for her to never have had a Black professor in university, a doctoral student responds:

> Has it made an impact? Um, yes. Yes. I was going to say no, but the truth is *yes*. Because when I want to bring up subjects that are culturally related, I think about it. I think about how I'm going to word it, and I think about how to make it the least hostile or the least hostile sounding, as possible. [*lowers the volume of her voice*] And you can see the discomfort in their faces. It is very, *very* obvious.

This student goes on to describe a professor in her department who "squirms, she *squiiiirms*" at the mention of Black people and culture, as an example of "the legitimacy problem" of non-Black professors who teach content or conduct research related to Black communities but are unable "to talk about it in the context of the culture from which it comes."

This was especially a concern in relation to white professors who teach about and conduct research in Africa, particularly those who do so without at all addressing colonialism and racism. Some people were careful to add that these white professors were "supportive," "wonderful" people and "great" professors, while expressing concern about the number of Black African scholars that could be hired in this area. One student says that as a person of African descent they found it "so crazy!" that Africa is "de-racialized" and treated solely as "a developing region" with focus placed on "the socio-economics, or the health issues or what have you":

> So how one can commit [their] entire life's work to talking about issues in developing regions in sub-Saharan Africa and never talk about Blackness and never talk about the implications of race blows my mind! But it is

done, and it's done without question or challenge. And for me, that's very problematic. Because there is a legacy of the colonial experience that is steeped in this race and racism. How you can talk about addressing issues that are a legacy of that history and not discuss or address race is beyond me.

This perception and critique of persistent colonial relations masquerading as academic liberal benevolence is common among Black students and faculty members. In a scathing article published in 2009, then law student Annamaria Enenajor powerfully critiques the conception of "global citizenship" among "McGill's socially conscious cosmopolitan elite," arguing that it represents an

approach to explaining development and legal work that normalizes power structures based in colonial history and grants permission to lack sensitivity, ignore politics, and tell the devastatingly incomplete story of Africa as a place of hopeless darkness and death.[35]

While the focus of Enenajor's critique is student internships, the issues she raises can as readily be applied to researchers, who may also be "well-meaning pluralists who '[fall] in love with Africa' and are ignorant of their own paternalism."[36] Exposing the ways in which such attitudes and engagements with Africa merely reproduce colonial power imbalances and are "steeped in assumptions of racial superiority," Enenajor argues that "race matters, history matters, wealth matters" and that without critical consciousness academics risk becoming "yet another cog in the wheel of foreign exploitation that has marred Africa's history for far too long."[37] That the majority of McGill professors teaching about and conducting research in Africa are white and not from African countries reinforces the idea that Africa and Africans are in need of Western saviours and experts. It leads some to conclude that, as one professor says, "if they're not going to hire the Black Africanist ... they're never going to hire us." This professor adds that because there are fields of study in which it is more or less likely that Black and other people of colour are working, the representation of Black professors is also a matter of what disciplines and specializations are valued, and consequently of constantly "fighting the [European] canonical tradition."

Students too are acutely aware of the ways in which professors' identities and interests influence what courses are offered. For example, CH states, "a lot of professors did not reflect who I was, and what I was interested in studying, and so I didn't get the courses that I desired." She had been seeking courses that explored Blackness in philosophy, particularly those that explored the "great genre of philosophy called

Black existentialism that McGill for some reason is sleeping on, or doesn't want to wake up to." CH feels that the significant number of white women teaching in her department has led to the inclusion of some feminist scholarship, but that in the absence of Black professors, the curriculum lacks critical race and Black philosophical perspectives. She says the feminist course material was "amazing, but feminist philosophy isn't only *white* feminist philosophy." CH adds that had she had the opportunity to study Black philosophers in addition to the European canon, she "would have been in academic heaven [and] probably would have never left university ... We could have studied Fanon side by side with Hegel and Merleau-Ponty and had an amazing class, but we never did that." It is noteworthy that, as in LR's call for a dialectical understanding of the university's history, CH does not call only for an engagement with Fanon, but for the study of the works of Fanon, Hegel, and Merleau-Ponty in relation to one another. Such a move requires more than an "objective" knowledge of the three philosophers and the ability to compare their work. It requires overcoming what Leonardo and Porter (indeed, drawing on the work of Fanon) so powerfully describe as white indulgence: "a gross attempt to understand the self through the self rather than through the other: narcissism par excellence."[38]

This point is echoed and developed further by JN, who in the 1970s had the opportunity to take a Caribbean literature class with Professor Lorris Elliott (1931–99). Elliott was born in Trinidad and Tobago and migrated to Canada in the late 1950s to attend university. He was a writer, actor, and educator and worked as a lecturer and professor at McGill for twenty-one years, from 1969 to 1990. As JN recalls:

> I was very privileged; I had Lorris Elliott. He was the *only* Black professor in the department at the time, and Lorris was an expert on Caribbean literature ...
>
> What made Lorris Elliott so important, for so many levels – he was a magnificent person, kind, generous, brilliant. What you get with a Black professor and can have as an opportunity, and I would say obviously this attaches to other racialized professors, is someone who can excavate or bring in forms of knowledge that only they can do. The most well-intentioned person tossing in a Caribbean author is not the same as someone who says, "I'm not only going to teach Caribbean literature through the lens of the West, but I'm going to say it has something, a resonance, a form, unique to itself and I see that." I would argue that you see to the spirit, to the structure of the knowledge. There is something about the experiential expertise we bring – and I say "we" because I've now become a professor – that we bring to our work. We legitimize the work by teaching it whole.

Suggesting the impact of cumulative educational experiences character-ized by whiteness, some students, particularly those from Canada, have a somewhat fatalistic view regarding the near-absence of Black professors and form their expectations of the university accordingly. As DN explains:

> I guess for me, I've always approached academia, and this might be because of the circumstances I've grown up in, ... I've always been used to having a certain demographic of teachers. So I've gotten used to having that. So, for me, the way I measure success is not whether or not I have someone to look up to, it's whether or not I can do my best in the circumstances that are given to me ...
>
> Y'know how Frantz Fanon talks about the internalization of an inferiority? I'm not saying I've internalized inferiority, but I've definitely, there's been an internalization of *circumstance* ... I'm used to the circumstances in which I have to thrive, and for me, I do think there are more ideal circumstances, but I guess that I've internalized that the environment can be as such. And for me that doesn't imply inferiority, it means that I need to do more. So, for me I'm internalizing that I need to do better, because of the environment around me. I guess I need to persevere *despite* not having [a Black academic] role model. Even though I think that in ideal circumstances you *would* have that.

Strong rootedness in local Black communities and access to mentorship outside of the university can mitigate both expectations of and depen-dency upon such relationships with professors, as suggested in XX's response to being asked if he received mentorship from his professors:

> I was a bit arrogant. So mentorship? Not necessarily mentorship per se. I was very determined, I was very driven, I knew what I wanted, I knew what I knew ... I wasn't necessarily looking for mentorship per se, and I think I'd already received it, when I was younger, with the McGill [Black Student Network] students because we'd set up a reading group and I was sufficiently grounded, at least from my perspective. So, mentorship no, but I wasn't necessarily looking for it.

This "not looking for it" reflects a belief that to do so would likely be fruitless. XX felt that any negative impact of lacking mentorship within the university had been pre-emptively undermined by the acceptance and emancipatory learning experiences he had as an adolescent with Black young adults in his community.[39] Prepared to carry forward a tradition of Black student activism, he came to McGill excited and pre-pared to assert himself.

If not looking to professors for mentorship is "a bit arrogant," as XX says, it is also a defense mechanism and response to what DN, in the comments quoted above, calls "an internalization of circumstance."

Another interviewee, DT, notes that throughout her schooling she

> always wrote about some perspective of either the Black community in Montreal, being Black in Canada, the African diaspora, something that related to who I was. And I also knew, even in university, that *I* was schooling *them* ... And that was often the comments I got, you know, "Oh, A+, great content!" "Very interesting read!" And I thought, "Yeh, because you didn't know anything before you read my paper."

As DT's comments highlight, Black Canadian students make learning in school meaningful through teaching ourselves and drawing knowledge and guidance from our communities. When I asked DT if she had sought and received any mentorship from her professors at McGill, she laughed heartily:

> Nahhh! [*laughs*] you mean *from them*? Why would I want mentorship from white people who hadn't a clue who I am? What would they be mentoring me about? What is it that they could tell me about myself that I didn't already know, which I got from my mum, and my aunts and my grandmothers and the women in my life and my other aunts and uncles and you know, the collective [Black] community? The wonderful people around me – people like Dolores [Sandoval], and other people like Juanita Westmoreland – these were the women that I looked up to. These were the women whose journey before me I took on as an example. Even people like Esmeralda Thornhill, who actually is my peer, but still, there are people who went into certain fields and certain areas, where I turned around and thought, "Y'know what? It's doable. It's definitely doable. Look at this. Look at this strength walking here." I didn't need to be schooled by these people [in the university], or mentored if that's the word you want to use.

It is important to note that such comments do not assume a dichotomy between university professors and Black elders and mentors; the three women DT mentions by name – Sandoval, Westmoreland, and Thornhill – have taught at universities. DT's point is that it is because of her deep family roots in Montreal that she grew up knowing these women and other mentors, and within her program of study at McGill there was no mentorship from Black professors available to her.

Largely responsible for constructing and guiding their own programs of study while accountable to the academic standards of the institution, many Black students, especially those working in the social sciences and education, are inspired and informed by a Black radical educational tradition of simultaneously working within and against the university and relations it upholds. As MR explains about her time as a student:

> They kind of couldn't touch me in a sense, because I wasn't just talking about race and then getting C's, not that people do that, but they couldn't – my shit was tight. And I was very intellectual about it, and I still maintain that that's my thing. This for me is like an intellectual project, it's not [just] personal feelings, it can be both – and, and personal feelings matter, and it's not fair that people feel like crap because these institutions are so racist, but this – there's a huge archive of [Black] *intellectual work*.

As the comments above suggest, a strong sense of identity and belonging within local, cultural, Black intellectual, or "back home" communities can protect students' self-esteem in lieu of seeing and learning from people who "look like us" in school. However, this should not be taken to suggest a lack of issue; students are also hurt and feel defeated by experiences of being ignored and devalued by professors. As one shares:

> I had the impression that they didn't even care to acknowledge the experiences of non-white students in their own class, because for them it was not an important topic. So they really didn't care. It's not to care; for me it's just as bad as discriminating ... I felt like they didn't really care about whether or not our experiences were heard or acknowledged, it wasn't what they valued, they didn't really give it a thought; that's what I felt.

Black students deserve to have access to the formal mentorship and informed guidance in their academic studies that can challenge them personally and intellectually and help to guide their work forward. Learning occurs through professors and students working together dialogically, with both acting as teachers and learners in this endeavour. As one professor states in underscoring the importance of continuing to learn from their mentors: "'I sit on their floor,' as we say back home, whether they're professors or not professors, I feel that they are the ones that teach me." Such understandings of teaching and learning stand in critical contrast with notions of individual masters and mastery, once again undermining the possessive individualism of the academy.

In a university environment where professors – particularly white men – are assumed to be all knowing, it can be daunting for students to assert counternarratives, which undermines the potential for critical thinking through problem posing and dialogue.[40] Black students thus often feel obliged – and are disproportionately required – to risk challenging such norms through the often taxing work of challenging professors' racism or compensating for their ignorance of Black intellectual thought. As one student states, "It was part of my radical approach to academia, I guess. And my understanding of what the role of the student is and scholarship kind of gave me that sense of empowerment to challenge." Another student describes the effect over time of being in a class with a white male professor he had been "challenging all year." One day the professor claimed that the notion "that racism is a form of violence is just ridiculous. It's got to the point that if I tell somebody I don't like their hair, we call me a racist." The student's further comments suggest the day-to-day emotional and intellectual labour that Black students regularly put into assessing when and when not to challenge their professors:

And he said this and I'm sitting beside my friend K and K's the only other Black person in the class and she's got these beautiful Bantu knots tied up on her head, and I'm sitting here with my locs and everything and I just started to laugh! I just started to laugh, y'know, and I was sitting there giggling in class and he's trying to keep, be serious, and be – I don't know *what* he's tryin to do. But I just like, it got to the point where it's just like, I'm not gonna' engage anymore, y'know? And I still don't know if that's a good or a bad reaction because, y'know, part of me is like, you *always* have to engage and you can never let something like that be uncontested, and then part of me is like, y'know, at a certain point after having contested him this whole time, at a certain point I just don't feel the need to prove anything to him. It's like, it gets to the point where you just realize that what you're experiencing is true, and needing to have validation from, y'know, some old white dude is like just a waste of breath at a certain point.

The Power of the Prof

Students face experiences of being made to feel invisible at some times, and at others of being made hyper-visible through racialized – and always simultaneously gendered – attention and racist microaggressions. While professors can be the perpetrators of such abusive behaviour, they are also understood as potentially powerful allies in their ability to set a respectful and inclusive tone in classroom interactions and to subtly reach out to racialized students. For example, RL explains that all of his professors at McGill were white and he felt ignored and devalued, until one professor "used her privilege to turn it around." He recalls:

> I always made sure to sit in the back of the class ... That was on purpose, because, I did that, because I didn't feel valued enough to speak up and say how and what I feel and speak my own mind, in general in the university setting, and especially here at McGill. So I just said, "might as well, if you're invisible, in general at McGill, you might as well stay invisible." So that's what I did. I always used to sit in the back of the class because I felt like other people, whether they be white students or professors, they wouldn't care to hear about what I think [or] how I feel.

He then took a class taught by a professor who was "conscious of the non-white experiences of students" and spoke about racism and systemic oppression in her lectures. RL says, "She really made me feel like I actually belonged at McGill for the first time in my life."

> She actually encouraged me to speak up in that class. And once I raised my hand once, she wouldn't let me go! And she'd ask me all these questions and so I feel that she was kind of a mentor to me. Someone I could really relate to and I could trust that she wouldn't just dismiss me because I'm not like her.

Other students similarly describe white women professors who have reached out to them and provided much-needed support. As one of these students recalls about a teacher of postcolonial literature and theory, "her being a feminist and her and I sharing similar ideologies ... I could talk to her about anything, I adore her."

While it cannot be assumed that women or feminist professors have racial literacy or a commitment to making the university a less hostile place for Black students, they may be more likely to be aware of institutional oppression and that racism is deeply intertwined with patriarchy. The preponderance and dominance of white men is difficult to ignore; women academics continue to be significantly under-represented in many academic disciplines, especially at the higher ranks of associate and full professor. Women continue to face striking wage gaps compared to their white male colleagues: 18.2 per cent for white women and an incredible 32.2 per cent for racialized women.[41] As a young male student explains of his Black women colleagues in law school, "because of their gender and their colour, ... they do double what I have to do, I think. Because they face adversity from two ways." Such inequity, reinforced by normalized patriarchal values and behaviours, is structurally embedded and reproduced within Canadian universities.[42] As one graduate student explains of the professoriate in her department:

> At the undergraduate level, at the very bottom I guess you could say, when you first start out, it's mainly females. And then as you get higher and higher to the graduate level, like the master's level, say, then there are more males. And then as you get to the PhD level there are even more males. So it's interesting to me, because for such a female-dominated field, in the higher levels there are definitely more males. I only know of one professor who's a visible minority, he's male, ... and I know of one other, there's one Black [male] professor on the Macdonald campus that I'm aware of.

Concentrated white male dominance and an emphasis on power, hierarchy, and individual competitiveness create conditions hospitable to interpersonal abuses of power in the form of sexual violence and harassment, which is a pervasive problem in universities throughout the country.[43] For Black and other racialized women – who are both more likely to experience sexual harassment and less likely than white women to be perceived as having been harassed – experiences of sexual harassment are always simultaneously experiences of racial discrimination.[44]

A Black woman graduate student describes a professor for whom she had worked as an undergraduate student in the early 2000s. She explains there was an "element of bonding" with this professor that she attributes in part to the fact that the professor was a person of colour from a working-class background:

> I think he just felt he could talk to me about that [his experiences of race and class] in ways that he couldn't talk about it in front of his other colleagues and students ... I definitely feel like there was definitely some element of this was a safe space for him because he didn't have to pretend he didn't want to talk about racism.

The student explains how this professor abused his power over her, highlighting the interlocking power relations that shaped their relationship:

> He was kind of fucked up and sexual harassing a little bit, like I was too young to understand what was going on, but I look back and there

were definitely moments where I was like, "No, I could get you fired right now if I was wearing a recording device." And I had an email where he was like, "If you get this to me by tonight you can have my second child." I don't know, if someone wrote that to me now, with what I know – are you *kidding me*? ... So, yeh, that was an issue. *And* he never paid me on time!

Even in hindsight and knowing what she knows now, as she reflects on the situation the student calls her own behaviour into question, questioning whether her willingness to be "very forthcoming" with her own experiences of racism at the university somehow encouraged the professor's behaviour. Her comments suggest the impact of what has been called "common bond bias" in shaping her understanding of a racial bond between herself and the professor as well as how she perceived and responded to the professor's sexual harassment within a broader context of white supremacy.[45] Such a sense of common bond further confuses racialized students as they seek to "make sense" of sexually suggestive behaviour by their professors that may also be strategically cloaked in ambiguous statements and gestures. In this student's case, the professor's comment about having his second child not only implies the student's presumed sexual availability – as his employee, as a young woman, as a Black woman – but also suggests her role is to breed, proposing the "opportunity" to produce his offspring as a reward for doing her job according to his scheduling needs. The ambivalence communicated in the student's final comments on the matter suggests how naturalized such power relations are in academia: "I don't know, he still wrote me a letter [of recommendation], even though I had to write him emails every day for like three weeks, he did eventually do it and like, I don't know."

The manner in which students and professors identify sexual harassment is filtered through the broader institutional culture of white hegemony, patriarchal male dominance, and competitive individualism.[46] The university environment naturalizes professors' power over students, men's power over women, white men's power over racialized men, and white women's power over racialized women.[47] In another example, BT describes a woman professor, Dr. R., and the particular attention she paid to him:

BT: I'm still looking for Dr. [R]; that was my sweetheart. She was an older lady; she had a thing about Blacks and Indians.

ROSALIND: She was a white woman?

BT: Yeh! [*imitating a woman's voice*] "I don't know why I have this skin, it's not nice. I wish I was like *you*" – She'd say it in class; a class of white Canadians and middle classes! That was a little kind of embarrassing for me [but] she didn't care, y'know? She had this thing and she used to spend all her time and all her holidays in India.

As a Black young man in an environment in which he often felt devalued, BT recalls Dr. R. with great fondness that suggests a schoolboy's crush, even fifty years later. He says, "That Dr. R. is still with me ... She wasn't typical at all, but she took a *real* interest in me." When later in our interview I ask BT if he had received mentorship from teachers at the university, his response is, "Only Dr. R. Dr. R. is the only one who would take the time."

The choice between relative invisibility and isolation on the one hand and subjection to a white fetishizing gaze on the other is, of course, not one that students should be forced to make. At the time of this writing, a new generation of McGill students – particularly Black and other women of colour – are amidst a highly public campaign pressuring the university to address the long-standing, pervasive culture of sexual violence. They join their peers at universities throughout the country and in the United States, asserting their experiences and analyses of sexual violence on campus in the context of a widespread movement of women sharing their experiences, naming sexual predators, and calling them to account.[48] At a 2018 rally on campus of a thousand McGill and Concordia students joined by faculty members and plenty of press, the important analysis that these women are insisting be incorporated into this struggle was evident. Their speeches linked sexual harassment at McGill to sexual violence in society more broadly, to racism and heteropatriarchy, to missing and murdered Indigenous women, and to ongoing settler colonial relations. In an example of this nuanced analysis, a Black student named Halle-Mackenzie Ashby, who had not planned to speak, was inspired by the moment and took the microphone to assert:

Just for women of colour who feel that their experiences aren't valid, I will tell you that they are. All the types of sexual violence that occur, it doesn't mean that you need to be touched or anything physical needs to happen. In my experience I was made to feel like a token, I was fetishized, I was made to feel special. And all the women of colour who are told by professors that they are there for them, they are their martyrs; that is not true. You have your own power. We have our own agency.[49]

Conclusion: Expectations Meet Experience

Students come to McGill University with expectations shaped by its history and reputation as an elite school. However, once they are within the university environment this institutional history and status are revealed as deeply racialized, causing many Black students and faculty members to feel marginalized and excluded. Several are disturbed by the university's celebration of its colonial origins and glorification of James McGill, a particularly disorienting experience for those accustomed to the typical denial of Canadian histories of colonialism and slavery. Black Canadian students also struggle with interlocking racialized and class-based disadvantages. On the other hand, people from middle- and upper-class backgrounds and those who had previous lived experiences of British colonial cultural norms tended to find the culture of the university more familiar and, as such, somewhat less destabilizing.

The comments of participants in this study highlight and lend further support to a body of research confirming the unpaid and unrecognized labour that Black, Indigenous, and other racialized scholars perform in the Canadian academy.[50] Black professors should not be hired in order to serve as role models for Black students, to serve as "race informants," or solely to meet "diversity" quotas at otherwise white universities. Rather, more Black professors should be hired to contribute to the range of teaching and research perspectives and methodologies, to expand the breadth and depth of knowledge production whatever their fields of interest and expertise. While thinking of Black professors as "role models" can promote tokenism and narrow conceptions of success, Black professors can and do provide essential mentoring for Black students. As professor of law Adelle Blackett argues, mentoring is a form of friendship. It is "very much about building relationships across differentials in age, experience, power with the explicit purpose of expanding the life options or advancing the career of the mentee."[51] As Blackett observes, in spotlighting the important role that mentorship has always played in academic success, we further expose the myth of meritocracy. While my argument is not that Black students cannot receive effective mentorship from non-Black professors, comments from interviewees demonstrate their desire for these sorts of relationships with Black professors and their understanding of how such relationships will aid them in their careers. Moreover, explicitly centring student needs and career interests in mentoring relationships provides a critical alternative to professor-student relationships based on the assertion and reproduction of professors' power and privilege.

The ongoing devaluing and exclusion of non-European knowledges and non-white professors and scholarship in university courses and curricula sends students the message that what they think, say, and write will not be valued either. This creates pressure on and in some cases motivates Black and other racialized scholars in the academy to focus our teaching and research on matters related to racialization and on revaluing non-European peoples and their experiences, only to then risk being characterized as preoccupied with race. As one professor describes, "We're [perceived as] hysterically identity-obsessed, and all these white scholars who do everything on whiteness and never name it are somehow just working neutrally." The assumed neutrality of whiteness lies at the centre of liberal conceptions of race. Black people's experiences demonstrate that the pervasive whiteness of the university and refusal to name it reinscribe racial categories and create a heightened awareness of one's Blackness; as African American writer and anthropologist Zora Neale Hurston wrote in 1928, "I feel most coloured when I am thrown against a sharp white background."[52] In the next chapter I ask, more specifically, what is this co-constitutional relation between "whiteness" and "Blackness"? I examine how processes of Black racialization function in constructing and maintaining the whiteness of the university.

5

Being and Becoming Black

Well, y'know, "Black" is definitely something that I learned here in Canada, because in Africa we don't call ourselves or each other Black, or I'm Black, you're Black, we're Black – this Western concept of African-descent people living in a white supremacist world. Because of the history of colonialism and slavery you had this distinction of white people, Black people, and they were put into boxes, and so we as African-descended people took on this word to define us in the face of adversity and the white supremacist world. So something that I learned here in Canada, but eventually I became kind of assimilated and ended up calling myself Black also after years. (RL)

This chapter highlights the dialectical construction of whiteness and Blackness within the university setting. I examine how Black students and faculty experience racialization through interpersonal relationships, academic curriculum, and institutional texts and discourses. Rather than suggesting one universal "Black experience" of the university, these varied experiences and conceptions of Blackness speak to the manner in which racialization is further shaped by differences in gender, class, and nationhood. I critically analyse these experiences of identifying and being identified as Black, particularly as they relate to Canadian settler nationalism and higher education. My analysis thus suggests the function of the category "Black" and the institutional imperative of maintaining – while simultaneously denying – this category and its significance. I discuss how, once racialized as Black, students and faculty manage the denigration of Blackness through avoiding and confronting racialized stereotypes shaped by class and gender. The last sections of this chapter highlight how Black people respond with what I term anticolonial identity work: deconstructing racism and racial tensions and barriers, reconstructing themselves as human, and redefining Blackness in politicized terms.

While the people I interviewed do not necessarily refer to themselves as activists, all of them self-identify as Black and most understand their racialized experiences and antiracist organizing as part and parcel of the "everyday life work" of being Black in the context of the academy.[1] This identification is complex and unstable, and not taking for granted the meaning of "being Black" reveals processes of racialization, how they function and to what ends. Race has been the primary lens through which many Black people in North America have historically defended ourselves against whiteness and understood our experiences of economic and other forms of oppression.[2] Hence, while there is and always has been an anticapitalist Black radical tradition,[3] many critical race theorists take issue with (most often white) Marxists' reduction of race to ideology and especially the suggestion that racialized identity represents a form of "false consciousness."[4] As Michael Dumas asserts, this tension "is not a matter of choosing between race and class but of how to best explain the relationship between race and class, and how to situate and engage race and racism within a critical social critique and political praxis."[5] Hence, examining whiteness and Blackness is part of elaborating a "critical *raceclass* theory"[6] that draws on the strengths of critical race and Marxist theories to formulate analysis that can effectively address the totalizing effects of white hegemony under neoliberal capitalism.[7]

A Word on Whiteness

Race is a category constructed by and for the benefit of particular people of European ancestry – deemed white – within specific historical, social, political, and geographic contexts. Racialization was and is intended to naturalize unearned privilege and an inequitable social order centring and normalizing whiteness and white people as that from which other "races" deviate. Black people have been constructed as the most not-white of all, as it is "through the negation of Blackness, or according Blackness only negative meaning" that whiteness is constructed and expressed.[8] In asking what specifically makes a university or a country "white," and how this relates to "white people," I understand whiteness as a racial discourse and social practice that posits white people as idealized subjects, superior to those who are understood as not-white. Whiteness is "primarily about the exercise of power."[9] As a way of knowing and worldview "supported by material practices and institutions," whiteness confers unearned privileges and structural advantages on white people, including the psychosocial, economic, and political power to define and to exclude Others.[10] Finally, whiteness grants white people the right to accumulate material resources from and at the expense of Indigenous peoples and people of colour.[11]

White people who embrace whiteness as their identity use "white racial knowledge" to maintain a self-perception of racial neutrality and innocence through a range of strategies that normalize and conceal the effects of race on their lives and on the lives of non-white people.[12] In so doing, they uphold and reproduce white dominance. Because society is already structured to reproduce white dominance, without the explicit acknowledgment, disruption, and refusal of that system and how it benefits them, white people contribute to upholding it.[13] While white people have choices about whether they attempt to maintain and reform whiteness or to abolish it, whiteness as ideology cannot be transformed into something that is not oppressive, or not racist – by definition it is always about racial domination.[14]

Socialization in a Culture of Whiteness

I think ... as a community we're kind of resisting some of what was the socialization that maybe we were supposed to be participating in, so I don't think it was ever something that we were trying to do, to be socialized by McGill. (VR)

"Socialization" refers to the formal and informal processes through which the culture of the university is communicated to individuals: how people become aware of the values, norms, and knowledge required for success within the institutional culture.[15] As William Tierney reminds us:

Insofar as socialization is a cultural act, ... it is an interpretive process involved in the creation – rather than the transmittal – of meaning. Culture is not discovered by unchanging recruits. Rather, socialization involves a give-and-take where new individuals make sense of an organization through their unique backgrounds and the current contexts in which the organization resides.[16]

While Tierney's position does not address the ways in which power intervenes to shape socialization, his critique of a modernist understanding of socialization is important: "socialization is not simply a planned sequence of learning activities" through which people are either assimilated and become "effective members of society" or not. Such a belief relies on "a unitary view of what it means to be effective,"[17] and suggests our only options are those of the dominant group.

Certainly, all participants in this study were aware of a dominant culture at the university and experienced pressure to accept and adopt its norms and values. Their stories demonstrate how in negotiating racialization and hegemonic whiteness, students and faculty members variously integrate into, resist, and refuse the dominant culture of the university depending on other aspects of their identities and backgrounds. Attending to these differences highlights that there is no essential "Black experience" of the university; what participants share is the common experience of social relations that are organized through institutional texts, discourses, and practices to (re)produce particular, historically developed social arrangements that include racialized, gendered, and class-based hierarchies.[18]

In addition to the work involved in coping with structural disadvantages and racism as a Black person at the university, being or becoming "Black" itself can also be understood as a form of labour. Racialization involves constant intellectual, psychological, and emotional work as one is viewed and categorized as racially different from the normative whiteness of the environment. Several participants faced racialization for the first time at McGill, as they had not identified as "Black" prior to coming to Canada to study. This was a significant difference from their peers from Canada and the United States who were born into a society in which they were already deemed and understood themselves as Black.

Naming Race and Racism

Well, I think people are a lot more comfortable talking about international students from different parts of the world, and talking about students who are from Africa and the particular issues that they may be dealing with as students in a new country and what not, and somehow talk about that, and do not. Talk. About the fact. That these. Students. Are *Black*! Black in Montreal! In a city that's had a number of issues of racism ... These African students are in this city where there are still enough unresolved issues with – I mean how do you ever resolve something like race? But it's not even talked about, not even whispered about. You know what I mean? So how do you talk about that and not acknowledge the context in which they exist? It's because they're not Black, they're African. You know what I mean? It's like being African is not Black, you're African ... And it's another way not to have to talk about [race]! I think that there is a conscious – because to me, you look at all areas and it's not talked about! This is not happenstance and it's not by accident. There has to be some kind of concerted effort to not acknowledge that it is something that should be addressed or spoken about, or even said, the word written, the issue of race. (Black Canadian student)

Whether or not people I spoke to were inclined to speak directly and explicitly about race and racism varied according to several other factors, including area of study – students and faculty who study race and racialization are much more inclined to use this language – as well as personality and national and cultural background. For example, BT and GR, who came to McGill as international students from the Caribbean between the late 1950s and early 1960s, speak indirectly about race and tend not to use the word "racism" in their narratives, finding other ways to frame their experience. GR suggests this is a conscious strategy for navigating race that he learned at McGill:

> What I learned in that period is … that you have to observe the world around you, and you have to – there are things you respond to, verbally, and things you don't. And you have to read people and you have to try to understand what are their motivations. In other words, if a professor treats you in a particular way, you have to be careful about attributing motives to him or her before you understand it. One of the things I still very strongly say to people within the Black community, outside the Black community, is be very careful about labelling someone as a racist or bigot. Because [if you do] it's the end of the discussion. There's nothing you can do … I think what I learned at McGill is that people do things for many different reasons, and you should be, as a Black person or a minority, you have to be very careful to try to really understand where they're coming from before you label them … Because there were people here who were very good to me, and there were people I suspected, you know, of being not so good – I couldn't prove it, and I had to sort of figure out how do I handle it, and I learned how to handle it.

GR also uses the term "Canadian students" to refer specifically to white Canadians, suggesting a broader avoidance of race as a primary framework. The collapsing of race and nation seems to be reinforced by his experience of entering McGill and Canada as an international student who understood himself and most of the other Black people he knew as foreigners to the university and the country:

> Part of that, I think, was that we were in an international university, and so people, even Canadian students after being here for a year were used to seeing foreigners, they were used to seeing Blacks.

He connects his success in navigating the culture of the university to his familiarity with living under British colonial rule in the Caribbean, recalling a previously quoted student's suggestion that the British architectural aesthetic sets "the tone of what they expect from us in a weird way." GR recalls:

McGill was very British in a lot of senses, and I guess those of us who came from British colonies – a lot of the Africans and Blacks that came here had come from some form of British colony – were actually quite used to that form of dealing with things: very non-confrontational, if you had a problem there were ways to deal with it, and you tended to avoid confrontation.

While also from the Caribbean, BT experienced McGill as less accommodating and easy to adjust to during this era than what GR describes. BT says he found the university to be "extremely conservative," adding "when I came here at first it was a big culture clash for me, man!" When I asked for an example of how he experienced this culture clash, BT points to the lack of value the university placed on track and field, his sport of choice. He describes other students and athletes laughing at him:

> They were laughing if you took a soccer ball and went trying to do some dribbling and they'd start laughing. It was really weird. The only thing here was hockey … So I found it in everything you wanted to try; it was very conservative, a very conservative approach to everything.

Given the manner in which hockey is such a part of Canadian national identity and even today Canadian professional hockey is strikingly dominated by white men, it is difficult not to detect a reference to whiteness in BT's use of "conservative." Likewise, in discussing the professoriate, BT repeatedly cuts himself off mid-sentence, creating breaks in his narrative within which I perceive unspoken references to interlocking relations of race and class:

> Some [professors] were very, very, very obviously anti – I mean, they had this – McGill had a really fantastic reputation, eh? At that time, the school was one of the international bodies you could find … But some of the teachers were very – that's what I mean by conservative. Like if you didn't fit a certain pattern and you didn't have a thing they could go and check and see how you did in high school and how you did in this, and if you didn't conform to all that stuff; they would never … spot talent from an unorthodox standpoint. If you were a guy that was coming up from the ghetto or some guy – but brilliant, they would never know.

BT's choice of words as he identifies professors' inability to recognize the "unorthodox standpoints" of racialized students is significant, focusing on the limitations of the faculty and of the curriculum, limitations that can render the knowledge and talent that Black students bring to academia invisible or illegible.[19]

People I interviewed whose experiences of McGill were after the mid-1970s are considerably more explicit in naming and critiquing racism, white hegemony, and the impact of institutional whiteness on their experience. RL, for example, offers the following critical analysis of "whiteness" and its value at the university as he describes his recent experiences:

> I really noticed that I felt like I was the Other, but people weren't doing it – like people around me here at McGill, people were not doing it on purpose to make you feel like you were different. It's just the way it's set up; the way McGill's set up, and the way the environment is, and the students, and the life at McGill, just makes you feel if you're not part of whiteness or if you don't value whiteness – 'cause that's one odd thing though: a lot of non-white people, whether they be students or professors, anyone at McGill, even if they're not white, I feel like if you can value whiteness and kind of put whiteness on a pedestal, then you can fit in. That's what I've noticed. But it's not me. I'm a really pro-Black person, pro-Black and … I like to see my people succeed, and not just be ignored and made to feel irrelevant. So I didn't feel comfortable doing that, but I noticed some other Black students and other non-white students have no problem fitting in here because they value whiteness above themselves.

When asked if he could explain this point further, RL describes encountering Black students who, due to "internalizing white supremacy," will not engage with their Black classmates, "they just ignore other Black students":

> So, this one guy would acknowledge everyone else, but not me. Which I thought was really, not self-hatred, but close to that. Okay? Because I guess I reminded him that he looks like me, and he didn't want to see this mirror reflection by looking at me, or acknowledging me. So it's like running away from yourself.

RL implies that in order to integrate and succeed in the university culture Black people need to demonstrate their willingness to value whiteness, and that for some students this involves a form of self-effacement that requires avoidance of other Black people. His analysis identifies race as a determining factor in whether not only white but also Black students will acknowledge and interact with him. Recent research examining blackface performances at Canadian universities supports this claim. Philip Howard similarly finds that for some Black students, proximity to whiteness entails distancing from Blackness. Howard refers to this as a "colonially motivated rejection" that reflects efforts by Black students "to be accepted as fully human by being one of the boys, who are normatively white," necessitating both "distance from Blackness" and overlooking its derision.[20]

"I Didn't Know I Was Black"

People kept on saying, "I didn't know I was Black 'til I came to McGill!" Even if they were born in Canada, they were like, "I didn't have this conception of myself as *Black* before coming to McGill." And to a certain degree that's true for me but not so much as it was for a lot of people in that room, coming from Africa, coming from the Caribbean, coming from everywhere – it seemed to be this sort of idea that you come to this space, where, in some senses your identity as a Black person is necessarily under threat, right? (KB)

The complex ways in which perceptions and experiences of Black racialization are shaped by culture, nationhood, class, and gender clearly emerged as I interviewed people from various backgrounds. As KB comments above, generally students from countries in which Black people form the majority say they had not thought of themselves as "Black" until they came to Canada or McGill. Expressing sentiments declared by several students raised in African or Caribbean countries, LG explains: "I was born in Africa, in [country], and race wasn't – well everyone looks the same, so race isn't a – it's not something I was ever aware of, to be honest." She says that studying law had made her more critical and aware "of the role of race in this society." Likewise, when I ask BR if he had thought of himself as Black when he was at home in the Caribbean, he laughs and says, "No, no, no! Of course not!" adding that "you really feel the difference" as part of a racial minority in Canada or the United Kingdom (where he had previously studied). On "becoming Black" in this way, he says:

I think it can be a bit unsettling. I think initially, especially in my experience, I mean it can be a bit unsettling. I guess it's not only the colour thing, but I guess it's also the other cultural norms … When I did my undergrad back home, I mean again, [in a] predominantly Black [environment], I mean the issue of race doesn't even come up. But here, I think it's often spoken about.[21]

Two students who had been raised in countries with majority Black populations report that it took a couple of years in Canada before they began to recognize racialization and how they were perceived as Black people. LR, originally from a country in the Caribbean, is clear that she "became a racialized woman at McGill" when she began teaching and faced racism from white students. After receiving comments about her race on course evaluations, LR says she "began to feel as if somehow the space was not welcoming to me anymore." However, rather than seeing this as confirming her subordination as a Black person in this society, which was not her usual understanding of herself or her place in the world, LR viewed her experience as an anomaly that she set out to understand:

> Because I figured this couldn't just be about me, it had to be something bigger than me, and so now I've done all this research and I understand, of course it's not about me. So now I kind of feel, I could say, back into my skin [*laughs*], back into my-self; that yes, these are spaces that do belong to me.

This approach allowed LR to empathize with her students, given that she had grown up in a relatively homogeneous environment herself: "So I understand how it is for them to see somebody who they don't expect to see in the position of authority representing the university. That is a big contrast to what they expect." Critically, this approach permitted LR to rechannel her feelings of hurt and anger into a critique of the university and the lack of preparation her degree program provided for her. For LR, both the silence around issues of race – "Nobody talks about the experience that you as a Black person are likely to have in a predominantly white institution" – and the lack of professors whose lived experiences would have made them able to anticipate this issue were responsible for "the most painful experience" she had at the university. Her experiences highlight the difficult, important work of depersonalizing and naming racism while focusing one's critical and analytical gaze on institutional practices and systemic critique. Moreover, her ability to do this work relied in part on her understanding that "this couldn't just be about *me*." This refusal to be identified with and by a colonial definition of Blackness reflects a self-awareness and confidence rooted in knowledge and experiences of her country of birth in the Caribbean and supported by her ability to research the gendered and racialized nature of course evaluations.[22]

Several participants believe that the erasure of Black histories and presence from Canadian school curricula and mainstream social-political discourses disadvantages Canadian Black youth and students.

One student who grew up in an African country expresses empathy for her North American colleagues, whom she describes as having had "more bitter experiences about race" and developed "hostile relations with this dominant group" in their "formative years," making them highly perceptive of and sensitive to racism. She notes:

> That's in contrast to me, who grew up without even thinking about race, and ... I'm only now realizing my race is important. Maybe people do treat me differently, but even when people treat me differently race isn't the first thing that comes to my mind.

To emphasize, the student does not suggest that the racism that her colleagues perceive is imagined. Rather, she acknowledges that due to their longer-term lived experiences of being racialized Black in Canada her colleagues are more perceptive of racism than she is. She considers herself privileged for having grown up without having to *even think* about race, which affects how she now perceives and responds to racialization as an adult.

Black Canadian "Identity Problems"

> If you think about education, it can be incredibly damaging. It can be incredibly damaging. And in terms of our culture, in terms of who we are, our identity, it can be incredibly damaging. It's ... constantly fracturing those messages that you get at home, that get undone on a daily basis at school. Then you go back [home], and you get whole again, you get knitted, and then you go back into school, and something is said again, and it's like a constant – it's just so hard to describe.
>
> My understanding of who I am is as a Black Canadian, not as a Caribbean, and I don't apologize for it. And I get annoyed with other Blacks who constantly want to pigeonhole me, I tell them no. I am Canadian, my mother's Canadian, my grandmother was Canadian, *her* mother was Canadian, her *grandmother* was a slave. I *am* Canadian, do not tell me I am other than that. And I am proud to be that. This is my country, this is who I am, this is my space. And so it's that kind of finality, that kind of – I don't know; I will not be moved from that ... Kids need to be grounded in their *Canadian* identity. And you have the whole system working against it! (DT)

As in any heterogeneous community, long-standing assumptions, perceptions, and tensions exist in Montreal Black communities regarding national, cultural, and political differences, often articulated along divisions between Canadian-born and Caribbean-born people.[23] These differences have been promoted and exploited by the Canadian state,[24] in ways that reinforce stereotypes about Black people, support national myths about Canada, and undermine Black antiracist organizing and resistance across ethno-cultural and class differences. However, as several people I interviewed argue, identity construction is relational, there are significant differences in how people perceive themselves within a Black majority population, and Black Canadian students continue to be disadvantaged by the historical and ongoing erasure of Black people's perspectives and experiences from dominant Canadian histories and social discourses.

In this sense, GR describes Black Canadian youth of the early 1970s as having had "real identity problems," explaining they had "no respect for their own history as Black people, and frankly in some ways had no respect for themselves as Black people. Because they didn't know their own history." RL, a student at the time of our interview, offers a similar comparison in relation to his interactions with other Black students at the university:

> I was born in Africa, I came here when I was ten years old, ... so I have this link, this attachment to Africa in my roots. I'm Black, but non-white students who were born here and were raised in this white supremacist country – and when I say white supremacy I don't mean in a racist or bad way, just the whiteness thing, white is valued. So, if you're born like that and raised like that and you see that in the media everywhere you go, it's easy for you to just fall into the trap, and just believe that okay, well, maybe white people *are* better than me, so let me also try to cater to them, or cater to this idea of whiteness to fit in in this country.

Even SB, born and raised in Canada, invokes these dynamics in describing herself as an undergraduate student in the early 2000s:

> I was very clear of my heritage and very proud so I didn't come in like other Black students who might have been confused, from Canada. I very much identified with the Caribbean and African students at McGill who were very proud of their heritage and knew who they were.

A strong sense of belonging and of cultural and/or national identity is indeed a determinant of postsecondary educational achievement,[25] and can provide Black students with an important foundation from which to navigate the university. Several first-generation Black Canadians said they grew up in "Caribbean homes" with a strong sense of self and of belonging to their parents' country of origin and to a Caribbean disapora community. DT, quoted at the opening of this

section, can trace her family's history in Montreal back several generations, and she attributes her confidence and resilience to her upbring-
ing and the opportunities for mentorship she had accessed within the
Little Burgundy Black community. This grounding helps to mitigate
the potentially destabilizing nature of experiences of racialization in
the university environment. As she argues, this is a crucial issue for
Black learners at all levels of education:

> I think it's so critical that we ground our youth. I cannot tell you how helpful
> that has been for me – or maybe this is what I've been saying – it's sooo
> critical to be grounded, and the younger the better. I think the community
> has done itself a disservice by not – by making the assumption that – I don't
> want to sound elitist, but the Eurocentric kinds of education that we have
> in our schools does not ground our children. What it does is create a mis-
> education of our youth. And some kids can ride over that, but that's a small
> minority. The rest really, really need to understand who they are, which
> Eurocentric education is just not going to give them. How do you create
> confident, well-structured adults? You ground them in who they are.

I contend that what is stake, what has always been at stake, is not
so much a matter of Black Canadian "identity problems" as it is about
"Black Canadian identity" problems. By this I mean to locate the origins of the problem being raised as within the construction of "Black
Canadian" (an oxymoron in the dominant construction of Canada as
a white settler nation) rather than within the psyches of Black Canadians. Erasing and obscuring the roles of European imperialism, settler
colonialism, slavery, and forced migrations in Canada's historical and
contemporary national development renders Black people in Canada
an anomaly, only explicable as always "recent" arrivals to the imagined   naturally-and-originally-white-but-now-multicultural   nation.
There is not a biological or psychosocial deficiency or problem inherent within the identities of Black Canadian people or Black people in
Canada. Rather, there is a problematic embedded in the ambivalent
and contentious construction of "Black Canadian identity." Within the
framing of Canadian liberal multiculturalism, Black racialization both
inscribes one's identity as (if not biologically, then socioculturally) predetermined by one's Blackness, while offering the "hope" that one, as
an individual, might subsequently "overcome" this Blackness through
emulating and aspiring to whiteness. Notably, what is offered is an
opportunity for mimicry, compliance, and deference, not for "becoming white" (and thus being perceived as a "real" Canadian), which is
never attainable from within the body racialized as Black.[26]

Managing Interlocking Stereotype Threats

Black students ... are constantly being invited to transcend their Blackness. Not to come with it, not to insist on it, not to assert it; but to transcend it, as the ultimate statement of colour blindness. And so some people struggle to do that and to live in these two worlds, and some people struggle to exist in these environments in spite of their Blackness – very rarely because of it.[27]

Constructed as a social "problem,"[28] Black people are left to manage, avoid, grapple with, challenge, or refute a range of preconveiced ideas and images associated with them, what Fanon called the "historicity" of Blackness.[29] People I spoke to share various strategies for maintaining one's sense of self and integrity through variously attempting to minimize or embrace racial differences, mirror or reject Eurocentric ideals. Some respond to the dominant culture of the university by emphasizing and asserting Black identities, cultural affiliations, and politics, while others put great effort into masking their differences from the dominant whiteness. Most, however, describe some concern about how their white peers, colleagues, and professors might read their bodies and behaviour through the lens of negative stereotypes, and several talked about navigating tensions between racialized visibility, invisibility, and hyper-visibility. In this way, students especially seem to be impacted by what researchers have described as stereotype threat,[30] the threat that their behaviour will confirm a negative stereotype about them and the group with which they are identified. While stereotype threats are complex phenomena beyond the scope of this research, what is significant here is that these threats can be experienced in relation to one's self-concept, one's perception of the group to which one belongs, one's reputation and the reputation or perception of the group with which one identifies.[31] Such threats can compromise Black students' sense of belonging and ability to succeed academically, regardless of how they respond.

Significant work can and does go into minimizing the visibility of racial difference and compensating for racial stereotype threats. Perhaps more aware of the potential and nature of racial stereotypes, Canadian students are particularly concerned about interlocking race and class differences, as they tended to be from less affluent backgrounds. One recent student in particular spoke extensively to me about how anticipating the perception of others shaped his behaviour at the university. He describes strategizing to avoid being identified as an athlete because of stereotypic assumptions about both Black people and athletes being less intelligent. He also talks about being "wary of saying I like rap or R&B all the time, because I think that brings with it certain stereotypes as well ... [and] I don't want to lead them down paths that they might conclude things." Although this student enjoyed the free vegan meals provided on campus by the Midnight Kitchen collective, he did not like for his peers to know this. If they were to find out, the student explains, he would declare that he was being "cheap," which he describes as putting a "disclaimer on it ... so that people don't frown upon it, so people can laugh about it." He says:

> I think [I'm concerned about] the assumption that I come from a poorer background, that I'm not *as* wealthy, and if not that assumption, then I think it's the assumption that maybe they do see me as coming from privilege and maybe I'm taking advantage [of the free food] – I guess I don't want them to have that dialogue, or to think about that, so I just put it out there immediately that I'm sort of a cheap person so that's all they can think about. So I don't want them having a dilemma [about] how to position me in their minds.

In other words, the student understands being stingy as more socially acceptable and normative among his colleagues than being in financial need. Furthermore, his comments suggest the subtle, racialized difference between the behaviour of stinginess and that of "taking advantage" of one's access to a situation. His nuanced analysis of how his racialized and gendered body is read and the consequences of these perceptions within various spaces and contexts in the university sometimes even led him to choose "to play up a stereotype, as opposed to fight against it" as a protective strategy, "almost like a shield." He explains:

> If you act, sometimes, the way people expect you to be, they'll leave it at that. So it's almost like a shield to use as well. If you accept the way people perceive you, and you know that's not who you are but you play it up so that they stop their commentary. I've done that in many circumstances as well.

The mental and emotional energy involved in such conscious self-policing in order to avoid fulfilling negative characterizations of Black people while attempting to "fit in" to the university environment should not be underestimated. Comments by another Canadian student, CH, reveal how interlocking stereotype threats associated with Blackness and Black womanhood kept her constantly aware of "the littlest things" she'd do:

I think that one thing that's really interesting is that for me, the experience of double consciousness in terms of my race – well, I guess even a triple or quadruple consciousness – of being Black, a woman, and also from a low-income neighbourhood. It would be the littlest things, … like I would always feel displaced if I was talking with my hands, or if I used slang, or if I got loud. That I couldn't do that at McGill [meant] that I couldn't *be me* at McGill.

As a Black young woman from a "low-income neighbourhood," CH describes moving through the university with a sharp awareness of how these aspects of her identity combined to call into question her "right" to be there. Moreover, her Blackness challenged dominant notions of ideal womanhood and her class background caused people, including Black students from more affluent backgrounds, to question her intelligence. As she explains,

I think that one thing that was very difficult in terms of being a Black woman who did come from a lower socio-economic status was the way in which I always felt like my intelligence was being questioned … So I always felt like I had to *perform* a certain Blackness that was not my own, in order to … be seen as an intelligent individual. And that can do a lot to an individual who goes to the same school as everyone else, but feels like her intelligence is constantly being questioned because she doesn't perform Blackness in the way that is acceptable, I guess, for the wider McGill community.

Describing her experiences with international Black students at the university as being most strongly affected by issues of class, CH says that they often corrected the way she spoke when she used "Black American vernacular," and they said things to her like "You're not Black like *us*, you're like, *Black*-Black!"

Regardless of their own gender identification, people I spoke to recognize the unique positioning of Black women in relation to patriarchal whiteness. Many identify Black women's hair as a remarkably persistent and consistent site of the "social devaluing" of Black women's aesthetics, [32] as part of broader practices of racial othering and fetishization that facilitate the repression and exploitation of Black women. [33] As one student, KB, puts it:

Definitely there's sexual elements to [it], y'know, talking to my Black friends who are women here, they're always having issues with people touching their hair, y'know, getting right up in there, y'know, very touchy-feely sort of thing.

Another student shares that they have noticed how many of the Black women in their faculty had changed their hairstyles since their first year at the university "to incorporate the weave, in order to have their hair look more like what has been normalized: the flowing hair." One can imagine this pressure on Black women students in relation to their hair and the attention it draws. Annette Henry writes about how as a Black woman professor, her unstraightened hair is a powerful racial signifier that is regularly seen as "transgressive and unruly," prompting comments such as "Isn't there something you can do with your hair? You know, to press it down a bit?"[34] Likewise, several students I interviewed comment on white people's preoccupation with their hair and report being asked what their hair feels like and whether it's "real." One woman says that in her experience, Black "hair is a point of reference" for white people that helps them to distinguish Black people from one another such that changing her hairstyle had caused some white people at the university not to recognize her.

KB links the obsession with Black hair to that of students dressing in blackface, as had happened at an undergraduate Halloween party on campus in 2012,[35] and further to regular occurrences of blackface performance in Québec and Canada.[36] He explains:

> It's almost as if *because* [the university is] an extra-white space, it's like those sort of things become even more popular – because they don't see Black people? I don't know, I'm still trying to work through it, in my own head, but absolutely, and what a disturbing thing to have happen, especially it's almost like it's a blackface renaissance that we're living through ... [Art historian and McGill professor] Charmaine Nelson writes about it as, there's a reason why blackface emerged after abolition, y'know, it has to do with a way of asserting power over the Black body, saying, "Okay you're not technically enslaved anymore but we can still lynch you, we can still make fun of you," right? And so I'm curious as to why now it seems to be emerging anew. But then again maybe that's just my perception that it's emerging anew, maybe it's just been going on the whole time and I just wasn't aware or noticing it, but because I'm here now, I'm noticing it.

KB's emerging analysis situates a preoccupation with Black hair within the broader project of locating, labelling, categorizing, controlling, and containing Black people. Racialization highlights skin colour and hair as reliable dominant signifiers of Blackness, marking the racial Other. It is in this way that Christiana Collison, writing in the *McGill Daily*, theorizes that to call the "'biological' realness" and "natural 'ownership'" of a woman's hair into question is to ask that she "affirm or deny ... the validity of [her] femininity and ... identity as a woman."[37] Such markers of physical Blackness are associated with a range of social and cultural behaviours that have historically been used to construct Black people as less human, less valuable, and less deserving than white people. If Black people are thought to overcome such behaviours through proximity to whiteness, anxiety around our presence in these "white" spaces evokes a desire to fetishize and contain. The persistence of incidents of blackface on Canadian university campuses (and elsewhere) can be understood in this way: as an exaggerated performance of Black racialization that reassures white people of racial difference and reminds Black people of our assigned social location at the bottom of the racial hierarchy.

As those subjected to what Claudia Jones called the "super exploitation" of interlocking relations of racism, patriarchy, and capitalism,[38] Black and Indigenous women are perceived as the bodies most out of place within the university environment.[39] Indeed, several Black women working as professors, course lecturers, and teaching assistants say that their knowledge and authority have been questioned by their students, especially by white male students.[40] In some cases these women felt that their racialized, gendered bodies in and of themselves had been disruptive to their teaching. As one explains:

> I think the stereotypes of Black femaleness are very much operative in the university. So I've gotten from students and from colleagues, either through direct statements or it's been implied, that I am the angry Black woman. And I could be whispering in front of the class, I could be crying up there, and I'll have students say, "She was yelling at us." ... Y'know what? My body is yelling at you. You see me, and you have an experience of what you *think* I am, through stereotypes from things like TV ... And so my body to you is alarming, or discomforting, or something, in a way that makes you fall back into the safe space for you, of seeing me as always already angry.

While Black people may understand the heterogeneity and fluidity of our various identities, racialization as Black within the university context is based on white settler colonial ideology that requires us to engage in what I think of as anticolonial identity work. This work involves an ongoing process of analysing how this ideology works in relation to how one is and is not seen,[41] anticipating how it is likely to affect and shape one's experiences, responding, and not responding. As a Black woman professor explains:

You end up performing this colonial surveillance on yourself, to be so sure that you never, y'know, do anything out of line, because you're so hyper-aware of the ways that they're going to come back and bite you. But again, that doesn't even work. Because a lot of times the perceptions are so false and so racist and they're not based on anything in terms of reality, in terms of what your actions actually are.

Such work is a deeply personal, political, and intellectual project including and extending beyond the maze of racial stereotypes related to how Black people dress, what Black people eat, the music we listen to, how we speak, our physical strength, our intellect, and how much money we do or do not have. Black students and faculty members engage in and manage an environment shaped and characterized by white hegemony while simultaneously participating in a range of interpersonal and institutional strategies to survive, resist, and redefine how Blackness is constructed, to promote change, and to construct social and political alternatives.

Construction Work

Navigating the highly racialized institutional environment not only requires constant self-examination and self-censorship, it also takes the form of rigorous compensatory social work and what I am referring to here as anticolonial "construction work." This work involves deconstructing racial tensions and barriers, and reaching across lines of racial difference to build interpersonal and collective working relationships, including with white people. While none of the participants suggest that Black people should be solely or even primarily responsible for initiating and maintaining such work, given racialized power dynamics most see it as in their interests, and some students and faculty approach it consciously and strategically. For example, LG describes her determination and strategies to overcome what her father explained would be her "handicap" in law school:

Being Black, trying to get a position in big law firms or in the government, you need to do something extra – my dad told me that. You have a handicap so don't just do what your peers are doing; go beyond. Because you need to go beyond to even be equal to them.

She therefore committed a great deal of time to serving in leadership positions, sitting on committees, and playing on sports teams, participating in "easily over ten extracurricular [activities] every year," for which she was recognized with awards and further opportunities. "Law school is like high school," she explains, "it's like cliques." For LG, the "old boys' club" represents little more than a white patriarchal clique that she navigates socially and through academic/professional networking. Consequently, her comments emphasize both her academic and social involvement: "I go to every party, I *plan* all the parties, I live with them, y'know?" – as her way of conditioning her peers to "see beyond colour ... and then they don't feel, for lack of a better word: guilt-tripped."

In addition to being an actively engaged colleague, LG strategically used her outgoing personality to become socially popular with her peers. From her perspective, her flurry of activity jarred her white peers into recognizing her as "one of them," thus permitting them to transcend their perceptions of Blackness. Illustrating this point, she explains how she took one of her best friends, a white man from her faculty, to a National Black Law Association event. Following the event, she recounts,

> he said to me, ... "I've known you for three years, and I've never thought of you as belonging to this community of Black people. Like I always just saw you as [LG], one of us, like, but you actually belong to this community!" He said that to me. After a whole weekend of Black empowerment, and Black! Black! Black! Black! He's like, "Wow, I did not know this kind of community existed. And that you're a part of it. Y'know, I always just saw you as one of us."

The comment by LG's friend appears to confirm her success in pushing her peers past preconceived notions about her racial identity, while it also points to the assumed benevolence of ignoring racial difference. Either way, in order for LG to be seen even by her close friend as "one of us" the "problem" of her Blackness must be overcome. The normative whiteness of the university creates an environment in which Black bodies *as* Black bodies appear out of place and cause discomfort. By bringing her friend to the National Black Law Association event, LG gave him an opportunity to experience Blackness as something other than a problem and as something he could not ignore. In doing so she set up the conditions for her friend to see her as a Black woman whose life extends beyond whiteness.

As Sara Ahmed demonstrates in her study of racism and diversity in universities in the United Kingdom and Australia, it is the one who inhabits the racialized body "who must work hard to make others comfortable":

You have to pass by passing your way through whiteness, by being seamless or minimizing the signs of difference. If whiteness is what the institution is oriented around, then even bodies that do not appear white still have to inhabit whiteness.[42]

The inherent contradiction of requiring Black bodies to "inhabit whiteness" in academia prevents some Black students from pursuing university and pushes others out. For others, however, the absurdity of this situation further roots us in our "Blackness" and pushes us to (re)define it for ourselves and on our own terms. In such cases, the palpable whiteness of the university can make tangible and identifiable social relations that may otherwise have been more difficult to understand and confront outside of the university.[43] The powerful potential of this process is in how such assertions of Blackness at the university can help prepare us to unsettle white settler possession of the nation, opening space for different understandings of nationhood and what it means to be Canadian.[44]

The experiences of law students in particular point to this dialectical relationship between constructions of Blackness and white settler nationalism in relation to the law in Canada. Several referred to the importance of both Black representation and critical race legal theory in combating systemic racism in Canada, and described collaborating with white colleagues in this regard. All law students I interviewed had been or were involved with the Black Law Students' Association (BLSAM). MK describes his participation in the BLSAM, emphasizing the importance of a range of Black organizing and activist pursuits:

The Black Law Students Association ..., I mean we looked at things like how to increase the Black population on campus in the faculty, where is outreach done, organizing high school visits and to particular high schools when we do that – it was focused on those kind of things ...

People are in law school for all different kinds of reasons, no matter where you're from and what background. So, you won't find a whole crew of people who want to change that system. They want to learn how to succeed in that system. How do I benefit, right? So part of the push [of BLSAM], which is also a valid push, is how do we increase representation in law firms, in *corporate* law firms? How do we get more Blacks in corporate law firms? Right? Which is a valid point, y'know. Is it where I'm going to, personally? No! [But] do I push and do I agree with that analysis? Yes, because the root of that analysis is racism. And y'know? How does the school deal with that and how do the firms deal with that? ...

And you would hear stories about people going in to interviews – I remember in particular, a person who was a year older than me, going in ... to hand in their CV a couple of weeks [before their interview] and the reception desk being, "Oh, good, the messenger boy's here, the messenger boy's here." And he was like, "I'm not the messenger boy. This is my application!" Do you know what I mean? That was the focus in law school, and having other Black law students also who had gone through the law school experience and also the firm experience (so they had the application experience), come talk to us and tell us what it was like and strategies that helped them. And all that stuff which some people would say, that's not political – it is political! That's very political; it's challenging racism. At different levels, but at the root of it it's challenging racism.

In his insistence that such work be understood as political, MK challenges notions of what forms and forums of activism are understood and valued as "Black." As Black Canadian scholar Carl James cautions, we may "hate the politicians," and they may not be talking to us, but our needs and expectations will not be placed on the political agenda if we totally disengage.[45]

Indeed, none of the people I interviewed equated a strong critique of the state with removing oneself from state politics and institutions. Even as many critiqued the university and called its authority into question, achieving success within the institution in ways that the institution values was not an option. Students and professors alike refer to the value placed on education in Black communities and a deep respect for intergenerational sacrifices that have enabled them entry into the university. Across disciplines, many of us share commitments to confronting racism and building more socially just societies from within state institutions such as education, health care, social service, and the law. Echoing MK, LG explains that helping to build racial literacy and an environment in which her white colleagues can feel comfortable enough to get involved in antiracist organizing is a form of career networking, a way of paving the way for other Black law students who will follow her, towards changing the law profession and ultimately, Canadian law. She concludes:

Black [people and] people of colour need to be involved in, for lack of a better word, more *mainstream* opportunities. Because otherwise, it's still going to be us versus them, and you're not getting more allies, and you won't be sought out for opportunities that – opportunities to make change.

In the pursuit of such "mainstream opportunities," a commitment to deep social change requires that we acknowledge and contend with the contradictions of "Black Canadian identity" and critically (re)situate ourselves in relation to the settler colonial capitalist nation state, in relation to Indigenous peoples, and our understandings of Indigenous sovereignty.[46] While racialized communities have relied on rights granted by the state in order to fight discrimination at all levels of society and to hold governments accountable, we must also think critically and question liberal assumptions about rights. Rights constructed by and requiring recognition from the state can validate inequitable power arrangements by setting up state-defined parameters of how we imagine justice.[47] As long as antiracism is conceived of solely in terms of a struggle for racial equality granted by the state, the broader settler colonial, capitalist social order that produced and reproduces racist social relations of domination and subordination remains unchallenged.[48] The goal, as Sandy Grande writes, is to "imagine political/pedagogical strategies that go beyond simply resisting settler relations of power and work instead to redefine the epistemological underpinnings through which the colonial world order is conceived."[49] We do so through engaging with and further developing radical Black and Indigenous knowledges that can facilitate deep social and political change.

Black as in Radical, Radical as in Rooted

I'd seen my father. Every time he had to deal with something having to do with racism and me, my father always took me. So I was always present when my father was dealing with another adult. Because, he said, "you need to learn how to do these things." He was highly conscious. So there I was, not because I was arrogant, but because my dad had told me, when he sent me off to university, that I was capable. (JN)

I guess it's a conscious decision, to just – I think the only way that change can happen is to be bold, right? (LG)

It is often through activist-academic organizing with other Black people and antiracist allies that Black students and faculty members find a sense of belonging and direction at the university. Organizing with student groups and working within the alternative campus community had provided many people I interviewed with a vital sense of social, cultural, and political belonging and purpose, and was understood to

have compensated for racialized and political gaps in formal education at the university. It is important to note that the activist community within and adjacent to the university is not free of racialized and
other oppressive power relations – of course it isn't. Rather, the political
commitments of some activists make them willing to be critically self-
reflexive and work towards building learning communities and political coalitions across differences.

Students who were at McGill in the 1990s and early 2000s in particular talked about what a powerful organizing base the Black Student
Network (BSN) had been for them. The BSN was formed in 1985, at
a time when race was being pushed into campus discourse through a
campaign opposing McGill's support for and investments in apartheid
South Africa. The campaign began in 1979, with the formation of the
McGill South Africa Committee to investigate the university's links with
South Africa.[50] By December 1979 the Students' Society of McGill University (SSMU) had passed a resolution calling for the divestment of all
McGill holdings from South Africa, and within a year had withdrawn
its own funds from the Canadian Imperial Bank of Canada because of
its links with that country. An article in the Canadian University Press
at the beginning of the 1980–81 school year reveals that McGill had over
ten million dollars invested in corporations with South African subsid-
iaries and in major banks supporting the apartheid regime, indicating
that "McGill may have [had] more invested in South Africa than any
other Canadian university."[51]

The divestment campaign was run by a multiracial coalition of student activists affiliated with SSMU and the McGill Daily, which grew
and gained prominence in 1985 as the broader anti-apartheid struggle spread and university students elsewhere took action.[52] Issues of
the Daily published that fall reflect the energy, visibility, and growing
breadth and depth of analysis by student activists participating in a
transnational movement. An editorial published at the beginning of the
school year asserts that "the most damning of all is the assumption that
we are more qualified to judge the interests of South African Blacks
than [they are] themselves," and quotes statements by Steve Biko and
the South African Congress of Trade Unions that call for international
divestment and dispute claims that divestment would negatively
impact Black South Africans.[53] Several articles in this issue of the Daily,
published 12 September 1985, the Day of Action against Apartheid,"
challenge common arguments used against divestment, and a piece
written by Mark Wynston Holder addresses the participation of Black
Canadians in the anti-apartheid movement. Holder's article draws on
interviews with local Black community workers Mary Robinson of the

Negro Community Centre and Ronald Rock of the Black Community Council of Québec, and attributes "low participation" among Blacks to severed connections with Africa, managing the day-to-day demands and stresses of poor and working class life, fear of repercussion from employers; and among the upper and middle classes, the desire to protect their "integration and status." Holder quotes Nigel Crawhall, then president of the South African Committee at McGill, as commenting that there "are too few Blacks in the university" and "many foreign Black students are rich and 'don't particularly care.'" Robinson challenges this last claim with an alternative theory: "foreign Black students are unable to participate in demonstrations of any kind because of a contract they have with the government. They buy your body, soul and mind."[54]

Enter the Black Students' Network. Two months later, in a statement published in the *Daily*, the coordinating committee of a newly formed BSN demand total divestment from South Africa, claiming "as members of the Black race" a "special concern" for the situation that had "thus far gone unrepresented."

> Members of the BSN feel a special responsibility to work constructively within their own community to achieve the abolition of Apartheid. While McGill continues to direct a large amount of monies towards the South African market, we, the Black student population, watch the transfer, in part, of our own monies to an oppressive regime, more notably a regime that oppresses our own peoples.

The BSN asserts that to use "the 'WHITE MAN'S BURDEN' as justification for Investment in South Africa [in arguing] that divestment would only serve to further injure Blacks is to veil the issue at hand and hide behind an attitude borrowed from the colonial days, while giving no economic justification for investment."[55] The statement concludes by identifying the anti-apartheid struggle as one to which Black students had both a responsibility to contribute and a unique contribution to make:

> As Blacks, we acknowledge our special role in respect to the South African situation and are prepared to fulfill that role. As Blacks at McGill our responsibility is to make apparent our dissatisfaction with McGill's present position on the issue of divestment and furthermore to employ our resources to effect change.
>
> Anti-Apartheid is not our sole concern, but in representing the interests of the Black community at McGill we occupy a stance against Apartheid

and subsequently against any McGill action in support of Apartheid. We intend to act upon this stance, for to remain inactive is to remain silent, to condone.[56]

From this point on, BSN members would maintain a strong and visible leading role in the years remaining of the divestment campaign. Following the end of the campaign, they formed their own Southern Africa Committee in the early 1990s to continue organizing popular education about South Africa and the apartheid regime.[57]

Black student organizing in the BSN as well as other ad hoc activist-academic groups and initiatives continues, often involving professors in various supportive roles both visibly and "behind the scenes." In the Black radical tradition, much of this work centres on critical race feminist analysis and activism. Blackness is understood broadly, in relation to ancestry, culture and politics, with an emphasis on understanding local, national, and international contexts and how they shape one another. The BSN mission is to attend to the interests and concerns of "Black students at McGill and in the greater Montreal community,"[58] and it is distinctive in being a group for all Black students regardless of national origins. For SB, who was a member as an undergraduate and again when she returned to McGill as a graduate student, this makes the BSN the best fit for a Black Canadian woman:

> I chose BSN because they were the umbrella group. I didn't want to be part of the Caribbean Student Society because I felt it only dealt with Caribbeans, and I didn't want to deal with MASS, which is McGill African Students' Society, because I felt that only dealt with African needs. But I felt like BSN was kinda' like the umbrella organization that was friends with everybody, so I preferred that. I've always been like that. I prefer an organization that can deal with everybody's needs as opposed to specific. Not that specific needs don't need to be addressed, but I preferred being in the commonality as opposed to the differences.

RL shares SB's assessment of these groups from his perspective as someone from an African country:

> Because I was really shocked to see this white crowd everywhere, it also led me to … join two student organizations here at McGill: the first is MASS, McGill African Students' Society, and BSN, Black Students' Network … Most Black people in MASS, I mean the people who are really involved in MASS, are Africans. And everything that we do is just really African. Even if we're not from the same country in Africa, we still understand each other – the ways, the ways of speaking sometimes, the conversations that

we have sometimes, it's really just *African*, globally, like in general. Which
is really different from the Black Students' Network.

These comments and others by members of these student groups refer
to distinctions between Canadian Black students' experiences and perspectives and those of students rooted in African and Caribbean countries, and suggest Blackness as an African-diaspora politics informed
by a deeply diverse network of people, experiences, and analyses.

Former students describe the BSN of the 1990s and early 2000s as
primarily a political education and activist group: "Very dynamic,
very engaged, very activist," as one former member recalls. Another
interviewee says, "The Caribbean Students Society were the ones who
had all the dances, they had the parties, and we were doing more
like education and activism stuff." This is not to suggest that the BSN
is not also a site of social support and communion, providing many
Black students with a beacon and collective site from which to come
together, develop analysis that connects their experiences on and off
campus, and act on social-political issues that inform and define their
sense of self and well-being. VR, who was not from Montreal, recalls
how she became more active in the BSN in the middle to late 1990s
after friends visited her from out of town and were denied entry into
a local nightclub:

> We were looking for what to do about it, and I met [a member of BSN] and
> he was like: "Here's the office, here's the fax machine." He was telling me
> about human rights complaints and it was kind of like somebody gave
> you the keys to a whole new situation. I think that's when I got more
> involved, versus just going to meetings and stuff like that.

She describes her involvement in the BSN as "the positive side of how
race impacted [her] experience" at McGill:

> I feel kind of more blessed than some [students from] communities that
> didn't have a place like the BSN to go to. I know a lot of people went to
> school and it was just going to school, they had some friends and that was
> it. But I came out with a lot more because of [the BSN] … I had the BSN to
> go to, I had a community.

Likewise, MK describes his organizing and activism outside of his formal studies as "almost like a lifesaver being thrown to me":

> And when I talk about that I'm talking about Black Students' Network, it
> ended up being my lifesaver. That's where we were *questioning* the system,

and we were questioning the system we were actually experiencing – we were questioning *McGill University*.

The effectiveness of the organizing and activism of the BSN during this era reveals how grounding and connections within local Black communities allows for ongoing learning from one generation of students to the next. BSN members of the early 1990s were mentored by Black student activists in the South Africa Committee as well as by former student-activists of the SGWU era.[59] Subsequently they prioritized popular education and mentorship initiatives in local Black communities and for incoming students, particularly in the local Little Burgundy community. The group established a Children's Day, inviting local Black youth onto the McGill campus to encourage them to pursue higher education, and an annual BSN Black History Month event that continues at the time of this writing. VR recalls that a lot of BSN members also served as tutors for children at a local community centre, "so there was kind of, like a piece that felt very BSN, where we'd all be volunteering at Tyndale in the afternoons and stuff like that and [we'd] take people who were not from Montreal down into the [Little Burgundy] community, so that was pretty special I think."[60]

One of the participants I interviewed, XX, was one of the Black youth who benefited from this local BSN outreach in the 1990s. He describes the BSN activists as having offered him access to popular education and opportunities to attend Black intellectual events as an adolescent that would not only encourage him to pursue university, but would powerfully shape his expectations, perceptions, and experiences of McGill when he became a student. As he recalls:

> My expectation [of McGill] was very much based on my experience when I was fourteen and older with the BSN. [I expected] that there would be a strong and activist student life that I would be able to immerse myself in and become an agent of change, both within the confines of the university but also beyond, within the broader Montreal community and perhaps even beyond that.

XX expresses a strong sense of gratitude towards the members of the BSN, not only for helping lay critical foundations that prepared him for university, but also for their attention to creating "accepting and pro-LGBT Black" learning spaces that were "particularly important and impactful" for him as someone who identifies as "gay or queer, depending on the day." Having previously been silenced when he tried to raise the issue of "discrimination faced by Black LGBTs" at a Black community centre, XX recalls how

> to be in this space [among Black university students] where there was this understanding of how homophobia intersects with racism and the importance of validating all of our experiences, that was very powerful for me, even if I had not even or did not identify at that time or realize that I was a queer person. So that was important. So very positive and an intellectually edifying experience with the McGill Black Student Network.

When XX became a student at McGill himself, he made the BSN – as a queer-positive, Black-centred space – his base of organizing:

> It was very vibrant; we were the movers and shakers and we were recognized. BSN was recognized at that point throughout the university student community and even by the senate and the president, as being a force to be reckoned with [and] that needed to be taken seriously.

The sense of empowerment produced through developing critical consciousness and becoming a political "force to be reckoned with" is very striking in students' descriptions of their activist work. This feeling helps students navigate the campus environment and academia overall, it enables them to claim space and make demands on the institutions, and it extends beyond the university as a sense of agency within the communities and the societies within which they live.

Community and Communing

With just one exception, everyone I interviewed talked about the importance of being involved in and maintaining links to local Black communities and community organizations. Underscoring Patricia Monture's assertion that academic assimilation "pressures us to stand outside of our communities,"[61] many of us find that academic norms of competitive individualism heighten the need to remain connected to and grounded within our non-academic communities. KB describes his preparation to "resist being assimilated into the McGill bubble" as having been based on earlier experiences of attending private school: "it's like it only takes [*snaps his fingers*] a couple years before you become totally alienated from your community, or at least distanced from your identity."

"Community" and "university" are not fixed, distinct, and separate realms, just as "activism" is not separate and distinguishable from "community work." To view "community" and "university" as binary oppositions is to normalize the racial-class hierarchy in which universities are deeply invested,[62] and for Black people it reinforces the notion of having to transcend one's Black identity in order to be an academic or to gain economic stability.[63] Popular education does not necessarily require the involvement of academics, and when students and academics are involved, they do not necessarily need to be – and often should not be – in roles of authority and understood as experts.[64] As critical scholars and activists have long argued, it is also crucial that we recognize the academy as part of the "real world,"[65] and that Black academics can still be understood as members of Black communities.[66] While this is central to personal well-being and academic survival for many Black people, it is also a critical foundation for challenging the competitive, possessive individualism that characterizes the "academic marketplace."[67] The community and political orientations of the Black student and faculty groups and initiatives thus reflect both a rejection of individualism and a refusal to be defined by and contained within the space and logics of McGill's "bubble."

Several Black students and professors I interviewed describe organizing conferences and other gatherings to maintain and continue to build community relationships, as well as to fill the void – or Black hole – in the curriculum and university experience. Expressing this aspect of their work, a professor describes organizing several conferences "about Black people that appealed to people that did not have anything to do with the university" because of a personal sense of responsibility to Black communities outside of academia:

> For me, the way I was raised, is that education is this privilege that opens certain doors for you, but I know where I came from and I know where my parents came from. So, I'm totally aware ... of the little shifts in someone's trajectory, that can make the difference between them accessing education and not ...
>
> I come from that understanding of how polluted and bankrupt Western education is. So what is the point of me being here [teaching at McGill] if I'm not trying to undo some of that damage?

In this way, for example, Black student activists campaigning for an Africana studies program at the beginning of the twenty-first century saw a Black Congress bringing together academics and community members as an obvious and important part of their struggle (see chapter 6). All participants in this research who had organized conferences, congresses, or similar events described a conscious effort to involve members of Black communities outside of the university. Some actively sought to decentre professional academic "expert" knowledge in these events, and to foreground the knowledge of various people who do not work or study in universities; others sought to highlight the academic work of Black scholars. Most integrated the arts and some form of performance within the event and formally provided time and space for dialogue and debate in both French and English.

In an example of such organizing, and marking the forty-fifth anniversary of the 1968 Congress of Black Writers, a Black-student-led group called Community-University Talks (C-Uni-T) organized and hosted "Create Dangerously: Congress of Black Writers and Artists" at McGill in October 2013.[68] The international event welcomed two hundred participants, was community oriented, and emphasized Black feminist, non-hierarchical organizing. There were no "keynote" or otherwise singled-out guests, transportation and accommodation were paid for all presenters, and all were offered the same modest honorarium. In addition to funding through university channels and a government grant, the event was supported by in-kind donations and discounts from campus and community-based groups and local businesses as well as the volunteer labour of student activists. Presenters were encouraged to donate honorariums to campus activist and local community groups, resulting in a $625 donation to a Black youth group in Little Burgundy. Finally, following the event a detailed summary report was prepared and circulated, making transparent how the event was organized and realized for the purposes of community accountability and in hopes of providing information that others would find helpful for future organizing.[69]

Collective organizing, community work, and political protest reveal emancipatory possibilities that remind us that another world is possible and make such work meaningful "in excess of political declarations or demands."[70] Most importantly, such experience can further prepare us to work towards realizing those possibilities. When the excitement of a campaign or mobilization is over, a large part of "what sticks" to and with us and resonates is the action itself, the emotional and embodied experiences that propelled learning in spite of what we knew (about power, about ourselves, about one another) and despite the outcome of stated goals and demands.[71] Those feelings of hope are essential to long-term struggles with which we are involved.

Conclusion: Navigating and Resisting Racialization and Colonial Ideology

For Black students and faculty, McGill can be a racialized and racializing environment within which Blackness is preconceived and denigrated as the antithesis to whiteness. Their comments highlight differences between African, Caribbean, and Canadian racial discourses and sensibilities, and point to the significance of identifying with an African or Caribbean nation/nationality and identifying as *Black* at the university. Moreover, differences in their experiences underscore the ways in which racialization interlocks with gender, sexuality, and class in ways that can leave Black people – and Black Canadian women in particular – feeling alienated and devalued. In this way, socialization within the culture of the university seems geared towards preparing Black students for social marginalization, for "never fitting in." As CH recounts:

> You're socialized in such a way that, for some, that socialization looks like preparation for the real world. And I guess that's essentially, scarily, what McGill did. It prepared you such that, for me, socialization looked like never fitting in. And it looked like difference. Looked like having to accept what was. Accept it or change it. But knowing that if you're seeking to change it, it's gonna be a long road; it's gonna be a difficult road and probably a very lonely road. But you make the choice. And so I feel like that's the socialization that I experienced. In terms of what a McGill graduate was supposed to look like, as in be? I don't know. That's a good question. I have no clue, but whatever a McGill student is, I guess I just don't feel like that student. So whatever they are, I feel like there are some people who went to McGill and can claim McGill, like: "that was my alma mater, that's my school." I can't do that. I don't have anything, I don't have any McGill memorabilia, my diploma is sitting in the same envelope that I received it in, in my suitcase, that I packed, when I left Montreal. Me and McGill – there's nothing. There's no love. Because I just don't feel that I am a reflection of what McGill is. At all. I feel like I am its antithesis. I feel like I am its, its darkness. And I like that.

While CH says she has "no clue" what a McGill graduate is supposed to "look like, as in be," her choice of words suggest significant connections between who can claim McGill, what one looks like and who one is; she suggests that unlike herself, the normative graduate is a "reflection of what McGill is." Her narrative speaks to coming to terms with social exclusion and recognizing her agency in choosing how to respond. Her unwillingness to aspire to the dominant culture of the university or to associate herself with it – she rejects the signifier of her "successful" engagement with the university by leaving her diploma in the envelope – is to take a stand firmly refusing to be socialized into whiteness. While many of us experience the sense of being haunted by the colonialism and slavery upon which McGill is founded, in embracing a role as the university's antithesis, its darkness, CH mobilizes a Black radical tradition that haunts the institution right back. Within this tradition, radical students and academics claim space in the university while refusing to "overcome" Blackness, using our positions instead to expose and exploit its contradictions and investments, to undermine the ruling relations it reproduces and upholds.[72] In the next chapter, I focus on students' and faculty members' work on formal and ad hoc university-based committees; I examine what it means to work to change the university from within and beyond the institution, both structurally and conceptually. Participants' experiences of working on committees in attempts to promote greater racial diversity and equity reveal how university texts and structures actively limit and foreclose the possibilities for and extent of change. Are there potential fault lines and strategies for surpassing these limitations? What are the possibilities and pitfalls of working within *and* against the university? How do we identify, avoid, and manage the "dangerous complicities implicit in our attempts to carve out sites of resistance from within the neoliberal university?"[73]

6

Academic Service and Resistance within the Neoliberal University

As I discussed in chapter 1, "neoliberal university" is a term commonly used to refer to the ways in which neoliberal policies are impacting higher education. Neoliberalism is a set of social, political, and economic practices based on the logic of free-market capitalism. It thus proposes that the most effective path to well-being is through individual responsibility and entrepreneurship rather than public social services and community building. The turn to neoliberalism represents a crisis in capital accumulation: the desire of the ruling classes of capitalist countries to abandon the model of embedded liberalism in order to create more markets and increase capitalist profit.

Embedded liberalism was a strategy to stabilize the economy and ensure domestic peace following the Second World War. It entailed the development of state-run social welfare systems such as public health care and education, while placing "social and political constraints and regulatory mechanisms on entrepreneurial and corporate activities."[1] By the 1980s, however, economic growth had slowed again due to the combined impact of rising inflation and unemployment, widespread discontent, social-political organizing and coalition building, and the increasing popularity of socialist and communist ideas.[2] Neoliberalism is thus about restoring the power and profit of the economic elite through freeing capital from the constraints of embedded liberalism. It means the privatization and corporatization of public and social services, but also the commodification of all that can be exploited as "natural resources" through the mining and destruction of land. Indigenous peoples around the world have thus experienced and continue to experience the most severe and immediate consequences of neoliberalism as part of an ongoing, centuries-old colonial, capitalist genocidal assault on their lives and sovereignty to gain access to land for the purposes of state formation and capitalist development.[3]

As I demonstrate in the first chapters of this book, the university has always been deeply imperialist and involved in building and expanding the Canadian settler nation through militarized state violence. The neoliberal university thus represents the continuation and expansion of colonial, capitalist investments within the logic that they set up. Reductions in public funding for higher education are met with strategies to adjust curricula and research agendas to better appeal to corporate and state military interests and funding.[4] Students are viewed as "customers," knowledge is seen as a commodity, and scholarship is judged according to "deliverables" and measures of "impact." Academics are increasingly pressured to "produce" under new regimes that increasingly surveil them and their work, auditing and quantifying their value according to market principles.[5]

Neoliberal universities retain fewer and fewer non-academic staff, and faculty members are therefore increasingly called upon to do more administrative work to maintain the university and uphold neoliberal interests.[6] Service work is largely framed as service learning and career building for students, professional service and democratic participation in one's workplace for professors. Such service is valued and indeed required by and for the institution:

> Without academics agreeing to help with administration, universities would grind to a halt. By default, we all must take a turn and step up to the plate (at least occasionally). There's a lot of karma in academia, and helping out with administration now and then certain can lead to good things and it's good to be tagged as a "team player."[7]

In sum, academic service is largely and increasingly required as part of academic life. And as one professor I interviewed emphasized, all forms of service are not valued equally by the institution; the institution recognizes service that meets its predetermined internal needs and priorities. These may appear to converge with our own interests, such as the need for structures that (at least appear to) involve faculty and students in decision making and the need to have committees and policies to address issues of equity and justice. It is within this context that Black students and faculty members describe taking up university committee work related to racial diversity as a potential way of challenging and changing institutional policies and governance.

In this final chapter, I discuss such efforts to effect change from within the structures of the neoliberal university. I focus specifically on the structure of committees, and do not address higher administrative appointments such as chairs, directors, and deans, although these also entail and are recognized as administrative service to the university. These "higher" forms of service are the most valued, and usually come with negotiated benefits and professional reward. Women, Indigenous, and racialized academics are deeply underrepresented in such senior positions,[8] and none of the participants in this study occupied such a position at the time of our interview. Two professors I interviewed describe having been blocked from serving in senior positions by white colleagues, and one of those professors was subsequently denied a promotion based on not having served in a senior position.

With a desire to influence and change institutional policies and practices that uphold the culture of whiteness of the university, then, students and professors especially serve on committees related to promoting racial diversity, and do so with varying degrees of belief in the capacities and good faith of their colleagues and of the institution. Given the university's foundations and role in society, is an "equitable and diverse" university possible? How do we respond to the expectation that Black, Indigenous, and other racialized people are the ones responsible for "diversifying" and "decolonizing" the university? For whom do we do such work? And how do we manage the potential for this work to be used to validate and further entrench the very relations it claims to undo?

"Diversity and Equity" Work

I never do this, but just out of my mouth, I said [to a colleague], "There isn't real diversity here." And he said to me, quick as a whatever the expression is, that "Oh but look, there are people from all over the world." So I said to myself, "Okay, [*self reference*], don't talk to people who don't know what you're talking about."

I got a little bit tired of that: "Oh we need to form, y'know, the kind of equity committee on blah blah," and y'know, everyone looks to me.

Many people I interviewed had worked on committees related to institutional diversity and equity in recent years, including on hiring committees. Several, like the two professors quoted above, find it aggravating that they are assumed to be the person responsible for institutional diversity and equity. Nevertheless, all of the professors and several of the students I interviewed had engaged in this work and expressed a sense of responsibility to do so. The consequences of refusing this role can mean (and at times has meant) that such positions remain vacant or such committees become dormant. The assumption

seems clear: racial injustice is racialized people's problem, and therefore it is the responsibility of racialized people to "solve" the problem
of institutional racism; if we don't agree to this role, if we're not willing to do this work, no one is going to do it "for us." As one student
comments:

> I think it's unfortunate that the onus has to be on us to make that change,
> but if I had just kept quiet and gone away when they said these stupid
> things ... there would be no change. Coming from the oppressed side,
> we want it to change, so we *have* to make the effort to change, nobody's
> going to say, "hey, here, take this!" It doesn't work that way, and that's
> just the way it is. And I have no problem being the one to kind of, push
> on that door to make that change, because I believe that the change is
> necessary, and again, I have a child. My son says he wants to be the mayor
> of Montreal, you know? What do I tell him? You can't be the mayor of
> Montreal because – No!

A sense of the structures within which we function and an obligation to those who come after us leads many to commit much time and
energy to discussing, researching, and generating reports and policy
recommendations while very much aware that such efforts may or may
not effect change. University committees and the policies they produce
and uphold are, by definition, intended to work for the university and
protect its determined interests. As existing power relations are challenged, committees are formed and reformed, claiming to address the
same concerns and demands for change again and again from one era
to the next. These cycles play out in various individual departments
while very little changes at that level, let alone within the broader culture of the university overall. One of the professors I interviewed made
this argument, describing how this decentralized approach to promoting racial diversity works against change at the institutional level:

> If every department has to change on their own, this will never happen.
> Because who's the chair that year? Who are the colleagues that year? Is
> there diversity that year? Who changes their mind next year? Department
> by department is department by department.

This professor argues that the only way to effect structural change "is
either from the very top, or from the very bottom"; that is, if "thousands
of undergrads" organized to pressure the institution the senior administrators would have to respond (lest the university suffer negative

press coverage and a subsequent decline in enrolment, for example). The other option, according to this professor, is for the principal to insist on the rigorous implementation of existing policies that this participant feels could genuinely "shift things overnight." Ultimately, this professor points to the ability but lack of will among senior administrators to use their power within the institution to bring about change. Institutional policies and practices that keep things the way they are, do just that – they maintain racial hierarchy and protect institutions and those who identify with them from having to acknowledge white hegemony and risk their own unearned benefits and power.

Based on her extensive research in colleges and universities in Australia and the United Kingdom, Sara Ahmed has written about the "non-performativity" that often characterizes institutional diversity and equity work. Non-performative speech fails to bring about the effects that it names; in Ahmed's model of the non-performative, this failure of the speech act is understood not to be "a failure of intent or even circumstance but is actually what the speech act is doing."[9] In other words, the function of non-performative institutional discourse is to (mis)represent naming as doing. Institutional declarations of a commitment to diversity and equity often work in this manner: a policy declares an institutional commitment – to racial or gender equity, for example – that subsequently stands in for actually practicing such equity. Reminding us that "the term 'committee' derives from 'commitment,'" Ahmed explains that it is through committees that organizations "distribute" institutional commitments. Subsequently, the tasks of forming, preparing for, and managing tensions within committees and committee meetings can become the work; the work becomes the committee and the committee becomes a routine, an "institutional habit."[10] In this way, "institutions can 'do committees' as a way of *not* being committed, of not following through."[11] As Black student and faculty experiences suggest, part of how this is achieved is through exploiting racialized students' and faculty members' sense of obligation and genuine commitment to change. Institutional consultations can function in this way as well: senior administrators arrange "consultations" that stall demands for change and demobilize and deflect resistance. The planning and scheduling of the consultation becomes the response such that when the "consultation" takes place, it represents the final stage of implementing a policy or decision rather than debating or even shaping one. As one professor comments:

> Of course [consultation] is the catch phrase of the upper administration! When it comes to anything to do with racism it's "we're going to consult."

And then they pray that you will go away … So that's the institutional bullshit that I've learned is a part of McGill's upper administration, who have no training and no desire to deal with issues of race and racism and just are wilfully blind to it.

The non-performativity of institutional discourse supports this wilful ignorance: "the self-perception of being good blocks the recognition of racism." In this way, the committee signifies the declared institutional "commitment" to antiracism, which on its own "can function as a perverse performance of racism" through which peoples' lived experiences of racism are denied.[12]

Not only can committees serve to block action by becoming the action themselves, they also signify the border between dominant/centred and marginal groups' concerns and interests. While speaking about her work for a campus labour union, LR makes comments that could apply to a range of committees considered to represent the interests of particular groups, arguing that committees can reify or re-establish the marginality of certain groups:

> What I see happening now and it's sad, within say, the union, is that it's become this patriarchal organization. So much so that one of the people called me to say, "We need to have a women's committee." I'm like: "we don't need any women's committee, we had a woman president – we had *two* women presidents! We just need people who are strong enough to tell those males to get out! And until you do that, no amount of having a women's committee to counteract people who are doing foolishness will help. Because you're bringing us in, in a subordinate position! Not in a position of power. And there's no way I'm going to be part of any women's committee – are you crazy? No! I'm sorry. A women's committee in *today's day*? No."

For LR, the solution to the organizational culture's becoming too patriarchal was the stronger representation of women, requiring pushing out some "males" from executive and representative positions. In her analysis, forming a women's committee is unnecessary and would cede space to the dominant group, men. Consequently, it would contain "women" as "an issue" and women as committee members in a subordinate position.

Other students and professors also describe being critically selective about committee work, according to their personal political assessments as well as time constraints and other commitments and priorities such as paid work and parenting. The personal and emotional investments involved in this work, of continuously running up against institutional "brick walls," particularly for racialized women, should not be under-estimated.[13] As a graduate student, RC, explains:

> There's a lack of analysis just about race, just about what does it do when this face walks through the door, to sit at a senate committee meeting, what does it do? What does my presence there mean when there's nobody else that looks like me? And you can sit in a meeting full of faculty and administrators and there's not one single Black person. Like what the hell? *Right*? And what does it do for and to me as a student to walk into those spaces when I am the only person of colour? Like really.

When I asked her what it did do, this student explained that such experiences generated a "hypersensitivity of who you are, and the perception of you in that space. Especially if you're there to deliver a message that you know is contrary to the running business of the day." She continues:

> These were spaces that I, of my own volition, put myself in because I thought it was important to do so for various reasons … These were spaces reserved for student representation, and then you get there and you realize that your face always belies you. You're never just a student, but you're a student and you're a Black student, and you're a woman. And you carry all of who you are. And obviously there are certain points where some of those aspects of your identity are more salient than others, y'know? So, definitely being in those areas and sitting on those committees and whatever – they didn't feel like safe spaces. At all …
>
> That was mean, putting myself in those spaces. And why I felt the need to do that [was that I was] wrapped up in what was going on at the moment but also me, I think, making a very active attempt to put myself in those spaces because I *knew* there would not be anybody else like me in those spaces. So I get there and there isn't. It wasn't like I was surprised, it was like: well, here we go again. And I think it's important to try. It felt important to me anyway, to try to trouble those waters a little bit.

The question of how to racially diversify universities and achieve more equitable practices is in no way unique to McGill. It bears repeating that the achievement of racial diversity and equity in academia, especially in relation to Black professors, is an issue across Canada,[14] in the United Kingdom,[15] the United States,[16] and in South Africa.[17] Given the role that the pervasive underrepresentation of Black professors plays in preserving and reproducing the whiteness of the university, I now turn to participants' experiences on hiring committees. In tandem with these experiences, I examine institutional texts related to hiring and employment equity, to understand the concrete conditions and actions necessary for this sort of committee work to lead to specific structural changes, if indeed it can.

Hiring Committees

Graduate students and professors sit on hiring committees in hopes of correcting the underrepresentation of Black, Indigenous, and other racialized professors. They find that these committees do achieve the "hiring" function they claim; however, non-performativity is again revealed when it comes to institutional commitments to diversity and equity in the selection process. One professor I interviewed describes the ongoing struggle to racially integrate the university faculty as "a very pitiful scenario," adding that to their knowledge there were at least two fewer Black professors in the faculty they worked in than when they had taken up their position more than a decade earlier.

LG says that through sitting on hiring committees, she learned that "when they say it's structural racism they mean it. Like *structural* – that's the key word. And it's hard to fight against the structure." She explains that structural advantages embedded in institutional criteria construct a "best" candidate as one that best reflects the institution's values and existing profile back to itself. LG's comments point to how hiring criteria privilege candidates from the dominant (white, middle-class, anglophone) group. Those who represent what is most familiar and comfortable to committee members will likely be perceived as the "best" match with a department. Thus, as Anthony Stewart observes, such hiring practices entail preferential decision making that does not *look* preferential to the majority: "These decisions look 'fair,' while diversity questions and diversity questions alone look like they (and only they) will somehow unlevel the proverbial playing field and wage an assault on the standards of merit that are otherwise so important."[18] Several of the professors I interviewed speak to this; for example:

> So when it comes to hiring, do I even get *let* on hiring committees? Not lately. Because if you're seen as threatening, they don't want your voice at the table. Because you might try to replicate yourself, instead of them replicating themselves, right? (ND)

Really, in no faculty meeting have people talked openly about looking at files that are Black professors. And then on one search committee that I was in – and they don't put me in a lot for a reason – they made sure to put weaker African scholars and Black scholars. I was there! I saw all the files. And the ones that they didn't choose got jobs at Harvard and Yale. [And] by weaker, I don't believe in this merit kind of discourse, by weaker I mean [the candidate is disadvantaged because] the [fluency in] English is not there, that kind of thing. (MT)

While those who had sat on hiring committees had not personally seen the shortlisting of Black candidates, all continue to believe that hiring committees remain strategic sites for students and professors to disrupt decision making based on "common-sense" assumptions about who is and is not the "best" candidate for a position. This strategy can be aided by shifting the idea of merit from an implicitly universal definition to one that is explicit and contextualized: "the best candidate available under the circumstances at this time."[19] Anthony Stewart's critical analysis of employment equity policies is helpful to explore here.

In his analysis of employment equity at Dalhousie University, Stewart observes how the employment equity policy functions to shift "all responsibility for actively pursuing candidates out of the hands of the department doing the hiring" and to make candidates from "designated groups" responsible for self-identification when they apply. He contrasts this with affirmative action "in which the onus is on the organization that is trying to change its composition to act affirmatively – recruiting candidates from 'designated groups' and setting timelines for the achievement of its goals."[20]

As Stewart argues:

Under the guise of "helping" the candidate, rather than improving the profession by actively integrating it, the equity policy holds the candidate to a restrictive standard to which non-designated-group candidates are not held. The "designated group member" must fill out an additional form in order for the university to "help" him or her ... There is nothing stopping the university from being proactive and taking on the responsibility of integration itself.[21]

McGill's employment equity policy includes a preamble that states the mission of the university, followed by a series of declarations of commitment, a list of objectives, and a list of actions through which "the University will ensure the implementation of this Policy."[22] "Designated groups" are identified as "historically disadvantaged groups in Canada": "indigenous peoples, visible minorities, ethnic minorities whose mother tongue is neither English nor French, persons with disabilities, women, and persons of minority sexual orientations and gender identities."[23]

The document takes up the neoliberal narrative of embracing diversity while "retaining individual merit and achievement as the prime criterion for all staffing decisions." As in Canada's Employment Equity Act, "employment equity means more than treating persons in the same way but also requires special measures and the accommodation of differences."[24] This language of same treatment with accommodation of difference forecloses the possibility of corrective or reparative responses to historical disadvantage, thus reproducing rather than deconstructing social hierarchy. As in response to other Canadian and Québec state narratives, we must ask: Who is being asked to accommodate and tolerate? Who is assumed to need accommodation? If we recognize that some groups are structurally disadvantaged and yet aim to treat disadvantaged and advantaged groups in the same manner, these structural positions are maintained. Emphasizing individual merit and achievement as "prime criterion" thus reasserts the logic of competitive individualism and works against the change – employment equity – that the document names.

Notably, the actions identified to "ensure the implementation of this Policy" focus almost exclusively on the development of further policy, raising awareness of policy, and reporting on policy. The policy fails to identify concrete practices that will eliminate "direct, indirect and systemic discrimination" and lead to the greater representation and "full participation and advancement" of members of designated groups. Indeed, the non-performativity of the text is quite explicit: "However, in its pursuit of employment equity it is understood that the University will not: Engage in **Reverse Discrimination** ... [or] Impose **Quotas**"[25] From the initial word "however" that begins this final paragraph of the document, the text functions to stabilize and re-centre the power of the dominant, non-designated groups. With "individual merit and achievement" emphasized in the university's commitment statements and twice in the stated objectives, there is still a perceived need to assert that the university will not "engage in reverse discrimination," which is defined as "when a less qualified candidate is hired over a better qualified one."[26] The decision to have the words "reverse discrimination" and "quotas" appear in boldface seems to contradict or at least establish the limits of an institutional commitment to "special measures and the accommodation of differences," suggesting the university's concern to reassure alumni and others from dominant groups. Such concerns are not exactly without cause. When McGill's medical school began to promote its intention to increase the diversity of its pool of student applicants in order to comply with altered accreditation standards in 2013, there was immediate public outcry about diversity "trumping excellence," and alumni threatened to withhold donations in response to the university's attempt.[27]

In 2010, after being required by the Federal Contractors Program to submit a workforce analysis, the university acknowledged "some under-representation in certain groups" and developed and submitted an employment equity plan to the FCP Compliance Management Board.[28] As of the fall of 2015, guidelines require departmental hiring committees to include "**at least** one member of a designated equity group" (not necessarily someone who is racialized) on their shortlist of candidates."[29] The university has launched a number of new employment equity committees and training and reporting initiatives related to hiring, and in 2017 put in place a new employee survey to collect disaggregated data about the workforce at the university. Data drawn from the previous employment equity survey indicate that the percentage of visible minority (academic and non-academic) employees at McGill increased by 1 per cent between 2008 and 2017. Visible minorities made up 14 per cent of the workforce in 2008 and 2013, and 15 per cent from 2014 to 2017.[30] McGill's 2017–2022 strategic plan "marks the first time that McGill has set targets in relation to employment equity."[31]

As diversity workers interviewed in Ahmed's study related, equity and diversity policies can be useful to the extent that they can be quoted when challenging decisions and actions that contradict stated institutional commitments and objectives. However, it is clear that policies alone do not ensure or bring about employment equity. The experiences of people I interviewed suggest that hiring and other committees are most effective in supporting or bringing about significant change when these goals are taken up as organizing and/or activist endeavours, with collective planning towards meeting clearly defined goals. I spoke to a professor who is not Black, who told me they have "given a lot of thought to how to hire more Black profs at McGill." This person describes their work on hiring committees and how they have seen racism – cloaked in "thinly veiled questions" about a candidate's accent or the merits of their curriculum vitae – prevent Black people from being hired. They also describe an experience that did lead to the hiring of a Black professor, included here for the valuable lessons it offers.

I anticipated resistance and worked very carefully and strategically with colleagues. This experience taught me that being strategic can pay off, but it is a lot of work and needs to be thought about in a lot of detail and carefully. A good knowledge of the kinds of openly and subtly racist cues and comments of colleagues should be anticipated and countered from the writing of the job advertisement. In this case, I also worked from the moment the committee was struck with colleagues who were good allies to subtly bring them over to thinking about race and hiring, pointing out statistics about faculty of colour at McGill first, for example, and then moving to the specific situation of Black profs and the specific situation of the faculty. Only then did I move to the department level. I worked to emphasize how positive it would be for students to have a Black prof in the department and how this would bring in more and different students potentially – and not just Black students. This was all done outside the meeting, and slowly. The strategies around the committee and the meetings were all very carefully planned, largely alone, some with the sympathetic members of the committee, at every level from drawing up short and long lists to the day of the interviews and so on. All of the usual counterarguments were expected and planned for, and the candidates who we brought and argued for were all ones who in different ways were able to challenge these typical roadblocks. We did experience different kinds of resistance, but in the end a strong short list of all candidates of colour made the hire of a Black prof possible and, because of this, the ways in which arguments for and against candidates were mobilized looked different.

My experience shows that it is worth it not to be discouraged however frustrating hiring committees are – and to me they are! The work is extensive and I probably spent about four to five times more time than others did working on reading every single file in great detail for all of its aspects, with for and against arguments for all of the candidates as well as thinking about how all of these issues fit in with the specific question of race and the goal of hiring Black profs. Then the practical and emotional work of having long talks with white colleagues that they do not really want to have and that make them deeply uncomfortable because they don't know how to have them, both in private and in meetings. I am convinced, though, that all of this work is what led to the successful hire.

This professor's experiences demonstrate the amount of work necessary to interrupt the processes through which the dominant majority is reproduced. This work is extensive and takes time, energy, and careful planning; as Sherene Razack puts it, academic "hiring is not just hiring but a political movement" with high political stakes that extend beyond the university.[32] Strategizing for hiring requires knowledge of the institution, racial literacy, and the ability to read the verbal and non-verbal cues of other committee members and to identify allies. Racially literate white and other non-Black professors are well placed to do this work, as Black professors describe having to contend with assumptions about their racial bias. Moreover, it seems that while students can be supportive of such a process, they do not hold significant power to coordinate such efforts.

Making informed decisions about which committees, groups, and struggles to take on is always a matter of personal and political strategy. Students are at the university temporarily with the specific goal of completing their degree, and some interviewees described feeling trapped between a sense of responsibility to work for institutional change and an increasing awareness of the ongoing, extensive (and at times futile) nature of such work. I conclude my discussion of committee work by returning to the issue of Black Studies, and the student-led struggle for a Black/Africana Studies program at McGill from the 1990s into the new millennium. With demands for Black Studies having been informally passed on through cohorts and generations of Black students since the late 1960s, in the 1991–92 school year members of the BSN escalated pressure on the university and submitted an extensive proposal to the history department, asking for a Black history course that would serve as a "forerunner of an Africana Studies program."[33] The history department refused to approve the proposal, claiming budgetary restraints.[34] The subsequent formation of the Africana Studies Committee provides an important case study for thinking about whether, under what conditions, and to what extent the potential of committees differs when they are formed and run by student organizers.

The Africana Studies Committee

In the spring of 1994, the university planned to convert the African Studies undergraduate major into a minor program, claiming the need to do so based on a lack of resources. Student protest prevented the cancellation of the major program; however, it remained desperately under-resourced and under-valued. For example, "the history of the entire African continent was condensed into a single course by the history department."[35] With billionaire Charles Bronfman having just donated ten million dollars for the creation of a new institute for Canadian Studies, as well as the expansion of East Asian Studies into a department, the lack of attention to African Studies was striking. In an article published in the *Daily*, Mebrat Beyene, the cultural coordinator of the BSN, describes African Studies at that time as not having the "bare minimums like a description in the Course Calendar, an office, a secretary, or even advisors capable of advising."[36] Concerned students and faculty felt that the university was deliberately trying to undermine the program, through "progressively eliminating the study of Africa from the curriculum."[37] The students rejected the university's claim that the situation was due to a shortage of funds, arguing that it was a matter of priorities. BSN political coordinator Astrid Jacques argued that Montreal was an ideal centre for African Studies given the number of African intellectuals in Montreal, particularly French West Africans.[38]

Building on and expanding a struggle by Black students stretching back over three decades, and after "numerous attempts" to "pull the plug" on the African Studies program and eliminate the African Studies major,[39] students in the program and members of the BSN formed the Africana Studies Committee (ASC) in 1994. Over the five years between 1994 and 1999, the vision of the committee grew from sustaining the African Studies major to expanding the program to include the African diaspora and to "reconsidering the notion of 'education'" in ways that would "surpass the teaching of ideas" and "extend beyond the campus."[40] While the university continued to claim that a lack of funds prevented them from responding positively, the extent of institutional resistance to Black Studies was understood to represent a "lack of political will" on the part of the university.[41]

Several people I interviewed had been among the multiple cohorts of student activists involved in extensive lobbying efforts, fundraising, press conferences, and meetings with administrators as part of this struggle. The BSN and ASC put at least another six to seven years into the campaign, which included the organizing of a congress, Africana 2000, held at McGill in February 2000. The congress was organized as a forum for students and community members to discuss the proposed program and how to create the conditions under which it could finally be realized.[42] The event included workshops and presentations by Black community members and educators, including McGill alumni Esmeralda Thornhill, by then a professor of law and the first James Robinson Johnson Chair at Dalhousie University, who spoke on the topic "The Double Challenge of Dismantling Privilege and Opening up the Academy."[43]

Discussing the Africana Studies campaign with one student who was involved in the early 2000s, I asked how the story ended, if the university ever officially and finally said "no." The student responded, "At least when I was on the front, there was never a no. It was never declined." They explained that they "passed on the file to [their] successors" at the BSN but realize in hindsight that it's not just Black community organizing, [it's] the mentorship piece: the need to mentor the future leaders. That's something I did not do, and I think [the campaign] may have suffered as a result of the fact that my successors did not necessarily have the fully developed skill set and leadership skills to really to bring that file forward, because it really required quite a lot of experience, and strategic know-how.

I asked if the student thought that the university had "waited out" the activist campaign.

Yeh, [the BSN] started leading [the campaign], and then I got on the file ten years later when I attended. So I think when I was there, there was a lot of, well, there seemed to be a lot of receptivity to it, both at the level of the dean and to a certain extent at the higher level, but again, there was development work that needed to be done, fundraising work. Developing a fundraising plan. And for that we almost needed to hire a professional development director, and so obviously that wasn't done. But again, I wasn't obviously physically there with the McGill administration, I don't know what their machinations were, but I do know where we had come to at that point.

When I say that it seems to me as though the university never took up the Africana/Black Studies as their responsibility, this student agrees, adding that for them personally, "there was never an expectation that they [the university administration] would take it on as a priority at the institutional level." The student concludes that this is why "from a pragmatic perspective," "whether or not that's ethical ... you need sustained engagement, otherwise it's going to be off the table."

At what point does such a sustained engagement no longer serve the interests of activists? The campaign for Africana Studies provided crucial organizing experiences and learning for those involved, and it seems clear that sustained student activism over the years has made it difficult for the university to abandon the African Studies program. However, it also seems that the ASC negotiations with the university over roughly a decade became a matter of "doing" the negotiations/ standoff. Having created the African Studies program in 1969, McGill had long positioned itself as having (already) responded to Black student and local community activism through the "raising of conscious- ness vis-à-vis the developing countries."[44] For McGill as an international university, being home to the country's first African Studies program is valuable in hailing international students from African countries with- out disrupting Canadian national narratives that posit Black people and racism as foreign. Finally, in keeping the BSN/ASC in an ongoing cycle of creating and submitting proposals, running campaigns, and searching for funding, the university administration maintained the appearance that Black/Africana Studies was being given serious consideration. I cannot help but recall the plight of Ralph Ellison's invisible man, who discovers that the president of his former college has sent him on a pointless mission in order to keep him away from the college from which, unbeknown to him, he has already been expelled: "hope him to death, and keep him running."[45]

Overlapping experiences of mapping, engaging, and challenging institutional power can generate invaluable insights into how various forms of oppression are interrelated and mutually constitutive, revealing how capitalist relations work through institutions.[46] What do we do (what *should* we do) when university policies and practices allegedly geared towards equity are revealed as non-performative texts and discourses standing in for – even guarding against – the actual changes we seek? How can we collectively avoid running in circles? A crucial part of this work is how we share and document our experiences, and the extent to which we are able to build intergenerational memories of resistance and struggle. In contrast to this strategic approach, pursuing change within the parameters and logics set up by the university, relying on institutional "good faith" claims and formal structures, can be a frustrating and exhausting experience of chasing power. As one student who sat on several institutional committees and initiatives at McGill recalls, "There just always seemed to be another fight. Something else. And I grew weary of it. Because it just felt like it was never ending." Chasing something, one cannot necessarily see it clearly and assess how it is moving. However, through mapping power we can learn how social relations are upheld and thus how to more effectively challenge domination and oppression through different ways of thinking and doing. Such a project can create a sense of individual and collective empowerment that allows people to work in solidarity to strategically challenge oppressive relations.

The neoliberal university requires that we remain all the more vigilant in assessing how race and practices of racialization are operationalized in the production of capital. What do increases in surveillance and precarity mean for Black people who, in the words of one professor quoted above, have always been surveilled and pressured to perform "colonial surveillance" on ourselves? Indeed, key aspects of academic work in the neoliberal university – surveillance, job precarity and disposability, too much work, time constraints and accompanying stress and anxiety – are conditions to which Black people and communities have always been subjected and continue to experience disproportionately.[47]

As the racial demographics of Canada change in response to global-ization and forced migration from the global South, universities seek new ways to derive social and economic value from associations with racialized people. Discourses of "diversity," like those of "multicultur-alism," are strategies of racial capitalism through which non-whiteness is "exploited for its market value."[48] If at all concerned about claiming diversity, the neoliberal university reduces notions of racial inclusivity to the numeric representation of "visible minority" students and faculty, ignoring historical context and erasing important qualitative differ-ences and nuances.[49] We continue the struggle to increase the presence of Black students and faculty in the Canadian university, and continue to develop and demand Black Studies as a crucial site of emancipatory research and pedagogy within and beyond the academy. Black radical praxis, as the politics and soul of Black Studies, insists that we reject and surpass limited notions of change. It calls upon us to repudiate the dictates of possessive individualism, and especially any offer to escape from, or overcome, Blackness.[50] It requires instead that we work col-lectively to undermine and undo the coloniality of the university, and that we vigilantly refuse visions of equity and justice that can easily be folded into the service of racial capitalism.[51]

Conclusion: Towards Informed Decision Making

It is not the inherent responsibility of racialized people to educate white people about race or to "fix" the university. Nor, recalling the questions of the youth quoted at the outset of this book, do we study and teach within "white" universities to "impress white people." Black people attend McGill for a variety of reasons reflecting the wide range of cultural, class, national, political, and personal interests, commitments, and ambitions that we bring to academia.

For well over half a century, universities have been sites of intense struggles, and Black students and teachers have often been at the forefront of social and political organizing and activism. The structures and practices of the Canadian university are deeply reflective of the settler colonial foundations of the nation, and the university remains deeply implicated in white settler nationalism and the transnational politics of globalization and neoliberalism. As this study demonstrates, the experiences and insights of Black students and faculty members across social, cultural, and political differences reveal the functioning of interlocking power relations of colonialism and racial capitalism, exposing the falsehoods of liberal ideology and myths of Canadian multiculturalism.

Rather than "getting" an imagined "plethora of knowledge" from experts at podiums within the classrooms of the idealized elite university, there is a Black radical tradition at McGill, however small in scale, of students, faculty members, and activists committed to social justice coming together in dialogue and action to co-construct knowledge across disciplinary interests and activist campaigns. This work happens in a countless range of collective settings: in the offices of student groups and professors and the offices of the *Daily*; at the campus-community radio station, in local parks and cafés; in local Black community centres; at conferences and congresses; in one another's homes; in street demonstrations, rallies, and direct actions; occasionally, in classrooms. As

XX describes, the most important education he received at the university was his "ability to critique society and the world [and] more conceptual tools to do that important work. To challenge received ideas." More specifically, he continues,

> I learned how to write grant proposals, I learned how to organize press conferences, I learned how to do outreach to the media, I learned how to create a movement of sorts; I learned how to advocate effectively. So I learned how to be a more effective activist.

Furthermore, this is what he expects from the university:

> [to contribute] to strengthening democracy in a society and globally, by creating aware citizens who are capable of reading through the lines, deconstructing and reconstructing, and challenging multiple forms of oppression, corruption, whether it happens at an institutional or state level or even interpersonally, because as people say, the personal is political. So really creating that heightened aware citizen.

Notably, across a wide range of personalities, politics, and experiences of and struggles within the university, participants generally do not regret studying or working at McGill overall, and several of the students had graduated with acknowledgments and awards of excellence. As noted, some people are left feeling "no love" for the university, and most understand their experiences in the broader context of structural racism and being Black in Canada. The participants who are parents, however, say they will not encourage their children to attend McGill, wishing their children not to have to endure the whiteness. One of these parents was quite adamant in communicating this point:

ROSALIND: So if [your son] asks you, if um –
PARENT: He could come to McGill?
ROSALIND: That's right.
PARENT: *No.* He will *not* come to McGill. He doesn't know that, and I've debated this. I would like [him] to go to a Black American college where there are a whole bunch of other Black people who are super smart just like he is. So it's not an *anomaly* because he's smart. I remember his teacher said, "What do you do?" I said, "I'm a student at McGill," and she said, "Ohhh, okay, that explains it!"
   Why couldn't I be some poor-ass person and my child is bright? You know what I mean? I had to be a student at McGill for my child to be doing so well in school. That's insane! That's so insane. And the teacher

didn't mean it in a bad way. They never mean it in a bad way! You understand? So he has to go in a space where everybody's bright like him, and everybody's Black like him, and everybody's achieving. Then when he's done, and he's really grounded, *then* he can come back to McGill and take over! But not before, not before!

But he doesn't know that, he's like, "Mom, I'm coming to McGill" and I'm like, "Mm-hmm, yeh, yeh, you'll go to McGill – at some point."

This parent is clearly connecting her child's experiences in school, her own at McGill, and the broader Canadian society in which they live. Another participant, not yet a parent, expresses similar concerns and links:

McGill is one thing, I think in a way I would say yes to McGill or any white institution at the university level if I'd prepared my child well enough to – and that's a big if – to know really solidly who they are because you have to come into these institutions and give yourself a counter-education. Because especially the undergrad degree is messed up. The undergrad degree is like, white whiteness. That's what they're trying to teach us. And then when you get to the MA, you can get the supervisor who's doing what you want to do, but the undergrad degree is *messed up* when you think about it. Like if you're not so powerful in your mind that you can ask the questions in the class, and ask the professor to do the paper topic that's slightly off from what they're teaching, you're going to get screwed as a Black person in any Canadian university.

Others, who were not parents, were more inclined to say they would support a young person's decision to study at McGill, primarily for the prestige associated with the university name. The following seven participants speak for themselves:

If a Black student asks me, because they want to go to McGill, I'd be brutally honest. I'd tell them I hated McGill, it was four treacherous years and I'd never go back in my entire life, but if you're going there at the end of the day, for prestige, then do it. Because I can say that I left, and I graduated from one of the top schools in Canada and I'm proud of that. But if we're talking happiness, look elsewhere.

I think the currency McGill affords you – and by currency, I mean "University of McGill" – you have that on your CV, I mean you can go anywhere … Let's say when I leave, although I'm going back to work when I go home but McGill has a very, very solid reputation worldwide.

And again, that's a really good currency to have. Although that currency may not necessarily translate into a – into you being a very savvy student, if you get through McGill people assume that you're very smart and intelligent. Maybe you're good at regurgitating, but people assume that you are very smart and intelligent.

I think I would still say yeh, you have to go. I don't know. I'm so old school, I'm still like education is freedom, even if it's shitty education! … I've actually helped a girl with her statement and she got accepted, and I felt really good about that, but I'm also like, once you're here, that doesn't absolve me of responsibility after I told them to go. If their prof is looking at them with contempt all the time, I should have to tell them about that beforehand so they can be prepared.

I do really encourage people to go to McGill. And I like the idea that it's something that does secure you in a sense, like every time I've gone, when I was younger, to job interviews, they'd be like, "Oh! You went to McGill!" So it has currency, you know, and I think that is important, for *anybody*, but especially for the Black community to carry that.

I encourage my students to go to McGill, because in my head, Concordia's great but you want your doors to open … If you go to Africa, people know it. McGill has never had to recruit. McGill has built up the perfect system of word-of-mouth recruitment and so they recruit individuals, not communities, and they don't care if nobody from Montreal comes here because everybody around the world will come here.

I would tell my brother or my sister: "Be strong and resilient and don't too much care about how you might be perceived. Because at the end of the day it's just that, a perception – you can't get kicked out of McGill because you're Black. They don't have that power over you." I wouldn't go so far as telling them not to go there, because that's also preventing yourself from growing – academically, career wise – just because of other people's bias and prejudice. That's too far; I wouldn't do that. Because at the end of the day we can still [claim] the space even though we're Black.

That space gave me an opportunity to see myself; the beginnings of this self. And I *recognized* her and I nurtured her so that I wasn't surprised to see in the mirror, in 2011, *that* woman. She's not a stranger to me. Had I done something different, had the experience been different at McGill, perhaps I would've been equally prepared. But equally so, perhaps not. I have a personal philosophy, that one's strength is not coming from moments of no disruption ... And I have never chosen to see my McGill experience through a lens of negativity. I have chosen to see that McGill was providing me with a range of experiences, none of which were wasted, all of which I've had to harvest in different ways. From pure knowledge, to how to challenge knowledge, how to assert myself, politics, all those things have come together in a way that I'm grateful [for].

Final Thoughts

We are only disadvantaged if you are using a white, middle-class yardstick. I quite frequently find that white middle-class yardstick is a yardstick of materialism [that measures] how valued you are by the size of your bank account or the number of degrees you can write after your name ... Disadvantage is a nice, soft, comfortable word to describe dispossession, to describe a situation of force whereby our very existence, our histories, are erased continuously right before our eyes. Words like disadvantage conceal racism.[1]

Blackness is the always already outside, but it also defines a space where things can happen.[2]

In this book I have shown how McGill, as a "particular corner" of the institution of the Canadian university, remains a contested site of learning and knowledge production, professional socialization, settler nationalism, and political struggle. The experiences of Black people spanning over the past fifty years offer insight into the university as it has shaped and been shaped by broader social-political circumstances over time. Through mapping these experiences in relation to institutional texts and discourses, I have highlighted how the university's consistent culture of whiteness has been actively maintained throughout the mid-twentieth century expansion of higher education and into the neoliberal era of corporatization and decreasing access. In the everyday activities of Black people at the university this whiteness is most notably experienced as a large white-majority student population, a near absence of Black professors and of racially literate mentors, Eurocentric curricula, institutional colonial nostalgia, racial microaggressions, stereotyping, competitive individualism, general insensitivity to the racialized experiences of Black people, and as the often passionate denial of the significance of race and persistence of racism. Differences in how the university culture affects Black people and shapes their activities confirm the ways in which the social construction of race is bound up with nationalism, class, and gender. Consistencies in these experiences speak to the roles of Black racialization and people racialized as Black in upholding relations of settler colonialism and racial capitalism. In my critical engagement with the origins story and histories of McGill, I have sought to fill in some of the lesser known and obscured events of the past – including the writing of institutional history itself – as a means of understanding the construction and reproduction of these ruling relations.

Black students and professors frequently – out of personal necessity and self-preservation, politics, and intellectual commitments – work within and against the university to undermine its function in the production and reproduction of racial capitalism and to produce emancipatory educational possibilities for themselves and those who follow them. Despite pervasive institutional hostility towards Black thought in Canadian academia, Black Canadian scholarship and educational organizing and activism persist as part of a Black radical tradition of education through which we seek to know systems of white supremacy not to buy into them, but to resist and dismantle them, to move towards new acts of building. In such a vocation, "all work is a pathway to the next stages of the struggle."[3]

Many Black students and faculty at McGill have claimed and continue to claim space in the institution to further Black Studies, including anticolonial, antiracist, anticapitalist, and feminist organizing and activism with and in local communities. Through building political alliances and coalitions, we take up Blackness in opposition to whiteness – systemic racial hierarchy and white domination, the accumulation of resources by white people at the expense of Indigenous peoples and people of colour, and the devaluing and denigration of racialized people and non-European knowledges – as well as to "whiteliness," a judgmental, self-righteous way of being in the world informed by the notion of white superiority.[4] Racialization and domination are always ongoing processes and as such remain contested and incomplete. In universities, these processes take place alongside and in tension with the potential for developing critical analyses and radical politics, for accessing institutional resources, for coalition building across differences, and for the use of institutional power despite itself to amplify oppositional politics and extend their impact.

This is certainly not to imply that one has to attend university or become an academic in order to develop Black radical thought and imagination. Quite the contrary can be and indeed has been argued given the ways in which universities reward possessive individualism and encourage distances between Black "communities" and Black "intelligentsia." Many Black academics have recognized and insisted upon the importance of remaining connected to grassroots communities – not merely based on notions of a responsibility to "uplift the race," but because these are our communities and they hold important collective memories and knowledge. For many of us, it is members of these communities who ultimately determine the value of our work, because it is with/in these communities that the shape of struggles for social change and social justice needs to be determined.

Black people in Canada experience racialization and discrimination as part of our daily lives, and under such conditions the potential socio-economic benefits of a university education or career are not quickly dismissed. I emphasize informed, wilful decisions in this regard and hope that this research contributes to analysis and tools that assist people in "becoming accountable to themselves ... rather than to the ruling apparatus of which institutions are part."[5] I add my voice to a collective call that has been reverberating for generations and traverses the boundaries of institutions and nation states. It is a call insisting upon the radical potential of people who converge within and beyond the university to imagine, theorize, and plot transformation; to build our collective power and defy the limitations of what is assumed to be possible in Black Studies and, more broadly, through Black study in Canada.

Notes

Prelude

1 Amadasun, "Black People"; Charland, "African American Youth"; Tyson, Darrity, and Castellino, "It's Not 'a Black Thing.'"
2 Inzlicht and Schmader, *Stereotype Threat*; Steele, *Whistling Vivaldi*.
3 Brand, *Bread*, 172.
4 Shahjahan, "Being 'Lazy'"; L.T. Smith, *Decolonizing Methodologies*.
5 Bakan and Dua, "Introducing the Questions," 8.
6 Fanon, *Black Skin*.
7 Martell, "Slow University," para. 16.
8 Mountz et al., "For Slow Scholarship," 8.
9 See also Sara Ahmed, *Willful Subjects*, 50–3, on the additional work of "being in time" with the institution that is required by some of us in order to appear cordially willing rather than wilful, difficult, and in the way.
10 See "Occupons McGill! A Letter from the Fifth Floor Occupiers," http:// rabble.ca/news/2011/11/occupons-mcgill-letter-fifth-floor-occupiers.
11 For more on the events of 10 November 2011 at McGill, see Sharp and Roberts, "Crisis at McGill"; and http://independentstudentinquiry. blogspot.ca/.
12 Choudry, "Avec Nous"; Collectif dix novembre, *This Is Fucking Class War*; hampton et al., "Fear and Violence"; Lamarre, "Outlaw Universities."
13 AGSEM Teaching Assistants' Unit Executive, "Travailleuses."
14 Likewise, the naming of the movement *Printemps d'érable* (Maple Spring) was a gesture towards revolutionary uprisings that had begun the previous year across the Arab world, known as the *Printemps Arabe* (Arab Spring). This gesture would be proven superficial, as increasingly open anti-Arab and Islamophobic sentiment characterized Québec political and popular discourses in the years following the movement. See hampton and Hartman, "Towards Language."

15 Mehreen, Bonin, and Hausfather, "Direct Democracy"; Sheppard, *Relationship*.

16 For anarchist analyses of the 2012 movement, see "Strike While the Iron Is Hot," Part 1, http://www.crimethinc.com/texts/recentfeatures/montreal1 .php, and Part 2, http://www.crimethinc.com/texts/recentfeatures /montreal2.php. See also Submedia TV, *Street Politics 101* (video), https:// sub.media/video/street-politics-101/.

17 Bigaouette and Surprenant, *Les Femmes*; Ferrer et al., "Building Solidarity"; hampton, Luxion, and Swain, "Finding Space"; Palacios et al., "Learning"; Pedneault, "Plan Nord Riot."

18 hampton, "Race, Racism" and "Claiming Space."

19 On the reproduction and challenging of racialized, settler relations within the Québec student movement since the 1960s, see hampton, "Nous Who?"

20 Affan, "Ethical Gestures"; hampton and Rochat, "To Commit and to Lead."

21 Hudson and Kamugisha, "On Black Canadian Thought"; Kitossa, "Black Canadian Studies."

22 G.W. Smith, "Political Activist."

23 Collins, "Learning from the Outsider Within" and *Black Feminist Thought*; hampton and Rochat, "To Commit and to Lead"; Henry, "African Canadian Women"; L. Simpson, *Dancing on Our Turtle's Back*.

24 Choudry, *Learning Activism*.

25 Reagon, "Coalitional Politics," 358.

26 Reagon, "Coalitional Politics," 358.

27 Reagon, "Coalitional Politics," 359.

28 Dhavernas, "Law"; Hurley, "In Anticipation"; Lamarre, "Outlaw Universities."

29 Choudry, "Avec Nous"; Foley, *Learning in Social Action*.

30 Bannerji et al., *Unsettling Relations*, 7.

1. Introduction: The University as a Site of Struggle

1 I have preserved the anonymity of interviewees by assigning each a two-letter pseudonym. In order to further protect their identities, at times I attribute a quote to a student or professor without using their pseudonym or identifying their gender. This is particularly the case for professors, given the small number of Black professors at McGill.

2 Ames, *City*, 165.

3 Ames, *City*; Westley, *Remembrance*; Williams, *Road to Now* and "Jackie Robinson Myth."

4 MacLeod, "Salubrious Settings."

5 Frost, *McGill University*, vol. 1; MacLennan, *McGill*; MacLeod, "Salubrious Settings"; Westley, *Remembrance*.

6 DeVault and McCoy, "Institutional Ethnography," 17.

7 Newson and Polster, *Academic Callings*.

8 Wilder, *Ebony*.

9 Miller, *Shingwauk's Vision*; Séminaire de Québec, "Vue d'ensemble."

10 Wilder, *Ebony*.

11 Trudel, *Canada's Forgotten Slaves*, 178.

12 Most slaves in what is now Canada were Indigenous. Black people account for approximately one-third of the forty-two hundred slaves identified in Marcel Trudel's study of two hundred years of slavery in Canada, *Canada's Forgotten Slaves*.

13 Thwaites, *Jesuit Relations*; Trudel, *Canada's Forgotten Slaves*.

14 Magnuson, *Brief History*; Milner, *Long Road*.

15 Magnuson, *Brief History*.

16 Regarding the 1837–38 rebellions that led to the union of Upper and Lower Canada, see http://www.thecanadianencyclopedia.ca/en/article/rebellions-of-1837/.

17 McRoberts, *Quebec*, 54.

18 Milner, *Long Road*.

19 Leslie, "Bagot Commission," 32. See also Miller, *Long Road*.

20 Lawrence, "Gender," 7.

21 Most notably, the 1844 report of the Bagot Commission established by the governor general of British North America; Superintendent for Education Egerton Ryerson's report of 1847; and following Confederation, Ebenezer McColl and Nicholas Flood Davin's 1879 "Report on Industrial Schools for Indians and Half-Breeds" commissioned by Prime Minister John A. Macdonald, http://www.canadianshakespeares.ca/multimedia/pdf/davin_report.pdf.

22 Haig-Brown, *Resistance*; Miller, *Shingwauk's Vision*; Ryerson University Aboriginal Education Council, "Egerton Ryerson"; Thomas, *Where Are the Children?*; TRC, "Canada."

23 The Residential Schools Settlement is available at http://www.residentialschoolsettlement.ca; the National Centre for Truth and Reconciliation website is at https://nctr.ca/map.php.

24 Backhouse, *Colour-Coded*; A. McLaren, "Stemming"; K. McLaren, "We Had No Desire"; Walker, *African Canadian Legal Odyssey*; Valverde, "Racial Purity."

25 Backhouse, *Colour-coded*; Hamilton, *Stories*; K. McLaren, "We Had No."

26 J. Bertley, "Role of the Black Community"; L.W. Bertley, "United Negro Improvement Association"; A. Cooper, "Black Women"; Hamilton, *Stories*; hampton and Rochat, "To Commit and to Lead"; K. McLaren, "We Had No Desire."

27 Axelrod and Reid, "Introduction"; Pietsch, *Empire*; Wilder, *Ebony*.

28 L.T. Smith, *Decolonizing Methodologies*; Wilder, *Ebony*.

29 Axelrod and Reid, "Introduction," xiv. See also H. Campbell, "Is It Possible."
30 Wilder, *Ebony*.
31 Westley, *Remembrance*.
32 J.I. Cooper, *James McGill*; Craig, "Strachan"; Frost, *McGill University*, vol. 1.
33 Axelrod and Reid, "Introduction," 13.
34 In 1852 the role of the Royal Institution changed to solely that of the McGill University Board of Governors. See Frost, *McGill University*, vol. 1.
35 MacKenzie, "History."
36 MacKenzie, "History," para. 8.
37 Pietsch, *Empire*.
38 Pietsch, *Empire*, 7.
39 Axelrod and Reid, "Introduction," xvii.
40 S. Fisher, *Boys and Girls*, 54.
41 S. Fisher, *Boys and Girls*, 51–62. For example, see Susan Fisher's discussion of articles appearing in *School: A Magazine Devoted to Elementary and Secondary Education*, published by the University of Toronto's Faculty of Education.
42 Axelrod and Reid, "Introduction," xviii.
43 Axelrod and Reid, "Introduction"; Bruneau, "Professors."
44 Whitaker and Marcuse, *Cold War*, 143.
45 Whitaker and Marcuse, *Cold War*, 278.
46 Whitaker and Marcuse, *Cold War*, 107.
47 Whitaker and Marcuse trace this sentiment back to the secularizing and radical politics in France during and following the Revolution (1789–99), which they describe as having "left Québec, as it were, a political and cultural orphan" (*Cold War*, 293).
48 Regarding continuing attempts to purge Marxist professors from McGill in the 1970s see Dixon, *Things Which Are Done*.
49 Bruneau, "Professors"; Jones, Shanahan, and Goyan, "University Governance"; Newson and Polster, *Academic Callings*.
50 McRoberts, *Quebec*; Milner, *Long Road*.
51 Magnuson, *Brief History*; McRoberts, *Quebec*. For a detailed description of Québec's contemporary postsecondary education system, see Trottier et al., "PSE Policy."
52 Bédard et al., "McGill Français"; Mills, *Empire Within*; Milner and Milner, *Decolonization*; Warren, "L'Opération."
53 Nevertheless, it is important to note that these events took place within a broader context of local social-political organizing and activism (including several other conferences and events) and decolonization movements around the world.
54 Affan, "Ethical Gestures"; Austin, *Fear*; Jacob and Shum, *Ninth Floor*; Ricci, "Searching."

55 Bayne and Bayne, "Quebec Board."

56 Beck, "Tired of Talk."

57 Bayne and Bayne, "Quebec Board"; Calliste, "African Canadians"; Williams, *Road to Now.*

58 Beck, "Tired of Talk," 1.

59 The TYP at University of Toronto also accepts students from working-class backgrounds.

60 Allen, "Transitional Year"; Arenburg, "Extended Family"; K.S. Brathwaite, *Access.*

61 K.S. Brathwaite, "Reflections"; C.E. James, "Contradictory Tensions."

62 K.S. Brathwaite, "Reflections."

63 K.S. Brathwaite, "Reflections," 76.

64 Ruggles and Rovinescu, *Outsider Blues,* 11.

65 K.S. Brathwaite, *Access*; Stewart, *Visitor.*

66 Kelley, "Black Study."

67 Biondi, *Black Revolution*; Rogers, *Black Campus Movement*; Rojas, *From Black Power.*

68 Carl Parris, quoted in Beck, "Tired of Talk," 1.

69 Hudson and Kamugisha "On Black Canadian Thought"; Walcott, "Shame."

70 Ash, "But Where"; Austin, "Narratives"; Bristow et al., *We're Rooted Here*; McKittrick, "Wait"; Pabst, "Mama"; M.S. Smith, "Race Matters"; Stewart, *Visitor*; Thobani, *Exalted Subjects*; Walcott, "Who Is She."

71 Statistics Canada, 2016 Census of Population, catalogue nos. 98–400-X2016190 and 98–400-X2016211.

72 Tattrie, "Dalhousie's Black and African Diaspora Studies."

73 Walcott, "Shame."

74 Walcott, "Into the Ranks."

75 Bascomb, "Productively Destabilized"; Harding, "Vocation"; Kelley, "Black Study."

76 Ervin and Woodhouse, "We Must Compete"; M. Horn, *Academic Freedom* and "Canadian Universities"; Schuetze, Bruneau, and Grosjean, *University Governance.*

77 Chatterjee and Maira, *Imperial University*; Downs and Manion, *Taking Back*; Kloet and Aspenlieder, "Educational Development"; Smeltzer and Hearn, "Student Rights."

78 Newson, "Corporate-Linked University."

79 Engler, "Harper"; Sears and Cairns, "Producing 'Intra-preneurs'"; Singh, "Ideological Roots."

80 Chatterjee and Maira, *Imperial University*; Goswami, "Neoliberalism"; Ochwa-Echel, "Neoliberalism"; Sears and Cairns, "Austerity U" and "Producing 'Intra-preneurs.'"

81 Chou, Kamola, and Pietsch, *Transnational Politics,* 2.

82 Belcourt, "Political Depression"; Chrisjohn and Wasacase, "Half-Truths"; Coulthard, *Red Skin*; A. Simpson, *Mohawk Interruptus*; L. Simpson, *Dancing on Our Turtle's Back* and "Indigenous Resurgence."

83 See Mathur, Dewar, and DeGagné, *Cultivating Canada*.

84 Walcott, "Into the Ranks," 346.

85 Dei, "African Scholar," 171.

86 Bobb-Smith, "We Get Troo"; Coulthard, *Red Skin*; L. Simpson, "Anticolonial Strategies," *Dancing on Our Turtle's Back,* and "Land as Pedagogy"; Dei, "African Scholar"; Spencer, "Spiritual Politics"; Wane and Neegan, "African Women's Indigenous Spirituality."

87 Grande, "Accumulation," 376.

88 Bisaillon, "Analytic Glossary"; M.L. Campbell, "Institutional Ethnography"; Campbell and Gregor, *Mapping Social Relations*; Choudry and Kuyek, "Activist Research"; D.E. Smith, *Everyday World*; *Texts*; *Writing the Social*; and *Institutional Ethnography*; G.W. Smith, "Political Activist."

89 Lubiano, "Like Being Mugged," 64.

90 Campbell and Gregor, *Mapping Social Relations*; D.E. Smith, *Institutional Ethnography*.

91 DeVault and McCoy, "Institutional Ethnography," 17.

92 Baszile, "Rhetorical Revolution," 1.

93 Baszile, "Rhetorical Revolution," 2.

94 Baszile, "Rhetorical Revolution," 9.

95 Baszile, "Rhetorical Revolution," 4.

96 Chioneso, "(Re)Expressions."

97 Birt, "Of the Quest."

98 Yosso, "Whose Culture," 79.

99 Mills, *Empire Within*, 144–6; Mowbray, "Journalism, Activism."

2. Colonial Legacies and Canadian Ivy

1 Quoted in Ertekin, "McGill is Delivered."

2 The Notice can be viewed at http://mohawknationnews.com/blog/wp-content/uploads/2015/09/mcgill-seizure-1.jpeg. Ertekin, "McGill is Delivered."

3 The audio recording of an interview with Kahentinetha conducted by Victoria Xie for CKUT News is available at https://ckutnews.wordpress.com/2015/09/23/mcgill-university-receives-notice-of-seizure-by-kahentinetha-horn-regarding-stolen-land/.

4 Frost, *McGill University*, vols. 1 and 2, and *James McGill*.

5 "Stanley Brice Frost."

6 "Best Man," 4.

7 Munroe-Blum, "Principal's Welcome," http://www.mcgill.ca/about /welcome. The message was removed from the website at the end of Munroe-Blum's term as principal in 2013.

8 The tapestry was designed by Kelvin McAvoy and woven in Scotland in 1969. See http://digital.library.mcgill.ca/fontanus/pdfs/Fontanus2010_ back_cover.pdf.

9 D.E. Smith, *Institutional Ethnography*, 112.

10 Lugones, "Toward a Decolonial Feminism," 743. See also Césaire, *Discourse*; Fanon, *Black Skin*; L.T. Smith, *Decolonizing Methodologies*; Wynter, "Unsettling the Coloniality."

11 MacKay, *Square Mile*.

12 McClintock, *Imperial Leather*, 250.

13 Coombes, *Rethinking Settler Colonialism*.

14 Frost, *James McGill*, 12.

15 Myers, *History*, 53.

16 Myers, *History*.

17 Abbott, "James McGill," 26; MacKay, *Square Mile*.

18 Trudel, *Canada's Forgotten Slaves*, 106.

19 Trudel, *Canada's Forgotten Slaves*, 238.

20 Trudel, *Canada's Forgotten Slaves*, 117.

21 Trudel, *Canada's Forgotten Slaves*, 117.

22 J.I. Cooper, *James McGill*, 29.

23 J.I. Cooper, *James McGill*, 122.

24 Frost, *James McGill*, 63. "Lafrenier" is an English spelling of the French "Lafrenière."

25 Frost, *James McGill*, 63, emphasis added.

26 Frost, *James McGill*, 64.

27 A. Cooper, *Hanging of Angélique*.

28 Mackey, *Done with Slavery*, 72.

29 Mackey, *Done with Slavery*, 74.

30 Mackey, *Done with Slavery*, 74.

31 Sharpe, *Monstrous Intimacies*, 83.

32 An Act for the Abolition of Slavery, art. 1, emphasis added.

33 An Act for the Abolition, art. 8.

34 An Act for the Abolition, art. 10.

35 An Act for the Abolition, art. 24.

36 Mackey, *Done with Slavery*.

37 Trudel, *Canada's Forgotten Slaves*, 93, emphasis added.

38 J.I. Cooper, *James McGill*, 17.

39 J.I. Cooper, *James McGill*, 38.

40 Abbott, "James McGill"; J.I. Cooper, *James McGill*.

41 J.I. Cooper, *James McGill*.

42 Trudel, *Canada's Forgotten Slaves*, 98.

43 Trudel, *Canada's Forgotten Slaves*, 118.

44 Trudel, *Canada's Forgotten Slaves*, 237.

45 Trudel, *Canada's Forgotten Slaves*, 238–9.

46 MacLeod, "Salubrious Settings," 32.

47 MacLeod, "Salubrious Settings."

48 Frost, *History of McGill*, 7.

49 Rosenfeld and Lukacs, "Six Nations"; Saul, "Century-Old Federal Debt."

50 This should not be mistaken for an equitable exchange of land for money; the initial land grant was partial compensation for millions of acres of lost homeland ("Six Nations Claim"; see also A. Simpson, *Mohawk Interruptus*, 37–65).

51 "Six Nations Claim," n.p.

52 "Six Nations Claim," n.p. *Windspeaker* is owned and operated by the Aboriginal Multi-Media Society of Alberta.

53 In today's terms the Golden Square Mile is roughly the central downtown area between Côte des Neiges and Aylmer streets, the base of Mount Royal, and Boulevard René Lévesque.

54 MacLeod, "Salubrious Settings." Where the escarpment was is now the Ville Marie Expressway/Autoroute 720.

55 Ames, *City*; Westley, *Remembrance*; Williams, *Road to Now* and "Jackie Robinson Myth."

56 Williams, *Blacks* and *Road to Now*.

57 MacLeod, "Salubrious Settings"; Williams, *Road to Now*.

58 Ames, *City*, 4.

59 Frost, *McGill University*, vol. 1; MacLeod, "Salubrious Settings."

60 Frost and Michel, "Macdonald."

61 Frost and Michel, "Macdonald," para. 8.

62 Frost and Michel, "Macdonald," para. 15.

63 Fong, "J.W. McConnell," 82. The McConnell Foundation, established in 1937, had made more than 120 million dollars in donations to McGill University by 2008. See http://www.mcgill.ca/channels/news/mcconnell-foundation-continues-its-legacy-supporting-mcgill-students-102268.

64 J.I. Cooper, *James McGill*.

65 Frost, *McGill University*, vol. 1; Kalbfleisch, "McGill Had a Rocky Start"; MacLeod, "James McGill Monument"; MacLennan, *McGill*.

66 MacLeod, "James McGill Monument."

67 Frost, *History of McGill*, 4.

68 Frost, *History of McGill*, 6.

69 "McGill University in the Past," 26.

70 Collard, "Sir William," 49.

71 Collard, "Sir William," 53.

72 Frost, *McGill University,* vols.1 and 2; Ryerson University Aboriginal Education Council, "Egerton Ryerson."

73 Collard, "Forgotten Cemetery," "Reburial," "Dufferin Park," and "Burial"; MacLeod, "James McGill Monument."

74 MacLeod, "James McGill Monument."

75 Frost, *History of McGill,* 8.

76 Pietsch, "Wandering Scholars," 379.

77 Pietsch, "Wandering Scholars," 377.

78 Pietsch, "Wandering Scholars," 379.

79 Melamed, "Racial Capitalism," 77.

3. Trying to Keep Canada White and the Power to Write History

1 Said, *Culture,* xiii, emphasis in original.

2 Hulan, *Northern Experience*; Berger, *Sense of Power.*

3 A. Cooper, "Constructing"; M.S. Smith, "Race Matters"; Stanley, "John A. Macdonald."

4 Stanley, "John A. Macdonald"; M.S. Smith, "Race Matters."

5 Haliburton, "Men," 2.

6 Berger, *Sense of Power*; Pitsula, *Keeping Canada British.*

7 Delisle, *Myths*; A. McLaren, *Our Own.*

8 Berger, *Sense of Power*; Pitsula, *Keeping Canada British*; Strong-Boag, "Independent Women." See also Leacock, "Canada," and "Woman Question"; Macphail, "The Immigrant."

9 Hulan, *Northern Experience*; Strong-Boag, "Independent Women."

10 Haliburton, "Men," 2.

11 Knowles, *Strangers*; Pitsula, *Keeping Canada British.*

12 For example, Canada was described as a "white man's country" by Canadian prime minister John A. Macdonald in 1867 (quoted in Dua, "Exclusion," 446. See also M.S. Smith, "Race Matters"). Future prime minister R.B. Bennett also argued that "British Columbia must remain a white man's country" in 1907 (quoted in Brown and Cook, *Canada,* 68). See also Pitsula, *Keeping Canada British*; Thobani, *Exalted Subjects.*

13 Woodsworth, *Strangers,* 278.

14 Dua, "Exclusion"; Yuval-Davis, *Gender and Nation.*

15 An Act Respecting Immigration, 1910, SC 9–10 Edward VII, chap. 27, art. 38c. See http://www.pier21.ca/research/immigration-history/immigration-act-1910.

16 An Act Respecting Immigration, chap. 27, arts. 3c–3e.

17 See Order in Council 1911–1324, https://pier21.ca/research/immigration-history/order-in-council-pc-1911-1324.

18 See Barrett, "Fascism"; Betcherman, *Swastika*; Perry and Scrivens, "Right-Wing Extremism"; Théorêt, *Blue Shirts*.

19 Bock, *Nation beyond Borders*; Delisle, *Traitor*.

20 Bock, *Nation beyond Borders*.

21 Bock, *Nation beyond Borders*, 5.

22 Trudel, *Mythes*.

23 Bannerji, *Dark Side*; Bell, "Canada's Racist Movement"; Galabuzi, *Canada's Economic Apartheid*.

24 Levine, *Reconquest*.

25 Levine, *Reconquest*, 33.

26 Levine, *Reconquest*, 31.

27 Bock, *Nation beyond Borders*, 11.

28 Levine, *Reconquest*, 40.

29 McGill University, "Brief," 84.

30 MacLennan, *McGill*, 17.

31 https://www.mcgill.ca/about/history/maclennan.

32 MacLennan, *McGill*, 17.

33 MacLennan, *McGill*, 21.

34 MacLennan, *McGill*, 27–9.

35 MacLennan, *McGill*, 7.

36 Austin, *Fear*, 38.

37 McGill University, "Brief," 84.

38 McGill University, "Brief," 85.

39 McGill University, "Brief," 88.

40 Dubinsky et al., *New World*; Lexier, "Backdrop"; Mills, *Empire Within*.

41 Edwards, "Historical Background"; Frost, *McGill University*, vol. 2; McGill University, "Brief"; Mills, *Empire Within*.

42 Ongoing coverage of this activism and the university's attempt to purge radical students and lecturer Stanley Gray can be found throughout the 1968–69 issues of *The McGill Daily*.

43 "Black Power," 1.

44 Boone, "Stokely," 6.

45 Austin, *Fear*.

46 Boone, "Stokely."

47 "Black Militants," 1. See also M. Smith, "CLR James."

48 Forsythe, *Let the Niggers Burn*.

49 The instructor, Perry Anderson, was teaching biology at SGWU while working on his PhD at McGill. In addition to racial discrimination, students alleged that Anderson was disorganized, unqualified, and was frequently unprepared for and cancelled lectures. Eber, *The Computer Centre Party*.

50 "Council Hits SGWU," 1.

51 "At Sir George."

52 "Anderson Hearings," 3. See also Walker and Jones, *Burnley "Rocky" Jones.*

53 I am intentionally refusing to join in the common use of the term "occupation" to describe this tactic of taking institutional space from those in power and refusing to leave, in recognition that Canada is located on occupied Indigenous land. See Danforth, "Occupy Wall Street"; Grande, "Accumulation"; Sztainbok, "Decolonize Together."

54 S. Horn, "Bail Denied," 1.

55 M.J. Alfred, "Revelations," 4.

56 "Council Comes Out," 3.

57 Bédard et al., "McGill Français"; Mills, *Empire Within*; Warren, "L'Opération."

58 Frost, *McGill University*, vol. 2, 284.

59 Frost, *McGill University*, vol. 2, 284.

60 Frost, *McGill University*, vol. 2, 405.

61 Cowen, "Africa," 7.

62 Black Caucus, quoted in Cowen, "Africa," 7.

63 Kassam, "Africa Conference," 1.

64 Cowen, "Africa"; Kassam, "Africa Conference."

65 Kassam, "Africa Conference."

66 Cowen, "Africa," 8.

67 Douglas and Parris, "Disruption," 6.

68 Douglas and Parris, "Disruption," 6.

69 Adeleke, "Africa"; Howe, *Afrocentrism.*

70 Mutamba, "Resisting Inclusion"; A. Smith, "Colonialism"; Tuck and Yang, "Unbecoming Claims."

71 Forsythe, "Black Studies," 4.

72 Forsythe, "Black Studies," 4.

73 "Senate Deliberates," 3.

74 Apouchtine, "Black Studies," 3.

75 Sally Cools, quoted in Beck, "Tired of Talk," 1.

76 See Frost, *McGill University*, vol. 2; and Taylor-Munro, "Frost."

77 Hugh MacLennan, quoted in CBC, "Distinguished Canadians."

78 McBride, "James McGill," A2.

79 McBride, "James McGill," A2.

80 "175th Anniversary."

81 See https://www.mcgill.ca/facultyclub/history/alfred.

82 "175th Anniversary."

83 See historical images at http://cac.mcgill.ca/campus/evolution.html.

84 Von Tunzelmann, "Rhodes."

85 Marschall, "Targeting Statues."

86 Von Tunzelmann, "Rhodes."

87 Carleton, "Life Beyond"; Tremblay, "Bursting the Bubble."
88 Hobsbawm, "Introduction: Inventing Traditions," 1.
89 Hobsbawm, "Introduction: Inventing Traditions," 2.
90 Hobsbawm, "Introduction: Inventing Traditions," 4.
91 Hobsbawm, "Introduction: Inventing Traditions," 9.
92 Sears and Cairns, *Good Book*, 150.
93 Césaire, *Discourse.*
94 Kinsman and Gentile, *Canadian War*, 21.
95 "McGill to Celebrate."
96 The following spring, the gesture was returned when McGill principal and vice-chancellor Heather Munroe-Blum was awarded an honorary degree by the University of Glasgow.
97 https://www.ontariocolleges.ca/en/apply/us-applicants.
98 https://www.timeshighereducation.com/student/news/canada-most-popular-destination-international-students.
99 https://www.topuniversities.com.

4. The Idealized Elite University

1 McGill and University of Toronto are ranked as the top two universities in Canada, McGill ranking first in 2011, 2012, and 2015–17; U of T ranking first in 2010, 2013, 2014, 2018, and 2019. See https://www.topuniversities.com.
2 Abada, Hou, and Ram, "Ethnic Differences." See also McMullen, "Postsecondary Education."
3 See Luxion, "Whose Campus?"
4 Gordon, *Ghostly Matters*, 8, and "Some Thoughts," 2, 3.
5 Gordon, "Some Thoughts."
6 Allahar, "Political Economy"; K.S. Moore, "Class Formations"; Waters, *Black Identities.*
7 K.S. Moore, "Class Formations," 504.
8 Galabuzi, *Economic Apartheid.*
9 Macdonald, "Outrageous Fortune," 5. See also Conference Board of Canada, "Income Inequality."
10 Galabuzi, "Creeping Economic Apartheid" and *Economic Apartheid.* See also Block, Galabuzi, and Weiss, "Colour-Coded Labour Market"; National Council of Welfare, "Snapshot."
11 Block, "Canada's Population."
12 Conference Board of Canada, "Racial Wage Gap."
13 http://www.univcan.ca/universities/facts-and-stats/tuition-fees-by-university/. Accessed 13 November 2019.
14 Nfah-Abbenyi, "Why (What)," 256, emphasis in original.

15 For examples, see J. Bertley, "Role of the Black Community"; L.W. Bertley, *Canada*; Hudson, "Research"; Israel, "Montreal Negro Community"; Potter, "Occupational Adjustments"; Williams, *Road to Now.*

16 See also my discussion in chapter 1 regarding objects and displays commemorating James McGill.

17 For example, https://mcgill.ca/about/history/features/mcgill-women.

18 Mackey, *Done with Slavery*, 186.

19 Gabourel, 1977; Williams, *Road to Now.*

20 Hudson and Kamugisha, "On Black Canadian Thought," 5.

21 McDonald and Ward, "Why So Many."

22 Mendelson, "McGill."

23 McGill University, "Student Demographic Survey," 8.

24 McGill University, "Student Demographic Survey," 20–1.

25 McGill University, "Student Demographic Survey," 24.

26 McGill University, "Student Demographic Survey," 2.

27 Terrence Ballantyne, a student at SGWU during this era, reported in a 1969 interview that when he first tried to rent a room upon his arrival in Montreal he was told: "I don't rent to niggers." Eber, *The Computer Centre Party*, p. 36.

28 For an example see *Macleans*, "Merit."

29 Choi, "Unlearning"; Guinier, *Tyranny*; Mijs, "Unfulfillable Promise"; Park and Liu, "Interest Convergence."

30 Stewart, *You Must Be a Basketball Player*, 54.

31 Cora-Lee Conway, discussion with the author, 6 May 2014.

32 Cora-Lee Conway, "White Hallways." In *Voices for Diversity and Social Justice: A Literary Education Anthology*, edited by Julie Landsman, Rosanna M. Salcedo, and Paul C. Gorski (Lanham: Rowman and Littlefield, 2015), 93–4. Reproduced with permission from the author.

33 CAUT, "Underrepresented." See also F. Henry et al., *Equity Myth.*

34 Carl E. James, discussion with the author, 12 March 2014.

35 Enenajor, "Second Look," 3.

36 Enenajor, "Second Look," 3. See also Tuck, "Suspending Damage"; Tuck and Yang "Unbecoming Claims."

37 Enenajor, "Second Look," 4. See also Engler, *Canada in Africa*; Rodney, *How Europe.*

38 Leonardo and Porter, "Pedagogy of Fear," 148.

39 These experiences are discussed further in chapter 5.

40 Boggs, "Education"; Freire, *Pedagogy.*

41 CAUT, "Underrepresented."

42 CAUT, "Underrepresented"; Monture, "Race, Gender"; Ng, "Woman Out of Control"; M.S. Smith, "Gender, Whiteness."

43 Chiose, "Justice"; Quinlan et al., *Sexual Violence.*

44 Richardson and Taylor, "Sexual Harassment."

45 Richardson and Taylor, "Sexual Harassment," 260.

46 Richardson and Taylor, "Sexual Harassment."

47 Gutiérrez y Muhs et al., *Presumed Incompetent.*

48 Harvey, "McGill Fails"; Pedram, "We Have Always Known." The Me Too movement was founded by a Black woman community worker in the United States named Tarana Burke. See http://justbeinc.wixsite.com/justbeinc/the-me-too-movement-cmml. See also Quinlan et al., *Sexual Violence.*

49 This quote is reproduced here with Halle's permission. The rally was held on 11 April 2018.

50 CAUT, "Underrepresented"; F. Henry, Choi, and Kobayashi, "Representation"; F. Henry et al., *Equity Myth*; Monture, "Doing Academia Differently"

51 Blackett, "Mentoring," 277. See also Delgado, "Affirmative Action," and Guinier, "Models."

52 Hurston, "How It Feels."

5. Being and Becoming Black

1 Regarding the everyday life work required to uphold social relations, see DeVault and McCoy, "Institutional Ethnography," 25.

2 hooks, *Where We Stand*; Dumas, "Doing Class"; Leonardo, *Race, Whiteness.*

3 For example, see Boyce Davies, *Left of Karl Marx* and *Claudia Jones*; Davis, *Women, Race*; Foner, *W.E.B. Dubois*; Johnson and Lubin, *Futures*; Kelley, *Freedom Dreams*; McDuffie, *Sojourning*; Robinson, *Black Marxism.*

4 Delgado, "Ethereal Scholar"; Omi and Winant, "On the Theoretical Status"; Roediger, *Wages*. Novels such as Chester Himes's (1947) *Lonely Crusade* and Ralph Ellison's (1952) *Invisible Man* offer layered analyses of these sorts of Black race-class tensions through their main characters' experiences with the Communist Party during the Cold War era in the United States.

5 Dumas, "Doing Class," 115.

6 Leonardo, *Race Frameworks*, 74.

7 Bannerji, "Marxism and Antiracism" and "Building from Marx."

8 Dei, "Race and the Production of Identity," 243.

9 Levine-Rasky, *Whiteness Fractured*, 4.

10 Leonardo, *Race, Whiteness*, 170. See also Frankenberg, *White Women*; Harris, "Whiteness as Property"; Levine-Rasky, *Whiteness Fractured.*

11 Dumas, "Contesting White Accumulation"; Harris, "Whiteness as Property."

12 Leonardo, *Race, Whiteness*, 110–18. See also Bonilla-Silva, *Racism*; Frankenberg, *White Women*; Frye, "White Woman Feminist"; Levine-Rasky,

Whiteness Fractured; Lipsitz, *Possessive Investment*; Schick, "Keeping the Ivory Tower White."

13 Ignatiev, "Abolitionism"; Leonardo, *Race, Whiteness*; Roediger, *Wages*.

14 Leonardo, *Race, Whiteness*; Roediger, *Wages*.

15 Boden, Borrego, and Newswander, "Student Socialization"; Mendoza, "Socialization."

16 Tierney, "Organizational Socialization," 7.

17 Tierney, "Organizational Socialization," 7.

18 D.E. Smith, *Everyday World*.

19 Yosso, "Whose Culture."

20 Howard, "Post-Racialism" and "On the Back."

21 Based on the context in which this comment was made, I understand BR to have meant that race is often spoken about among Black people in Canada.

22 See Bunjun, "Racialized Feminist"; Lazos, "Are Student Teaching Evaluations."

23 Israel, "Montreal Negro Community"; Handleman, "West Indian Associations"; Potter, "Occupational Adjustments."

24 Affan, "Ethical Gestures"; Austin, *Fear*.

25 Abada, Hou, and Ram, "Ethnic Differences."

26 This in contrast to French Canadians, who were able to "become white" Québécois and gain access to unearned advantages associated with white privilege. See Scott, "How French Canadians."

27 Grace-Edward Galabuzi, discussion with the author, 13 March 2014.

28 DuBois, *Souls*.

29 Fanon, *Black Skin*; Keeling, "In the Interval."

30 Inzlicht and Schmader, *Stereotype Threat*; Steele, *Whistling Vivaldi*.

31 Shapiro, "Types of Threats."

32 Collison, "Is Your Hair Real?"

33 Lawson, "Images."

34 A. Henry, "We Especially Welcome," 598.

35 Corbeil, "Blackface."

36 Dauphin, "Why the Hell"; P.S.S. Howard, "On the Back"; Nelson, "Challenging Blackface."

37 Collison, "Is Your Hair Real?" n.p.

38 Jones, "End to the Neglect."

39 Bannerji et al., *Unsettling Relations*; Carty, "African Canadian Women"; A. Henry, "Thoughts"; Mogandine, "Black Women"; Monture, "Introduction – Surviving the Contradictions," "In the Way," and "Doing Academia Differently"; Samuel and Wane, "Unsettling Relations"; Wagner, Acker, and Mayuzumi, "Introduction"; Wane, Deliovsky, and Lawson, *Back to the Drawing Board*.

40 See Bunjun, "Racialized Feminist"; Douglas, "Black/Out"; Nelson, "Toppling the 'Great White North.'"

41 For further discussion about how the image of the Black woman is mobilized in various ways in the context of racial neoliberalism, see hampton, "By All Appearances."

42 Ahmed, *On Being Included*, 41.

43 Grace-Edward Galabuzi, discussion with the author, 13 March 2014.

44 Walcott, *Black Like Who?* and "Who Is She."

45 Carl James, discussion with the author, 12 March 2014.

46 Day, "Being or Nothingness"; Mutamba, "Resisting Inclusion"; A. Smith, "Colonialism"; Thobani, *Exalted Subjects*.

47 Delgado, "Ethereal Scholar"; D'Souza, "Rights" and *What's Wrong*; Matsuda, "Looking."

48 Bannerji, "Marxism and Antiracism"; Lawrence and Dua, "Decolonizing Antiracism."

49 Grande, "Accumulation," 376.

50 Canadian University Press, "McGill"; van Eyken, "Student's Society."

51 Canadian University Press, "McGill," 6; Wittstock, "McGill's Apartheid Links."

52 Canadian University Press, "McGill"; Sheppard, "Relationship"; van Eyken, "Student's Society."

53 Weston, Tomlins, and Wittstock, "South Africa."

54 Crawhall, and Robinson, quoted in Holder, "Canadian Blacks," 10.

55 de Gannes, Flemmings, and Warner, "BSN," 4.

56 de Gannes, Flemmings, and Warner, "BSN," 4.

57 Hudson, "Research."

58 de Gannes, Flemmings, and Warner, "BSN," 4.

59 Hudson, "Research."

60 VR is referring here to Tyndale Community Centre, http://www.tyndale stgeorges.com.

61 Monture, "Doing Academia Differently," 95

62 Orr, "Challenging."

63 hooks, *Where We Stand*.

64 For analysis of the strengths and limitations of student activists organizing in local poor and working-class communities in the United States in the 1960s and 1970s, see Sonnie and Tracy, *Hillbilly Nationalists*.

65 Orr, "Challenging."

66 Kitossa, "Nuances."

67 Hudson and Kamugisha, "On Black Canadian Thought."

68 C-Uni-T was co-founded by Cora-Lee Conway and myself, and organized events bringing together local Black community members, students, and academics from 2011 to 2016. The congress took its name from Haitian author Edwidge Danticat's book *Create Dangerously: The Immigrant Artist at Work*, with inspiring encouragement from the author.

69 hampton, "Créer dangereusement"; Sarvi, "Create Dangerously."
70 S. Moore, "Taking Up Space," 11.
71 Choudry, *Learning Activism*; S. Moore, "Taking Up Space."
72 Harney and Moten, *Undercommons*.
73 Oparah, "Challenging Complicity," 101.

6. Academic Service and Resistance within the Neoliberal University

1 D. Harvey, *A Brief History*, 11. See also my discussion in chapter 1 of the nature of these shifts in Québec.
2 H. Campbell, "A Response to Austerity"; Harvey, *A Brief History*.
3 Coulthard, *Red Skin*.
4 Regarding student resistance to military research at McGill in recent years, see O'Neal and Steeves, "Demilitarize," and Binks-Collier, "McGill Releases."
5 Luka et al, "Scholarship," 191.
6 CBC, "Wilfrid Laurier"; Gill, "Academics"; Wilton, "McGill University."
7 Buddle, "In Praise."
8 DiversityLeads, "Women and Visible Minorities"; McGill University, "McGill University Workforce Analysis"; Misra et al., "Ivory Ceiling."
9 Ahmed, *On Being Included*, 117.
10 Ahmed, *On Being Included*, 121–3.
11 Ahmed, *On Being Included*, 124, emphasis in original.
12 Ahmed, "Non-Performativity," para. 11.
13 Ahmed, *On Being Included* and *Willful Subjects*; Gutiérrez y Muhs et al., *Presumed Incompetent*.
14 CAUT, "Underrepresented"; F. Henry et al., *Equity Myth*.
15 Grove, "Black Scholars"; Hunt, "Racism."
16 Flaherty, "Demanding 10 Percent"; Gutiérrez y Muhs et al., *Presumed Incompetent*.
17 Mangcu, "Decolonizing"; "Why Are There So Few."
18 Stewart, *Visitor*, 80.
19 Stewart, *You Must Be a Basketball Player*, 54.
20 Stewart, *You Must Be a Basketball Player*, 35.
21 Stewart, *You Must Be a Basketball Player*, 37–8.
22 McGill University, "Employment Equity Policy," 2.
23 McGill University, "Employment Equity Policy," 1.
24 McGill University, "Employment Equity Policy," 1.
25 McGill University, "Employment Equity Policy," 2, boldface in original.
26 McGill University, "Employment Equity Policy," 2.
27 Reiter and Aalamian, "External Review"; Seidman, "Changing Face" and "Stabbed."

28 This information was initially shared in a July 2010 "Message to Employees" published on the McGill Human Resources website and is no longer available online. A summary report of the workforce analysis conducted in 2010 is available at https://www.mcgill.ca/hr/files/hr/summary_report.pdf.

29 https://www.mcgill.ca/equity/employment-equity/human-resources-information/guidelines-academic-recruitment; boldface in original. See also A. Campbell, "Employment Equity," p. 8. According to this report the policy also anticipates the possibility of there being no woman, person with a disability, Indigenous person, racialized person, ethnic minority, *or* LGBTT2SQ* person among the top-ranked applicants for an appointment. It states that if a designated group member is not shortlisted, "the chair of the search committee must provide assurance that no candidate among the top ten members of a recruitment pool is a member of a designated equity group."

30 A. Campbell, "Employment Equity," p. 5, table 2a.

31 A. Campbell, "Employment Equity," p. 9. Specifically, the plan states: "We will deepen our commitment to excellence and diversity in faculty recruitment and career progression. To this end, McGill aims to increase the proportion of women at the rank of full professor to 25% in five years, and to increase the proportion of all tenured and tenure-track staff self-identifying as members of all other equity groups to 20%."

32 Razack, "Racialized Immigrant Women," 58.

33 Golding, "McGill History Department," 1. See also Perelle, "African Studies."

34 Black Students' Network, "Mis-Education"; Golding, "McGill History Department."

35 Perelle, "African Studies," 22.

36 Perelle, "African Studies," 4.

37 Perelle, "African Studies," 22.

38 Perelle, "African Studies," 22.

39 Perelle, "African Studies"; Cook, "Planted"; Pyne, "Member."

40 Cook, "Planted," 1.

41 Aziz Fall, quoted in Cook, "Planted," 12.

42 Gordon and Jones, "Congress Rallies," 5.

43 Dean, "Rethinking Freedom," 5.

44 Hinkson, "McGill's African Studies," 20.

45 Ellison, *Invisible Man*, 194.

46 Choudry, *Learning Activism*, 23.

47 Gill offers important analysis identifying corporate "cultures of performativity and surveillance" as gendered, but does not attend to how they are also profoundly racialized. See Gill, "Academics."

48 Leong, "Racial Capitalism," 2154. See also Tuck and Yang, "R-Words."
49 Park and Liu, "Interest Convergence," 53.
50 Harding, "Black Students."
51 Melamed, *Represent and Destroy.*

Conclusion: Towards Informed Decision Making

1 Monture, "Ka-Nin-Geh-Heh-Gah-E-Sa-Nonh-Yah-Gah," 161. See also Tuck, "Suspending Damage."
2 Bascomb, "Productively Destabilized," 150.
3 Harding, "Vocation," 17.
4 Fox, "Race to Truth"; Frye, "White Woman Feminist."
5 D.E. Smith, *Everyday World,* 178.

Bibliography

Abada, Teresa, Feng Hou, and Bali Ram. "Ethnic Differences in Educational Attainment among Children of Canadian Immigrants." *Canadian Journal of Sociology* 34, no. 1 (2009): 1–28. https://doi.org/10.29173/cjs1651.

Abbott, Lewis W. "James McGill of Montreal (1744–1813)." *International Review of Scottish Studies* 12 (1982): 26–39.

Adeleke, Tunde. "Africa and Afrocentric Historicism: A Critique." *Advances in Historical Studies* 4, no. 3 (2015): 200–15. DOI: 10.4236/ahs.2015.43016.

Affan, Samah. "Ethical Gestures: Articulations of Black Life in Montreal's 1960s." Master's thesis, Concordia University, 2013.

AGSEM Teaching Assistants' Unit Executive [Sunci Avlijas, Cora-Lee Conway, rosalind hampton, Justin Marleau and Megan Mericle]. "Travailleuses, Étudiant-es: Même Combat!" *McGill Journal of Education* 48, no. 3 (2013): 587–96. https://mje.mcgill.ca/article/view/8989.

Ahmed, Sara. "The Non-Performativity of Antiracism." *Borderlands* 5, no. 3 (2005). http://www.borderlands.net.au/vol3no2_2004/ahmed _declarations.htm.

–. *On Being Included: Racism and Diversity in Institutional Life*. Durham: Duke University Press, 2012.

–. *Willful Subjects*. Durham: Duke University Press, 2014.

Alfred, Marguerite J. "Revelations." *McGill Daily* 58, no. 76 (20 February 1969), 4, 5.

Allahar, Anton, L. "The Political Economy of 'Race' and Class in Canada's Caribbean Diaspora." *American Review of Political Economy* 8, no. 2 (2010): 54–86.

Allen, Keith. "The Transitional Year Programme at the University of Toronto: A Life-Line for Seeking a University Education." In *Educating African Canadians*, edited by Keren S. Brathwaite and Carl E. James, 234–50. Toronto: James Lorimer, 1996.

Amadasun, David Osa. "'Black People Don't Go to Galleries': The Reproduction of Taste and Cultural Value." *Media Diversified,* 21 October 2013. https://mediadiversified.org/2013/10/21/black-people-dont-go-to-galleries-the-reproduction-of-taste-and-cultural-value/.

Ames, Herbert Brown. *The City Below the Hill: A Sociological Study of a Portion of the City of Montreal, Canada.* Montreal: Bishop Engraving and Printing, 1897.

An Act for the Abolition of Slavery Throughout the British Colonies for Promoting the Industry of the Manumitted Slaves and for Compensating the Persons Hitherto Entitled to the Services of Such Slaves. London, 1833.

"Anderson Hearings Closed to Public." *McGill Daily* 58, no. 65 (4 February 1969), 1, 3.

Apouchtine, Nathalie. "Black Studies Priority Is Low." *McGill Daily* 59, no. 95 (5 March 1970), 3.

Arenburg, Patricia Brooks. "An Extended Family through Dal's Transition Year Program." *Dal News* (9 January 2012). http://www.dal.ca/news/2012/01/09/an-extended-family-through-dals-transition-year-program.html.

Ash, Melanie C.T. "But Where Are You REALLY From? Reflections on Immigration, Multiculturalism, and Canadian Identity." In *Racism Eh? A Critical Inter-Disciplinary Anthology of Race and Racism in Canada,* edited by Camille A. Nelson and Charmaine A. Nelson, 398–409. Concord, ON: Captus, 2004.

"At Sir George …" *McGill Daily* 58, no. 64 (3 February 1969), 1, 3.

Austin, David. *Fear of a Black Nation: Race, Sex and Security in Sixties Montreal.* Toronto: Between the Lines, 2013.

–. "Narratives of Power: Historical Mythologies in Contemporary Québec and Canada." *Race and Class* 52 no. 19 (2010): 19–32.

Axelrod, Paul. "The Student Movement of the 1930s." In *Youth, University and Canadian Society: Essays in the Social History of Higher Education,* edited by Paul Axelrod and J.G. Reid, 216–36. Montreal/Kingston: McGill-Queen's University Press, 1989.

Axelrod, Paul, and John G. Reid. Introduction to *Youth, University and Canadian Society: Essays in the Social History of Higher Education,* edited by Paul Axelrod and J.G. Reid. Montreal/Kingston: McGill-Queen's University Press, 1989.

Backhouse, Constance. *Colour-Coded: A Legal History of Racism in Canada, 1900–1950.* Toronto: Osgoode Society for Canadian Legal History/University of Toronto Press, 1999.

Bakan, Abigail B., and Enakshi Dua. "Introducing the Questions, Reframing the Dialogue. In *Theorizing Anti-Racism: Linkages in Marxism and Critical Race Theories,* edited by Abigail B. Bakan and Enakshi Dua, 5–13. Toronto: University of Toronto Press, 2014.

Bannerji, Himani. *The Dark Side of the Nation: Essays on Multiculturalism, Nationalism and Gender.* Toronto: Canadian Scholars' Press, 2000.

–. "Building from Marx: Reflections on Class and Race." *Social Justice* 32, no. 4 (2005): 144–60. https://www.jstor.org/stable/29768341.

–. "Marxism and Antiracism in Theory and Practice: Reflections and Interpretations." In *Theorizing Antiracism: Linkages in Marxism and Critical Race Theories,* edited by Abigail B. Bakan and Enakshi Dua, 127–41. Toronto: University of Toronto Press, 2014.

Bannerji, Himani, Linda Carty, Kari Dehli, Susan Heald, and Kate McKenna. *Unsettling Relations: The University as a Site of Feminist Struggles.* Toronto: Women's Press, 1991.

Barrett, Stanley R. "Fascism in Canada." *Contemporary Crises* 8, no. 4 (1984): 345–77. https://doi.org/10.1007/BF00728847.

Bascomb, Lia T. "Productively Destabilized: Black Studies and Fantastic Modes of Being." *Souls* 16, no. 3–4 (2014): 148–65. https://doi.org/10.1080/10 999949.2014.968957.

Baszile, Denise T. "Rhetorical Revolution: Critical Race Counterstorytelling and the Abolition of White Democracy." *Qualitative Inquiry* 21, no. 3 (2014): 239–49. https://doi.org/10.1177/1077800414557830.

Bayne, Edina, and Clarence Bayne. "The Quebec Board of Black Educators: An Innovator." Revised April 2009. https://bscportal.wordpress.com /the-quebec-board-of-black-educators-an-innovator/.

Beck, Ellen. "Tired of Talk … McGill Blacks Rally." *McGill Daily* 60, no. 3 (23 September 1970), 1.

Bédard, Éric, John Provart, Stanley Gray, Gilles Dostaler, Charles Gagnon, Claude Ryan, Pierre Bélanger, and Ginette Lamontagne. "McGill Français: 30 Ans Après." *Cahiers du PÉQ* no. 20 (January 2001). https://www.mcgill .ca/qcst/fr/publications/cahiers-du-peq.

Belcourt, Billy-Ray. "Political Depression in a Time of Reconciliation." *Active History,* 15 January 2016. http://activehistory.ca/2016/01 /political-depression-in-a-time-of-reconciliation/.

Bell, Stewart. "Canada's Racist Movement: A History of Violence." *Global News,* 20 August 2017. https://globalnews.ca/news/3678021/canada-racist -movement-history-violence/.

Berger, Carl. *The Sense of Power: Studies in the Ideas of Canadian Imperialism, 1867–1914.* Toronto: University of Toronto Press, 2013.

Bertley, June. "The Role of the Black Community in Educating Blacks in Montreal, from 1910 to 1940, with Special Reference to Reverend Charles Humphrey Este." Master's thesis, McGill University, 1982.

Bertley, Leo W. *Canada and Its People of African Descent.* Pierrefonds, QC: Bilongo, 1977.

–. "The United Negro Improvement Association of Montreal: 1917–1979." PhD
diss., Concordia University, 1980.

"The Best Man for Principal." *McGill Daily* 59, no. 4 (4 March 1970), 4.

Betcherman, Lita-Rose. *The Swastika and the Maple Leaf: Fascist Movements in
Canada in the Thirties*. Toronto: Fitzhenry and Whiteside, 1975.

Bigaouette, Mylène, and Marie-Eve Surprenant, eds. *Les Femmes Changent la
Lutte: Au Cœur du Printemps Québécois*. Montreal: Les Éditions du Remue-
Ménage, 2013.

Binks-Collier, Max. "McGill Releases 600 Pages of Documents to Demilitarize
McGill." *McGill Daily* (10 July 2016).

Biondi, Martha. *The Black Revolution on Campus*. Berkeley: University of
California Press, 2012.

Birt, Robert E. "Of the Quest for Freedom as Community." In *The Quest for
Community and Identity: Critical Essays in Africana Social Philosophy*, edited
by Robert E. Birt, 87–104. Lanham, MD: Rowman and Littlefield, 2002.

Bisaillon, Laura. "An Analytic Glossary to Social Inquiry Using Institutional
and Political Activist Ethnography." *International Journal of Qualitative
Methods* 11, no. 5 (2012): 607–27. https://doi.org/10.1177/160940691201100506.

Blackett, Adelle. "Mentoring the Other: Cultural Pluralist Approaches to
Access to Justice." *International Journal of the Legal Profession* 8, no. 3 (2001):
275–90. https://doi.org/10.1080/09695950220141052.

"Black Militants and Red Guards." *McGill Reporter* 1, no. 7 (4 November 1968), 1.

"Black Power Is Coming." *McGill Daily* 58, no. 2 (27 September 1968), 1.

Black Students' Network. "Mis-education at McGill." *McGill Daily* 81, no. 64 (3
February 1992), 3.

Block, Sheila, 2017. "Canada's Population Is Changing but Income
Inequality Remains a Problem." *Behind the Numbers* (blog),
27 October 2017. http://behindthenumbers.ca/2017/10/27
/population-changing-income-inequality-remains/.

Block, Sheila, Grace-Edward Galabuzi, and Alexandra Weiss. *The Colour
Coded Labour Market by the Numbers: A National Household Survey Analysis*.
Toronto: Wellesley Institute, 2014. http://www.wellesleyinstitute.com
/wp-content/uploads/2014/09/The-Colour-Coded-Labour-Market-By
-The-Numbers.pdf.

Bobb-Smith, Yvonne. "'We Get Troo…': Caribbean Canadian Women's
Spirituality as Strategy of Resistance." In *Theorizing Empowerment: Canadian
Perspectives on Black Feminist Thought*, edited by Notisha Massaquoi and
Njoki N. Wane, 55–71. Toronto: Inanna, 2007.

Bock, Michael. *A Nation beyond Borders: Lionel Groulx on French Canadian
Minorities*. Translated by Ferdinanda Van Gennip. Ottawa: University of
Ottawa Press, 2014.

Boden, Daniel, Maura Borrego, and Lynita K. Newswander. "Student Socialization in Interdisciplinary Doctoral Education." *Higher Education: The International Journal of Higher Education Research* 62, no. 6 (2011): 741–55. https://doi.org/10.1007/s10734-011-9415-1.

Boggs, Grace Lee. "Education: The Great Obsession." In *Education and Black Struggle: Notes from the Colonized World*, edited by Institute of the Black World, 61–81. Cambridge, MA: Harvard Educational Review, 1974.

Bonilla-Silva, Eduardo. *Racism without Racists: Color-Blind Racism and the Persistence of Racial Inequality in the United States*. 2nd ed. Lanham, MD: Rowman and Littlefield, 2006.

Boone, Mike. "Stokely Preaches Violent Revolution." *McGill Daily* 58 no. 12 (15 October 1968), 1.

Boyce Davies, Carole, ed. *Claudia Jones: Beyond Containment*. Banbury, UK: Ayebia Clarke, 2011.

–. *Left of Karl Marx: The Political Life of Black Communist Claudia Jones*. Durham: Duke University Press, 2008.

Brand, Dionne. *Bread Out of Stone*. Toronto: Vintage Canada, 1994.

Brathwaite, Keren S., ed. *Access and Equity in the University: A Collection of Papers from the 30th Anniversary Conference of the Transitional Year Program, University of Toronto*. Toronto: Canadian Scholars' Press, 2003.

–. "Reflections on My Years in TYP: Lessons in Education Equity." In *Access and Equity in the University: A Collection of Papers from the 30th Anniversary Conference of the Transitional Year Program, University of Toronto*, edited by Keren S. Brathwaite, 59–78. Toronto: Canadian Scholars' Press, 2003.

Brathwaite, Keren S., and Carl E. James, eds. *Educating African Canadians*. Toronto: James Lorimer, 1996.

Bristow, Peggy, Dionne Brand, Linda Carty, Afua Cooper, Sylvia Hamilton, and Adrienne Shadd. *We're Rooted Here and They Can't Pull Us Up: Essays in African Canadian Women's History*. Toronto: University of Toronto Press, 1994.

Brown, Robert Craig, and Ramsay Cook. *Canada 1896–1921: A Nation Transformed*. Toronto: McClelland and Stewart, 1976.

Bruneau, William. "Professors in Their Places: Governance in Canadian Higher Education." In *University Governance and Reform: Policy, Fads, and Experience in International Perspective*, edited by Hans G. Schuetze, William Bruneau, and Garnet Grosjean, 47–62. New York: Palgrave Macmillan, 2012.

Buddle, Christopher. "In Praise of University Administration." *University Affairs*, 24 March 2014. http://www.universityaffairs.ca/career-advice/careers-cafe/in-praise-of-university-administration/.

Bunjun, Benita. "The Racialized Feminist Killjoy in White Academia: Contesting White Entitlement." In *Exploring Race in Predominantly White*

Classrooms: Scholars of Color Reflect, edited by George Yancy and Maria del Guadalupe Davidson, 147–61. New York: Routledge, 2014.

Calliste, Agnes. "African Canadians Organizing for Educational Change." In *Educating African Canadians,* edited by Keren S. Brathwaite and Carl E. James, 87–106. Toronto: James Lorimer, 1996.

Campbell, Angela. "Employment Equity." Biennial Report to Senate. May 2017. https://mcgill.ca/senate/files/senate/11._d16-66_report_on_employment_equity.pdf. Accessed 25 November 2019.

Campbell, Horace. "Is It Possible to Have Access and Equity in University Education in the Twenty-First Century? Lessons from the Transitional Year Program at the University of Toronto." In *Access and Equity in the University: A Collection of Papers from the 30th Anniversary Conference of the Transitional Year Program, University of Toronto,* edited by Keren S. Brathwaite, 35–58. Toronto: Canadian Scholars' Press, 2003.

–. "A Response to Austerity Measures Requires Audacity Not Timidity." *Souls: A Critical Journal of Black Politics, Culture, and Society* 14, no. 3–4 (2012): 240–64. https://doi.org/10.1080/10999949.2012.768080.

Campbell, Marie L. "Institutional Ethnography and Experience as Data." *Qualitative Inquiry* 21, no. 1 (1998): 55–73.

Campbell, Marie, and Frances Gregor. *Mapping Social Relations: A Primer in Doing Institutional Ethnography.* Toronto: University of Toronto Press, 2008.

Canadian University Press. "McGill, U of Winnipeg Student Associations Act to Protest Investments in South Africa." *McGill Daily* 70, no. 1 (8 September 1980), 6.

Carleton, Audrey. "Life beyond the McGill Bubble: Stepping into the Real World." *McGill Tribune,* 29 September 2015. http://www.mcgilltribune.com/student-living/life-beyond-the-mcgill-bubble-2901941/.

Carpenter, Sara, and Shahrzad Mojab. "Adult Education and the 'Matter' of Consciousness in Marxist-Feminism." In *Marxism and Education: Renewing the Dialogue, Pedagogy and Culture,* edited by Peter E. Jones, 117–40. New York: Palgrave Macmillan, 2011.

Carty, Linda. "African Canadian Women and the State: 'Labour Only Please.'" In *We're Rooted Here and They Can't Pull Us Up: Essays in African Canadian Women's History,* by Peggy Bristow, Dionne Brand, Linda Carty, Afua P. Cooper, Sylvia Hamilton, and Adrienne Shadd, 193–229. Toronto: University of Toronto Press, 1994.

–. "Black Women in Academia: A Statement from the Periphery." In *Unsettling Relations: The University as a Site of Feminist Struggles,* by Himami Bannerji, Linda Carty, Kari Dehli, Susan Heald, and Kate McKenna, 13–44. Toronto: Women's Press, 1991.

–. "A Genealogy of Marxist Feminism in Canada." *Studies in Political Economy* 94 (2014): 177–84. https://doi.org/10.1080/19187033.2014.11674960.

CAUT (Canadian Association of University Teachers). "Underrepresented and Underpaid: Diversity and Equity among Canada's Post-Secondary Education Teachers." April 2018. https://www.caut.ca/sites/default/files /caut_equity_report_2018-04final.pdf.

CBC. "Distinguished Canadians: Hugh MacLennan." 12 June 1972. http:// www.cbc.ca/archives/entry/distinguished-canadians-hugh-maclennan.

CBC. "Wilfrid Laurier University to Cut 22 Jobs in Face of $25M Deficit." 10 March 2015. http://www.cbc.ca/news/canada/kitchener-waterloo /wilfrid-laurier-university-to-cut-22-jobs-in-face-of-25m-deficit-1.2989357.

Césaire, Aimé. *Discourse on Colonialism*. New York: Monthly Review Press, 2000. First published as *Discours sur le colonialisme*, 1950.

Charland, William. "African American Youth and the Artist's Identity: Cultural Models and Aspirational Foreclosure." *Studies in Art Education* 51, no. 2 (2010): 105–33. https://doi.org/10.1080/00393541.2010.11518796.

Chatterjee, Piya, and Sunaina Maira, eds. *The Imperial University: Academic Repression and Scholarly Dissent*. Minneapolis: University of Minnesota Press, 2014.

Chioneso, Nkechinyelum A. "(Re)Expressions of African/Caribbean Cultural Roots in Canada." *Journal of Black Studies* 39, no. 1 (2008): 69–84.

Chiose, Simona. "Justice on Campus." *Globe and Mail*, 1 April 2016. https:// www.theglobeandmail.com/news/national/education/canadian -universities-under-pressure-to-formalize-harassment-assaultpolicies /article29499302/.

Choi, Jung-ah. "Unlearning Colorblind Ideologies in Education Class." *Educational Foundations* 22, no. 3–4 (2008): 53–72.

Chou, Meng-Hsuan, Isaac Kamola, and Tamson Pietsch, eds. *The Transnational Politics of Higher Education: Contesting the Global/Transforming the Local*. London: Routledge, 2016.

Choudry, Aziz A. "Avec Nous, Dans la Rue: Pedagogy of Mobilization, University of the Streets." *Wi: Journal of Mobile Media*, 19 June 2012. http:// wi.mobilities.ca/avec-nous-dans-la-rue-pedagogy-of-mobilization -university-of-the-streets/.

–. *Learning Activism: The Intellectual Life of Contemporary Social Movements*. Toronto: University of Toronto Press, 2015.

Choudry, Aziz, and Devlin Kuyek. "Activist Research: Mapping Power Relations, Informing Struggles." In *Organize! Building from the Local for Global Justice*, edited by Aziz Choudry, Jill Hanley, and Eric Shragge, 23–4. Oakland/Toronto: PM Press/Between the Lines, 2012.

Chrisjohn, Roland, and Tanya Wasacase. "Half-Truths and Whole Lies: Rhetoric in the 'Apology' and the Truth and Reconciliation Commission." In *Response, Responsibility and Renewal: Canada's Truth and Reconciliation Journey*, edited by Gregory Younging, Jonathan Dewar, and Michael DeGagné, 217–29. Ottawa: Aboriginal Healing Foundation, 2009.

Collard, Edgar A. "Forgotten Cemetery." *Montreal Gazette,* 17 July 1965.

–. "Burial on the Campus." *Montreal Gazette,* 21 May 1983.

–. "Dufferin Park – Once Protestant Cemetery." *Montreal* Gazette, 17 April 1971.

–. "The Reburial of James McGill." *Montreal Gazette,* 24 July 1965.

–. "Sir William Dawson's Principalship, 1855–1893." In *McGill: The Story of a University,* edited by Hugh MacLennan, 49–72. London: Allen and Unwin, 1960.

Collectif dix novembre, ed. *This Is Fucking Class War: Voices from the 2012 Québec Student Strike,* 2014. http://luxgoodcreative.com/classwar/home.html.

Collins, Patricia Hill. *Black Feminist Thought.* 2nd ed. New York: Routledge Classics, 2009.

–. "Learning from the Outsider Within: The Sociological Significance of Black Feminist Thought." *Social Problems* 33, no. 6 (1986): S14–S32. https://doi .org/10.2307/800672.

Collison, Christiana. "'Is Your Hair Real?' Don't Fucking Ask Me if My Hair Is Real." *McGill Daily* 101, no. 38 (16 March 2012). https://www.mcgilldaily .com/2012/03/is-your-hair-real/1347115062000/.

Conference Board of Canada. "Income Inequality." Ottawa. Last updated April 2017. http://www.conferenceboard.ca/hcp/provincial/society /income-inequality.aspx.

–. "Racial Wage Gap." Ottawa. Last updated April 2017. http://www .conferenceboard.ca/hcp/Provincial/society/racial-gap.aspx.

Cook, Verda. "Planted in Frozen Earth: McGill's Africana Studies Committee Celebrates 30 Years of Survival." *McGill Daily* 88, no. 52 (18 February 1999), 12.

Coombes, Annie E., ed. *Rethinking Settler Colonialism: History and Memory in Australia, Canada, Aotearoa New Zealand and South Africa.* Manchester: Manchester University Press, 2006.

Cooper, Afua. "Black Women and Work in the Nineteenth-Century Canada West: Black Woman Teacher Mary Bibb." In *Back to The Drawing Board: African-Canadian Feminisms,* edited by Njoki N. Wane, Katerina Deliovsky, and Erica Lawson, 117–28. Toronto: Sumach, 2002.

–. "Constructing Black Women's Historical Knowledge." *Atlantis* 25, no. 1 (2000): 39–50.

–. *The Hanging of Angélique: The Untold Story of Canadian Slavery and the Burning of Old Montréal.* Toronto: Harper Collins, 2006.

Cooper, John I. *James McGill of Montreal: Citizen of the Atlantic World.* Ottawa: Borealis, 2003.

Corbeil, Laurent Bastien. "Blackface and Other Costumes Stir Controversy at 4Floors." *McGill Daily* 102, no. 17 (1 November 2012). http://www.mcgill daily.com/2012/11/blackface-and-other-costumes-stir-controversy -at-4floors/.

Coulthard, Glen. *Red Skin, White Masks: Rejecting the Colonial Politics of Recognition*. Minneapolis: University of Minnesota Press, 2014.

"Council Comes Out Against Violence." *McGill Daily* 58, no. 75 (19 February 1969), 3.

"Council Hits SGWU." *McGill Daily* 58, no. 63 (31 January 1969), 1.

Cowen, Harry. "Africa for the Africans." *McGill Reporter* 2, no. 8 (November 1969), 6–8.

Craig, G.M. "Strachan, John." In *Dictionary of Canadian Biography*, vol. 9. Toronto/Québec City: University of Toronto/Université Laval, 2003. http://www.biographi.ca/en/bio/strachan_john_9E.html.

Crawhall, Nigel. "Some Arguments for Divestment." *McGill Daily* 75, no. 4 (12 September 1985), 12.

Danforth, Jessica Yee. "Occupy Wall Street: The Game of Colonialism and the Left." *Rabble*. http://rabble.ca/columnists/2011/10/occupy-wall-street-game-colonialism-and-left.

Dauphin, Nydia. "Why the Hell Are Québec Comedians Wearing Blackface?" *Huffington Post Canada*, 16 May 2013. http://www.huffingtonpost.ca/nydia-dauphin/blackface-in-quebec_b_3276801.html.

Davis, Angela. *Women, Race and Class*. New York: Vintage, 1983.

Day, Iyko. "Being or Nothingness: Indigeneity, Antiblackness and Settler Colonial Critique." *Critical Ethnic Studies* 1, no. 2 (2015): 102–21.

Dean, Michelle. "Rethinking Freedom, Privilege in Today's Universities." *McGill Daily* 89, no. 49 (10 February 2000), 5.

de Gannes, Gillian, Randy Flemmings, and Mark A.A. Warner. "BSN Calls for Total Divestment." *McGill Daily* 75, no. 27 (11 November 1985), 4.

Dei, George J.S. "The African Scholar in the Western Academy." *Journal of Black Studies* 45, no. 3 (2014): 167–79. https://doi.org/10.1177%2F0021934714525198.

–. "Race and the Production of Identity in the Schooling Experiences of African-Canadian Youth." *Discourse: Studies in the Cultural Production of Education* 18, no. 2 (1997): 241–57. https://doi.org/10.1080/0159630970180206.

Delgado, Richard. "Affirmative Action as a Majoritarian Device: Or, Do You Really Want to Be a Role Model?" *Michigan Law Review* 89, no. 5 (1991): 1222–31.

–. "The Ethereal Scholar: Does Critical Legal Studies Have What Minorities Want?" *Harvard Civil Rights-Civil Liberties Law Review* 22, no. 2 (1987): 301–22.

Delisle, Esther. *Myths, Memory and Lies: Québec's Intelligentsia and the Fascist Temptation, 1939–1960*. Westmount, QC: R. Davies Multimedia, 1998.

–. *The Traitor and the Jew: Anti-Semitism and the Delirium of Extremist Right-Wing Nationalism in French Canada from 1929–1939*. Outremont, QC: Robert Davies, 1993.

DeVault, Marie, and Liza McCoy. "Institutional Ethnography: Using Interviews to Investigate Ruling Relations." In *Institutional Ethnography as Practice*, edited by D.E. Smith, 15–44. Lanham, MD: Rowman and Littlefield, 2006.

Dhavernas, J. "Law, Preventative State, and Dissent." In *This Is Fucking Class War: Voices from the 2012 Québec Student Strike*, edited by Collectif dix novembre, 267–79, 2014. http://luxgoodcreative.com/classwar/dhavernas.html.

DiversityLeads. "Women and Visible Minorities in Senior Leadership Positions: A Profile of Greater Montreal." Diversity Institute, Ryerson University, and Desautels Faculty of Management, McGill University, 2012–13. http://www.ryerson.ca/content/dam/diversity/reports /DiversityLeads_Montreal_EN_2012-13.pdf.

Dixon, Marlene. *Things Which Are Done in Secret*. Montreal: Black Rose, 1976.

Douglas, Delia D. "Black/Out: The White Face of Multiculturalism and the Violence of the Canadian Academic Imperial Project." In *Presumed Incompetent: The Intersections of Race and Class for Women in Academia*, edited by Gabriella Gutierrez y Muhs, Yolanda Flores Niemann, Carmen G. González, and Angela P. Harris, 50–64. Logan: Utah State University Press, 2012

Douglas, Rosie, and Carl Parris. "Disruption as a Means of Self-Determination for Black People." *McGill Daily* 59, no. 30 (27 October 1969), 6.

Downs, Jim, and Jennifer Manion, eds. *Taking Back the Academy: History of Activism, History as Activism*. New York: Routledge, 2004.

D'Souza, Radha. "Rights, Action, Change: Organize for What?" In *Organize! Building from the Local for Global Justice*, edited by Aziz Choudry, Jill Hanley, and Eric Shragge, 71–81. Toronto/Oakland: Between the Lines/PM Press, 2012.

–. *What's Wrong with Rights? Social Movements, Law and Liberal Imaginations*. London: Pluto, 2017.

Dua, Enakshi. "Exclusion Through Inclusion: Female Asian Migration in the Making of Canada as a White Settler Nation." *Gender, Place & Culture* 14, no. 4 (2007): 445–66. https://doi.org/10.1080/09663690701439751.

Dubinsky, Karen, Catherine Krull, Susan Lord, Sean Mills, and Scott Rutherford. *New World Coming: The Sixties and the Shaping of Global Consciousness*. Toronto: Between the Lines, 2009.

DuBois, W.E.B. *The Souls of Black Folk*. New York: Bantam, 1989.

Dumas, Michael J. "Contesting White Accumulation in Seattle: Toward a Materialist Antiracist Analysis of School Desegregation." In *The Pursuit of Racial and Ethnic Equality in American Public Schools: Mendez, Brown and Beyond*, edited by Kristi L. Brown, 291–311. East Lansing: Michigan State University Press, 2014.

–. "Doing Class in Critical Race Analysis in Education." In *Handbook of Critical Race Theory in Education*, edited by Marvin Lynn and Adrienne D. Dixon, 113–25. New York: Routledge, 2013.

Eber, Dorothy. *The Computer Centre Party: Canada Meets Black Power.* Montreal: Tundra, 1969

Edwards, Reginald. "Historical Background of the English-Language CEGEPs of Quebec." *McGill Journal of Education* 25, no. 2 (1990): 147–74.

Ellison, Ralph. *Invisible Man.* New York: Vintage International, [1952] 1995.

Enenajor, Annamaria. "A Second Look at McGill's Intrepid Global Citizens." *Quid Novi* 31, no. 2 (20 October 2009), 3–4.

Engler, Yves. *Canada in Africa: 300 Years of Aid and Exploitation.* Black Point, NS: Fernwood, 2015.

Engler, Yves. "Harper Promotes Canadian Militarism: Introducing University Undergraduates to a Form of Military Service on Campus." *Global Research: Centre for Research on Globalization,* 16 August 2013. http://www.globalresearch.ca/harperpromotes-canadian-militarism-introducing-university-undergraduates-to-a-form-ofmilitary-service-on-campus/5346493.

Ertekin, Cem. "McGill Is Delivered Notice of Seizure." *McGill Daily,* 13 September 2015. http://www.mcgilldaily.com/2015/09/mcgill-is-delivered-notice-of-seizure/.

Ervin, Alexander, and Howard Woodhouse. "'We Must Compete': Corporate Elite Leveraging Public Universities into Private Profit." *Rabble,* 10 July 2014. http://rabble.ca/blogs/bloggers/campus-notes/2014/07/we-must-compete-corporate-elite-leveraging-public-universities-p.

Fanon, Frantz. *Black Skin, White Masks.* Translated by C.L. Markmann. New York: Grove, 1967.

Ferrer, Ilyan, Farha Najah Hussain, Edward Ou Jin Lee, and Lena Palacios. "Building Solidarity: Searching for Racial and Migrant Justice within the Québec Student Movement." In *This is Fucking Class War: Voices from the 2012 Québec Student Strike,* edited by Collectif dix novembre, 2014. http://luxgoodcreative.com/classwar/ferrer.html.

Fisher, Susan. *Boys and Girls in No Man's Land: English-Canadian Children and the First World War.* Toronto: University of Toronto Press, 2011.

Flaherty, Colleen. "Demanding 10 Percent." *Inside Higher Ed,* 30 November 2015. https://www.insidehighered.com/news/2015/11/30/student-activists-want-more-black-faculty-members-how-realistic-are-some-their-goals.

Foley, Griff. *Learning in Social Action: A Contribution to Understanding Informal Education.* London: Zed Books, 1999.

Foner, P.S. *W.E.B. Du Bois Speaks: Speeches and Addresses, 1920–1963.* Atlanta: Pathfinder, 2008.

Fong, William. "J.W. McConnell and the Chancellorship of McGill University, 1942–3." *Fontanus* 13 (2013): 81–94.

Forsythe, Dennis. "Black Studies Night." *McGill Daily* 59, no. 85 (18 February 1970), 4.

–. ed. *Let the Niggers Burn: The Sir George Williams University Affair and Its Caribbean Aftermath.* Montreal: Black Rose Books/Our Generation Press, 1971.

Fox, Catherine. "The Race to Truth: Disarticulating Critical Thinking from Whiteliness." *Pedagogy* 2, no. 2 (2002): 197–212. https://muse.jhu.edu /article/26394.

Frampton, Caelie, Gary Kinsman, A.K. Thompson, and Kate Tilleczek, eds. *Sociology for Changing the World.* Halifax: Fernwood, 2006.

Frankenberg, Ruth. *White Women, Race Matters: The Social Construction of Whiteness.* Minneapolis: University of Minnesota Press, 1993.

Freire, Paulo. *Pedagogy of the Oppressed.* London: Bloomsbury, 2000.

Frost, Stanley B. *The History of McGill in Relation to the Social, Economic and Cultural Aspects of Montreal and Quebec.* N.p.: Commission d'étude sur les universités, 1979.

–. *James McGill of Montreal.* Montreal/Kingston: McGill-Queen's University Press, 1995.

–. *McGill University, for the Advancement of Learning, Volume 1: 1801–1895.* Montreal/Kingston: McGill-Queen's University Press, 1980.

–. *McGill University, for the Advancement of Learning, Volume 2: 1895–1971.* Montreal/Kingston: McGill-Queen's University Press, 1984.

Frost, Stanley B., and Robert H. Michel, "Macdonald, Sir William Christopher." In *Dictionary of Canadian Biography*, vol. 14. Toronto/Quebec City: University of Toronto/Université Laval, 2003–. Accessed 14 April 2018. http://www.biographi.ca/en/bio/macdonald_william_christopher_14E .html.

Frye, Marilyn. "White Woman Feminist: 1983–1992." In *Willful Virgin: Essays in Feminism, 1976–1992*, 146–69. Freedom, CA: Crossing, 1992.

Gabourel, Rev. F. "Charles Humphry Este Will Never Be Forgotten by Montreal Blacks." *Montreal Oracle* 2, no. 1 (20 January 1977): n.p.

Galabuzi, Grace-Edward. "Canada's Creeping Economic Apartheid: The Economic Segregation and Social Marginalisation of Racialised Groups." Toronto: Centre for Social Justice Foundation for Research and Education, 2001. http://www.socialjustice.org/pdfs/economicapartheid.pdf.

–. *Canada's Economic Apartheid: The Social Exclusion of Racialized Groups in the New Century.* Toronto: Canadian Scholars' Press, 2006.

Gill, Rosalind. "Academics, Cultural Workers and Critical Labour Studies." *Journal of Cultural Economy* 7, no. 1 (2014): 12–30.

Golding, Audrea. "McGill History Department Refuses Black Studies." *McGill Daily* 81, no. 42 (18 November 1991), 1.

Gordon, Avery. *Ghostly Matters: Haunting and the Sociological Imagination.* Minneapolis: University of Minnesota Press, 2008.

–. "Some Thoughts on Haunting and Futurity." *Borderlands* 10, no. 2 (2011): 1–20.

Gordon, Ricky C., and Chantelle Jones. "Congress Rallies for a Stronger African Studies Program." *McGill Daily* 89, no. 49 (10 February 2000), 5.

Goswami, Marami. "Neoliberalism and Higher Education in India." *Journal of Research in Humanities and Social Science* 1, no. 3 (2013): 32–7. http://www .questjournals.org/jrhss/papers/vol1-issue3/F133237.pdf.

Grande, Sandy. "Accumulation of the Primitive: The Limits of Liberalism and the Politics of Occupy Wall Street." *Settler Colonial Studies* 3, nos. 3–4 (2013): 369–80. https://doi.org/10.1080/2201473X.2013.810704.

Griffin, Philip J. "What Happens to a Dream Deferred?" *The Georgian* 32, no. 32 (28 January 1969), 6.

Grove, Jack. "Black Scholars Still Experience Racism on Campus." *Times Higher Education*, 14 March 2014. https://www.timeshighereducation.com /news/black-scholars-still-experience-racism-on-campus/2012154.article.

Guinier, Lani. "From Racial Liberalism to Racial Literacy: Brown v. Board of Education and the Interest-Divergence Dilemma." *Journal of American History* 91, no. 1 (2004): 92–118. https://ssrn.com/abstract=2023994.

–. "Models and Mentors." In *Becoming Gentlemen: Women, Law School and Institutional Change*, edited by Lani Guinier, Michelle Fine, and Jane Balin, 85–97. Boston: Beacon, 1997

–. *The Tyranny of Meritocracy: Democratizing Higher Education in America*. Boston: Beacon, 2015.

Gutierrez y Muhs, Gabriella, Yolanda Flores Niemann, Carmen G. González, and Angela P. Harris, eds. *Presumed Incompetent: The Intersections of Race and Class for Women in Academia*. Logan: Utah State University Press, 2012.

Haig-Brown, Celia. *Resistance and Renewal: Surviving the Indian Residential School*. Vancouver: Arsenal Pulp Press, 2006.

Haliburton, Robert Grant. *The Men of the North and Their Place in History*. Montreal: J. Lovell, 1869.

Hamilton, Sylvia. "Stories from 'The Little Black Schoolhouse.'" In *Cultivating Canada: Reconciliation through the Lens of Cultural Diversity*, edited by Ashok Mathur, Jonathan Dewar, and Michael DeGagné, 91–112. Ottawa: Aboriginal Healing Foundation, 2011.

hampton, rosalind. "By All Appearances: Thoughts on Colonialism, Visuality and Racial Neoliberalism." In "Crucibles of Creativity: Reimagining Relations under Multiple Colonialisms," edited by Dia DaCosta and Alex DaCosta, special issue, *Cultural Studies* 3, no. 3 (2019): 370–90. https://doi .org/10.1080/09502386.2019.1584909.

–. "Claiming Space in Québec's Social Movements." *Community Contact* 22, no. 13 (17 July 2012), 23.

–. "Créer Dangereusement: Congrès des Écrivain·e·s et Artistes Noir·e·s."
    À Bâbord: Revue Sociale et Politique 52 (December 2013/January 2014): 41.
    https://www.ababord.org/Creer-dangereusement.
–. "Nous Who? Racialization and Québec Student Movement Politics." In *The
    University and Social Justice: Struggles across the World,* edited by Aziz A.
    Choudry and Salim Vally. London: Pluto Press, forthcoming.
–. "Race, Racism and the Québec Student Movement." *New Socialist Webzine,* 8
    July 2012. http://newsocialist.org/race-racism-and-the-quebec-student
    -movement/.
hampton, rosalind, and Michelle Hartman, Michelle. "Towards Language
    and Resistance: A Breaking Manifesto." In *Manifestos for World Thought,*
    edited by Lucian Stone and Jason Bahbak Mohaghegh, 115–28. London:
    Rowman and Littlefield, 2017.
hampton, rosalind, Michelle Hartman, Adrienne Hurley, and Tom Lamarre.
    "Fear and Violence in Québec: Why Solidarity with a Diversity of Tactics
    Matters." *Wi: Journal of Mobile Media,* 19 June 2012. http://wi.mobilities
    .ca/fear-and-violence-in-quebec-why-solidarity-with-a-diversity-of-tactics
    -matters/.
hampton, rosalind, Mona Luxion, and Molly Swain. "Finding Space in the
    Student Movement for Both/And Identities." In *This Is Fucking Class War:
    Voices from the 2012 Québec Student Strike,* edited by Collectif dix novembre,
    188–202, 2014. http://luxgoodcreative.com/classwar/hampton.html.
hampton, rosalind, and Desirée Rochat. "To Commit and to Lead: Black
    Women Organizing across Communities in Montreal." In *African Canadian
    Leadership: Continuity, Transition and Transformation,* edited by Tamari
    Kitossa, Philip S.S. Howard, and Erica Lawson, 149–69. Toronto: University
    of Toronto Press, 2019.
Handleman, Don. "West Indian Associations in Montreal." Master's thesis,
    McGill University, 1964.
Harding, Vincent. "Black Students and the Impossible Revolution." *Journal of
    Black Studies* 1, no. 1 (1970): 75–100. DOI: 10.1177/002193477000100106.
–. "The Vocation of the Black Scholar and the Struggles of the Black
    Community." In *Education and Black Struggle: Notes from the Colonized World,*
    edited by Institute of the Black World, 3–29. Cambridge, MA: Harvard
    Educational Review, 1974.
Harney, Stefano, and Fred Moten. *The Undercommons: Fugitive Planning and
    Black Study.* Wivenhoe: Minor Compositions, 2013.
Harris, Cheryl I. "Whiteness as Property." *Harvard Law Review* 106, no. 8
    (1993): 1707–91. DOI: 10.2307/1341787.
Harvey, Alexandra. "McGill Fails to Protect against Sexually Abusive
    Professors, Students Say." *Maclean's,* 18 April 2018. http://www.macleans

.ca/education/mcgill-fails-to-protect-students-from-sexually-abusive
-professors-students-say/.

Harvey, David. *A Brief History of Neoliberalism*. Oxford: Oxford University Press, 2005.

Henry, Annette. "African Canadian Women Teachers' Activism: Recreating Communities of Caring and Resistance." *Journal of Negro Education* 61, no. 3 (1992): 392–404. DOI: 10.2307/2295256.

–. "Thoughts on Academic Leadership: A Letter to African Canadian Women Professors." In *African Canadian Leadership: Continuity, Transition and Transformation,* edited by Tamari Kitossa, Philip S.S. Howard, and Erica Lawson, 170–89. Toronto: University of Toronto Press, 2019.

–. "'We Especially Welcome Applications from Members of Visible Minority Groups': Reflections on Race, Gender and Life at Three Universities." *Race Ethnicity and Education* 18, no. 5 (2015): 589–610. https://doi.org/10.1080/136 13324.2015.1023787.

Henry, Frances, Andrea Choi, and Audrey Kobayashi. "The Representation of Racialized Faculty at Selected Canadian Universities." *Canadian Ethnic Studies* 44, no. 2 (2012): 1–12. DOI: 10.1353/ces.2012.0008.

Henry, Frances, Carl James, Peter S. Li, Audrey Kobayashi, Malinda Sharon Smith, Howard Ramos, and Enakshi Dua. *The Equity Myth: Racialization and Indigeneity at Canadian Universities*. Vancouver: UBC Press, 2017.

Himes, Chester. *Lonely Crusade*. New York: A.A. Knopf, 1947.

Hinkson, Kamila. "McGill's African Studies Program Leads Canada." *The Link* 30, no. 23 (16 February 2010), 20.

Hobsbawm, Eric. "Introduction: Inventing Traditions." In *The Invention of Tradition*, edited by Eric Hobsbawm and Terence Ranger, 1–14. Cambridge: Cambridge University Press, 2004.

Holder, Marc Wynston. "Canadian Blacks Protest Apartheid." *McGill Daily* 75, no. 4 (12 September 1985), 10.

hooks, bell. *Where We Stand: Class Matters*. New York: Routledge, 2000.

Horn, Michiel. *Academic Freedom in Canada: A History*. Toronto: University of Toronto Press, 1999.

–. "Canadian Universities, Academic Freedom, Labour and the Left." *Labour/ Le Travail* 46 (Fall 2000): 439–68. http://www.lltjournal.ca/index.php/llt /article/view/5214.

Horn, Simon. "Bail Denied 97 Arrested Students." *McGill Daily* 58, no. 72 (13 February 1969), 1.

Howard, Philip S.S. "On the Back of Blackness: Contemporary Canadian Blackface and the Consumptive Production of Post-Racialist, White Canadian Subjects." *Social Identities* 24, no. 1 (2018): 87–103. https://doi.org /10.1080/13504630.2017.1281113.

–. "Post-Racialism and the Production and Negotiation of Blackness at University." Presentation at the annual meeting of the Canadian Society for the Study of Education (CSSE), Congress of the Humanities and Social Sciences, University of Calgary, 30 May 2016.

Howe, Stephen. *Afrocentrism: Mythical Pasts and Imagined Homes*. London: Verso, 1998.

Hudson, Peter J. "Research, Repression and Revolution – On Montreal and the Black Radical Tradition: An Interview with David Austin." *CLR James Journal* 20, no. 1–2 (2014): 197–232. DOI: 10.5840/clrjames201492319.

Hudson, Peter J., and Aaron Kamugisha. "On Black Canadian Thought." *CLR James Journal* 20, no. 1–2 (2014): 3–20. https://www.jstor.org/stable/26752055.

"Hugh MacLennan (1907–1990)." McGill University. http://www.mcgill.ca/about/history/mcgill-pioneers/maclennan.

Hulan, Renée. *Northern Experience and the Myths of Canadian Culture*. Montreal/Kingston: McGill-Queen's University Press, 2014.

Hunt, Sally. "Racism in Universities: 'There Is a Sense that Your Face Doesn't Fit.'" *The Guardian*, 4 February 2016. http://www.theguardian.com/higher-education-network/2016/feb/04/racism-in-universities-there-is-a-sense-your-face-doesnt-fit.

Hurley, Adrienne. "In Anticipation of an Unleashed Professoriate." In *This Is Fucking Class War: Voices from the 2012 Québec Student Strike*, edited by Collectif dix novembre, 246–55, 2014. http://luxgoodcreative.com/classwar/hurley.html.

Hurston, Zora Neale. "How It Feels to Be Colored Me." In *I Love Myself When I'm Laughing … And Then Again When I'm Looking Mean and Impressive*, edited by Alice Walker, 152–5. New York: Feminist Press at the City University of New York, 1979.

Ignatiev, Noel. "Abolitionism and the White Studies Racket." *Race Traitor*, no. 10 (1999): 3–7. https://libcom.org/library/racetraitor-journal-new-abolitionism-winter-1999.

Inzlicht, Michael, and Toni Schmader. *Stereotype Threat: Theory, Process, and Application*. New York: Oxford University Press, 2012.

Israel, Wilfred Emmerson. "The Montreal Negro Community." Master's thesis, McGill University, 1928.

Jacob, Selwyn, prod., and Mina Shum, dir. *Ninth Floor*. National Film Board of Canada, Montreal, 2015.

James, Carl E. "Contradictory Tensions in the Experiences of African Canadians in a Faculty of Education with an Access Program." *Canadian Journal of Education/Revue canadienne de l'éducation* 22, no. 2 (1997): 158–74. DOI: 10.2307/1585905.

Johnson, Gaye Theresa, and Alex Lubin. *Futures of Black Radicalism*. London: Verso.

Jones, Claudia. "An End to the Neglect of the Problems of Negro Women." *Claudia Jones: Beyond Containment*, edited by Carole Boyce Davies, 74–86. Banbury, UK: Ayebia Clarke, [1949] 2011.

Jones, Glen A., Theresa Shanahan, and Paul Goyan. "University Governance in Canadian Higher Education." *Tertiary Education and Management* 7, no. 2 (2001): 135–48.

Kalbfleisch, John. "McGill Had a Rocky Start." *Montreal Gazette*, 25 June 2006, A16.

Kassam, Amin. "Africa Conference Disrupted." *McGill Daily* 59, no. 25 (20 October 1969), 1.

Keeling, Kara. "In the Interval: Frantz Fanon and the 'Problems' of Visual Representation." *Qui Parle* 13, no. 2 (2003): 91–117. https://www.jstor.org /stable/20686152.

Kelley, Robin D.G. "Black Study, Black Struggle." *Boston Review*, 7 March 2016. http://bostonreview.net/forum/robin-d-g-kelley-black -study-black-struggle.

–. *Freedom Dreams: The Black Radical Imagination*. Boston: Beacon, 2002.

Kinsman, Gary William, and Patrizia Gentile. *The Canadian War on Queers: National Security as Sexual Regulation*. Vancouver: UBC Press, 2010.

Kitossa, Tamari. "Black Canadian Studies and the Resurgence of the Insurgent African Canadian Intelligentsia." *Southern Journal of Canadian Studies* 5, no. 1 (2012): 255–84. https://doi.org/10.22215/sjcs.v5i1.298.

–. "Nuances of Blackness: Testimony, Scholarship and Black Academics." Presentation at 2nd Biennial Black Canadian Studies Association Conference, Dalhousie University, Halifax, 24 May 2015.

Kloet, M.V., and E. Aspenlieder. "Educational Development for Responsible Graduate Students in the Neoliberal University." *Critical Studies in Education* 54, no. 3 (2013): 286–98. https://doi.org/10.1080/17508487.2013.826706.

Knowles, Valerie. *Strangers at Our Gates: Canadian Immigration and Immigration Policy, 1540–2015*. Toronto: Dundurn, 2016. http://www.deslibris.ca /ID/450074.

Lamarre, Thomas. "Outlaw Universities." *Theory and Event* 15, no.3 (2012): n.p. https://muse.jhu.edu/article/484448.

Lawrence, Bonita. "Gender, Race, and the Regulation of Native Identity in Canada and the United States: An Overview." *Hypatia* 18, no. 2 (2003): 3–31. https://doi.org/10.1111/j.1527-2001.2003.tb00799.x.

Lawrence, Bonita, and Enakshi Dua. "Decolonizing Antiracism." *Social Justice*, 32, no. 4 (2005): 120–43.

Lawson, Erica. "Images in Black: Black Women, Media and the Mythology of an Orderly Society." In *Back to the Drawing Board: African-Canadian Feminisms*, edited by Njoki N. Wane, Katerina Deliovsky, and Erica Lawson, 199–223. Toronto: Sumach, 2002.

Lazos, Sylvia R. "Are Student Teaching Evaluations Holding Back Women and Minorities? The Perils of 'Doing' Gender and Race in the Classroom." In *Presumed Incompetent: The Intersections of Race and Class for Women in Academia*, edited by Gabriella Gutierrez y Muhs, Yolanda Flores Niemann, Carmen G. González, and Angela P. Harris, 164–85. Logan: Utah State University Press, 2012.

Leacock, Stephen. "Canada and the Immigration Problem." *National Review* 57 (1911): 316–27.

–. "The Woman Question." *Maclean's* 28, no. 12 (1 October 1915), 7–9.

Leonardo, Zeus. "The Race for Class: Reflections on a Critical Raceclass Theory of Education." *Educational Studies* 48, no. 5 (2012): 427–49. https://doi.org/10.1080/00131946.2012.715831.

–. *Race Frameworks: A Multidimensional Theory of Racism and Education*. New York: Teachers College Press, 2013.

–. *Race, Whiteness and Education*. New York: Routledge, 2009.

Leonardo, Zeus, and Ronald K. Porter. "Pedagogy of Fear: Toward a Fanonian Theory of 'Safety' in Race Dialogue." *Race Ethnicity and Education* 13, no. 2 (2010): 139–57. https://doi.org/10.1080/13613324.2010.482898.

Leong, Nancy. "Racial Capitalism." *Harvard Law Review* 126, no. 8 (2013): 2151–226. https://harvardlawreview.org/wp-content/uploads/pdfs/vol126_leong.pdf.

Leslie, John. "The Bagot Commission: Developing a Corporate Memory for the Indian Department." *Historical Papers/Communications historiques* 17, no. 1 (1982): 31–52. https://www.erudit.org/en/journals/hp/1982-v17-n1-hp1117/030883ar.pdf.

Levine, Marc V. *The Reconquest of Montreal: Language Policy and Social Change in a Bilingual City*. Philadelphia: Temple University Press, 1990.

Levine-Rasky, Cynthia. *Whiteness Fractured*. Farnham, UK: Ashgate, 2013.

Lexier, Roberta. "'The Backdrop Against Which Everything Happened': English-Canadian Student Movements and Off Campus Movements for Change." *History of Intellectual Culture* 7, no. 1 (2007): 1–18. https://www.ucalgary.ca/hic/issues/vol7/3.

Lipsitz, George. *The Possessive Investment in Whiteness*. Philadelphia: Temple University Press, 1998.

Lubiano, Wahneema. "Like Being Mugged by a Metaphor: Multiculturalism and State Narratives." In *Mapping Multiculturalism*, edited by Avery F. Gordon and Christopher Newfield, 64–75. Minneapolis: University of Minnesota Press, 1996.

Lugones, María. "Toward a Decolonial Feminism." *Hypatia* 25, no. 4 (2010): 742–59. https://www.jstor.org/stable/40928654.

Luka, Mary Elizabeth, Alsion Harvey, Mél Hogan, Tamara Shepherd, and Andrea Zeffiro. "Scholarship as Cultural Production in the Neolibereal

University: Working Within and Against 'Deliverables.'" *Studies in Social Justice* 9, no. 2 (2015): 176–96. https://doi.org/10.26522/ssj.v9i2.1138.

Luxion, Mona. "Whose Campus? Our Campus? Life on Campus and Who Fits In." *McGill Daily* 102, no. 8 (27 September 2012). http://www.mcgill daily.com/2012/09/whose-campus-our-campus/.

Macdonald, David. *Outrageous Fortune: Documenting Canada's Wealth Gap.* Canadian Centre for Policy Alternatives, 3 April 2014. https://www .policyalternatives.ca/sites/default/files/uploads/publications /National%20Office/2014/04/Outrageous_Fortune.pdf.

MacKay, Donald. *The Square Mile: Merchant Princes of Montreal.* Vancouver: Douglas and McIntyre, 1987.

MacKenzie, N.A.M. "The History of the University." University of British Columbia Archives, 1957. http://www.library.ubc.ca/archives/history.html.

Mackey, Frank. *Done with Slavery: The Black Fact in Montreal, 1760–1840.* Montreal/Kingston: McGill-Queen's University Press, 2010.

Macleans. "Merit: The Best and Only Way to Decide Who Gets into University," 25 November 2010. http://www.macleans.ca/general /who-gets-into-university/.

MacLennan, Hugh, ed. *McGill: The Story of a University.* London: Allen and Unwin, 1960.

MacLeod, Roderick. "James McGill Monument – 1813." *The Identity of English-Speaking Quebec in 100 Objects.* http://100objects.qahn.org/content /james-mcgill-monument-1813.

–. "Salubrious Settings and Fortunate Families: The Making of Montreal's Golden Square Mile, 1840–1895." PhD diss., McGill University, 1997.

Macphail, Andrew. "The Immigrant." *Canadian Club Year Book 1919–1920.* Ottawa, 1920.

Magnuson, Roger. *A Brief History of Quebec Education: From New France to Parti Québécois.* Montreal: Harvest House, 1980.

–. *Education in New France.* Montreal/Kingston: McGill-Queen's University Press, 1992.

Mangcu, Xolela. "Decolonizing South African Sociology: Building on a Shared 'Text of Blackness.'" *Du Bois Review* 13, no. 1 (2016): 45–59. https://doi.org/10.1017/S1742058X16000072.

Marschall, Sabine. "Targeting Statues: Monument 'Vandalism' as an Expression of Sociopolitical Protest in South Africa." *African Studies Review* 60, no. 3 (2017): 203–19. https://doi.org/10.1017/asr.2017.56.

Martell, Luke. "The Slow University: Inequality, Power and Alternatives." *Forum: Qualitative Social Research* 15, no. 3 (2014): art. 10. http://sro.sussex .ac.uk/50389/1/2223-8942-2-PB.pdf.

Matsuda, Mari J. "Looking to the Bottom: Critical Legal Studies and Reparations." *Harvard Civil Rights-Civil Liberties Law Review* 22, no. 2 (Spring 1987): 323–99.

Mathur, Ashok, Jonathan Dewar, and Michael DeGagné, eds. *Cultivating Canada: Reconciliation through the Lens of Cultural Diversity.* Ottawa: Aboriginal Healing Foundation, 2011.

McBride, Eve. "James McGill Strides by the Roddick Gates Today." *Montreal Gazette,* 6 June 1996.

McClintock, Anne. *Imperial Leather: Race, Gender, and Sexuality in the Colonial Contest.* New York: Routledge, 1995.

McDonald, Jeremy, and Ward, Lori. "Why So Many Canadian Universities Know So Little about Their Own Racial Diversity." CBC, 21 March 2017. http://www.cbc.ca/news/canada/race-canadian-universities-1.4030537.

McDuffie, Erik S. *Sojourning for Freedom: Black Women, American Communism, and the Making of Black Left Feminism.* Durham: Duke University Press, 2011.

"McGill to Celebrate Its Scottish Antecedents." *McGill Reporter,* 23 May 2012. https://reporter.mcgill.ca/mcgill-to-celebrate-its-scottish-antecedents/.

McGill University. "Brief to the Royal Commission on Education of the Province of Quebec: Submitted under the authority of the Board of Governors, with the approval of the Senate, November 29, 1961." Montreal, 1961.

–. "Employment Equity Policy." 2007. https://mcgill.ca/secretariat/files /secretariat/employment-equity-policy.pdf.

–. "McGill University Workforce Analysis Summary." 2010. http://www .mcgill.ca/hr/files/hr/mcgill_university_wfa_summary.pdf.

–. "Student Demographic Survey: Final Report." 2011. https://www.mcgill .ca/studentlifeandlearning/files/studentlifeandlearning/final_report_1 .pdf.

"McGill University in the Past." In *Old McGill* (McGill Annual), 25–35. McGill University yearbooks (1898). http://yearbooks.mcgill.ca/viewbook.php? campus=downtown&book_id=1898#page/1/mode/2up.

McKittrick, Katherine. "Wait Canada Anticipate Black." *CLR James Journal* 20, no. 1–2 (2014): 243–9. DOI: 10.5840/clrjames2014984.

McLaren, Angus. *Our Own Master Race: Eugenics in Canada, 1885–1945.* Toronto: McClelland and Stewart, 1990.

–. "Stemming the Flood of Defective Aliens." In *The History of Immigration and Racism in Canada: Essential Readings,* edited by Barrington Walker, 189–204. Toronto: Canadian Scholars' Press, 2008.

McLaren, Kristin. "'We Had No Desire to Be Set Apart': Forced Segregation of Black Students in Canada West Public Schools and Myths of British

Egalitarianism." *Social History Ottawa* 37, no. 73 (2004): 27–50. https://hssh
.journals.yorku.ca/index.php/hssh/article/view/4373.

McMullen, Kathryn. "Postsecondary Education Participation among
Underrepresented and Minority Groups." Statistics Canada, 2011. http://
www.statcan.gc.ca/pub/81-004-x/2011004/article/11595-eng.htm.

McRoberts, Kenneth. *Quebec: Social Change and Political Crisis.* Toronto: Oxford
University Press, 1993.

Mehreen, Rushdia, Hugo Bonin, and Nadia Hausfather. "Direct Democracy,
Grassroots Mobilization and the Québec Student Movement." In *This is
Fucking Class War: Voices from the 2012 Québec Student Strike,* edited by
Collectif dix novembre, 53–68, 2014. http://luxgoodcreative.com/classwar
/mehreen.html.

Melamed, Jodi. "Racial Capitalism." *Critical Ethnic Studies* 1, no. 1 (2015): 76–58.

–. *Represent and Destroy: Rationalizing Violence in the New Racial Capitalism.*
Minneapolis: University of Minnesota Press, 2011.

Mendelson, Morton. "McGill University Student Diversity Survey:
Preliminary Report." Montreal: McGill University, 2011. https://www
.mcgill.ca/studentlifeandlearning/files/studentlifeandlearning/2011-02-16
.SLL.Report.Diversity.Survey.Senate.FINAL.pdf.

Mendoza, Pilar. "Socialization to the Academic Culture: A Framework of
Inquiry." *Revista de Estudios Sociales,* no. 31 (2008): 104–17. http://www
.scielo.org.co/scielo.php?script=sci_arttext&pid=S0123-885X2008000300008.

Mijs, Jonathan J.B. "The Unfulfillable Promise of Meritocracy: Three Lessons
and Their Implications for Justice in Education." *Social Justice Research* 29,
no. 1 (2016): 14–34. https://doi.org/10.1007/s11211-014-0228-0.

Miller, J.R. *Shingwauk's Vision: A History of Native Residential Schools.* Toronto:
University of Toronto Press, 1996.

Mills, Sean. *The Empire Within: Postcolonial Thought and Political Activism in
Sixties Montreal.* Montreal/Kingston: McGill-Queen's University Press, 2010.

Milner, Henry. *The Long Road to Reform: Restructuring Public Education in
Quebec.* Montreal/Kingston: McGill-Queen's University Press, 1986.

Milner, Henry, and Sheilagh Hodgins Miller. *The Decolonization of Quebec: An
Analysis of Left-Wing Nationalism.* 3rd ed. Toronto: McClelland and Stewart,
1977.

Misra, Joya, Jennifer Hickes Lundquist, Elissa Holmes, and Stephanie
Agiomavritis. "The Ivory Ceiling of Service Work." *Academe* 97, no. 1 (2011):
22–6. https://www.jstor.org/stable/i25799856.

Mogandine, D. "Black Women in Graduate Studies: Transforming the
Socialization Experience." In *Back to the Drawing Board: African-Canadian
Feminisms,* edited by Njoki N. Wane, Katerina Deliovsky, and Erica Lawson,
129–57. Toronto: Sumach, 2002.

Monture, Patricia. "'Doing Academia Differently': Confronting 'Whiteness' in the University." In *Racism in the Canadian University: Demanding Social Justice, Inclusion and Equity*, edited by Frances Henry and Carol Tator, 76–105. Toronto: University of Toronto Press, 2009.

–. "Introduction – Surviving the Contradictions: Personal Notes on Academia." In *Breaking Anonymity: The Chilly Climate for Women Faculty*, edited by The Chilly Collective, 11–28. Waterloo: Wilfrid Laurier University Press, 1995.

–. "Ka-Nin-Geh-Heh-Gah-E-Sa-Nonh-Yah-Gah." *Canadian Journal of Women and the Law* 2, no. 1 (1986): 159–71.

–. "Race, Gender and the University: Strategies for Survival." In *States of Race: Critical Race Feminism for the 21st Century*, edited by Sherene Razack, Malinda Smith, and Sunera Thobani, 23–36. Toronto: Between the Lines, 2010.

–. "In the Way of Peace: Confronting Whiteness in the University." In *Seen but Not Heard: Aboriginal Women and Women of Colour in the Academy*, edited by Rashmi Luther, Elizabeth Whitmore, and Berrnice Moreau, 29–49. Ottawa: CRIAW/ICREF, 2001.

Moore, Keesha S. "Class Formations: Competing Forms of Black Middle-Class Identity." *Ethnicities* 8, no. 4 (2008): 492–517. https://doi.org /10.1177/1468796808097075.

Moore, Sheehan. "Taking Up Space: Anthropology and Embodied Protest." *Radical Anthropology*, no. 7 (2013): 6–16. http://radicalanthropologygroup .org/sites/default/files/journal/ra_journal_nov_2013_6-16.pdf.

Mountz, Alison, Anne Bonds, Becky Mansfield, Jenna Loyd, Jennifer Hyndman, Margaret Walton-Roberts, Ranu Basu, Risa Whitson, Roberta Hawkins, Trina Hamilton, and Winifred Curran. "For Slow Scholarship: A Feminist Politics of Resistance through Collective Action in the Neoliberal University." *ACME: An International E-Journal for Critical Geographies* 14, no. 4 (2015): 1235–59. https://acme-journal.org/index.php/acme/article /view/1058.

Mowbray, Mike. "Journalism, Activism, Alternative Media: The Link and the McGill Daily, 2000–2010." Master's thesis, McGill University, 2010.

Mutamba, Moyo Rainos. "Resisting Inclusion: Decolonial Relations between Peoples of Afrikan Descent and Original Peoples." *Decolonization: Indigeneity, Education & Society*, 18 June 2014. https://decolonization.word press.com/2014/06/18/resisting-inclusion-decolonial-relations-between -peoples-of-afrikan-descent-and-original-peoples/.

Myers, Gustavus. *History of Canadian Wealth*. Chicago: Charles H. Kerr, 1914. https://archive.org/details/historyofcanadia00myerrich.

National Council of Welfare. "A Snapshot of Racialized Poverty in Canada." Ottawa: Employment and Social Development Canada, 2013. https://

www.canada.ca/content/dam/esdc-edsc/migration/documents/eng
/communities/reports/poverty_profile/snapshot.pdf.

Nelson, Charmaine. "Challenging 'Blackface' Is Not Québec-Bashing."
Huffington Post Canada, 28 May 2013. http://www.huffingtonpost.ca
/charmaine-nelson/blackface-in-quebec_b_3348561.html.

–. "Toppling the 'Great White North': Tales of a Black Female Professor in the
Canadian Academy." In *The Black Professoriate: Negotiating a Habitable Space
in the Academy*, edited by Sandra Jackson and Richard Greggory Johnson,
108–34. New York: Peter Lang, 2011.

Newson, Janice. "The Corporate-Linked University: From Social Project to
Market Force." *Canadian Journal of Communication* 23, no. 1 (1998). https://
www.cjc-online.ca/index.php/journal/article/view/1026/932.

Newson, Janice A., and Claire Polster, eds. *Academic Callings: The University We
Have Had, Now Have, and Could Have*. Toronto: Canadian Scholars' Press, 2010.

Nfah-Abbenyi, Juliana M. "Why (What) Am I (Doing) Here: A Cameroonian
Woman?" In *Our Own Agendas: Autobiographical Essays by Women Associated
with McGill University*, edited by Margaret Gillett and Ann Beer, 250–61.
Montreal/Kingston: McGill-Queen's University Press, 1995.

Ng, Roxana. "'A Woman Out of Control': Deconstructing Sexism and Racism
in the University." *Canadian Journal of Education* 18, no. 3 (1993): 189–205.
DOI: 10.2307/1495382.

"Occupons McGill! A Letter from the Fifth Floor Occupiers." *Rabble*, 16
November 2011. http://rabble.ca/news/2011/11/occupons-mcgill-letter
-fifth-floor-occupiers.

Ochwa-Echel, James R. "Neoliberalism and University Education in Sub-
Saharan Africa." *Sage Open* (July–September 2013), 1–8. http://sgo.sagepub
.com/content/3/3/2158244013504933.

Omi, Michael, and Howard Winant. "On the Theoretical Status of the Concept
of Race." In *Race, Identity, and Representation in Education*, edited by Cameron
McCarthy and Warren Crichlow, 3–10. New York: Routledge, 1993.

O'Neal, Cadence, and Nauss Steeves. "Demilitarize McGill." *Canadian
Dimension*, 9 June 2014. https://canadiandimension.com/articles/view
/demilitarize-mcgill.

"175th Anniversary Garden Party." *McGill Reporter* 28, no. 18 (10 July 1996).
http://reporter-archive.mcgill.ca/Rep/r2818/garden.htm.

Oparah, Julia C. "Challenging Complicity: The Neoliberal University and the
Prison-Industrial Complex." In *The Imperial University: Academic Repression
and Scholarly Dissent*, edited by Piya Chatterjee and Sunaina Maira, 99–125.
Minneapolis: University of Minnesota Press, 2014.

Orr, Catherine M. "Challenging the 'Academic/Real World' Divide." In
Teaching Feminist Activism: Strategies from the Field, edited by Nancy Naples
and Karen Bojar, 36–53. New York: Routledge, 2002.

Pabst, Naomi. "'Mama, I'm Walking to Canada': Black Geopolitics and Invisible Empires." In *Globalization and Race: Transformations in the Cultural Production of Blackness,* edited by Kamari Maxine Clarke and Deborah A. Thomas, 112–29. Durham: Duke University Press, 2006.

Palacios, Lena, rosalind hampton, Ilyan Ferrer, Elma Moses, and Edward Ou Jin Lee. "Learning in Social Action: Students of Colour and the Québec Student Movement." *Journal of Curriculum Theorizing* 29, no. 2 (2013): 6–25.

Park, Julie J., and Amy Liu. "Interest Convergence or Divergence? A Critical Race Analysis of Asian Americans, Meritocracy, and Critical Mass in the Affirmative Action Debate." *Journal of Higher Education* 85, no. 1 (2014): 36–64.

Pedneault, Joël. "The Plan Nord Riot." In *This is Fucking Class War: Voices from the 2012 Québec Student Strike,* edited by Collectif dix novembre, 225–41, 2014. http://luxgoodcreative.com/classwar/pedneault.html.

Pedram, Arno. "We Have Always Known about McGill's Predatory Professors." *McGill Daily,* 13 April 2018. https://www.mcgilldaily.com/2018/04/we-have-always-known-about-mcgills-predatory-professors/.

Perelle, Robin. "African Studies on Losing Side of the Resource Game." *McGill Daily* 84, no. 55 (1995), 1, 22.

Perry, Barbara, and Ryan Scrivens. "Right-Wing Extremism in Canada: An Environmental Scan." Ottawa: Public Safety Canada, 2015. https://joeclark.org/rwa/perry-scrivens/PerryRWE-tagged.pdf.

Pietsch, Tamson. *Empire of Scholars: Universities, Networks and the British Academic World, 1850–1939.* Manchester: Manchester University Press, 2013.

–. "Wandering Scholars? Academic Mobility and the British World, 1850–1940." *Journal of Historical Geography* 36, no. 4 (2010): 377–87. https://doi.org/10.1016/j.jhg.2010.03.002.

Pitsula, James M. *Keeping Canada British: The Ku Klux Klan in 1920s Saskatchewan.* Vancouver: UBC Press, 2013.

Potter, Harold H. "The Occupational Adjustments of Montreal Negroes, 1941–48." Master's thesis, McGill University, 1949.

Pyne, Pohanna. "A Member of Africana Studies Speaks Her Mind." *McGill Daily* 88, no. 52 (18 February 1999), 12.

Quinlan, Elizabeth, Curtis Fogel, Andrea Quinlan, and Gail Taylor. *Sexual Violence at Canadian Universities: Activism, Institutional Responses, and Strategies for Change.* Waterloo: Wilfrid Laurier University Press, 2017.

Ramos, Howard. "Does How You Measure Representation Matter? Assessing the Persistence of Canadian Universities' Gendered and Colour Coded Vertical Mosaic." *Canadian Ethnic Studies* 44, no. 2 (2012): 13–37.

Razack, Sherene. "Racialized Immigrant Women as Native Informants in the Academy." In *Seen but Not Heard: Aboriginal Women and Women of Colour in the Academy,* edited by Ramshi Luther, Elizabeth Whitmore, and Bernice Moreau, 51–60. Ottawa: CRIAW/ICREF, 2001.

Razack, Sherene, Malinda Smith, and Sunera Thobani. *States of Race: Critical Race Feminism for the 21st Century.* Toronto: Between the Lines, 2010.

Reagon, Bernice Johnson. "Coalitional Politics: Turning the Century." In *Home Girls: A Black Feminist Anthology*, edited by Barbara Smith, 356–68. New York: Kitchen Table Press, 1983.

Reiter, Harold, and Armand Aalamian. "External Review." Office of Admissions, Equity and Diversity Program, Faculty of Medicine, McGill University, 8 October 2013. https://www.mcgill.ca/medadmissions/files /medadmissions/mcgill_external_review_2013_admissions_office_final .pdf.

Ricci, Amanda. "Searching for Zion: Pan-African Feminist Thought and Practice in English-Speaking Black Montreal (1967–1977)." *Left History* 17, no. 1 (2013): 43–74. https://doi.org/10.25071/1913-9632.39214.

Richardson, Brian K., and Juandalynn Taylor. "Sexual Harassment at the Intersection of Race and Gender: A Theoretical Model of the Sexual Harassment Experiences of Women of Color." *Western Journal of Communication* 73, no. 3 (2009): 248–72.

Robinson, Cedric J. *Black Marxism: The Making of the Black Radical Tradition.* Chapel Hill: University of North Carolina Press, 2000.

Rodney, Walter. *How Europe Underdeveloped Africa.* London: Bogle-L'Ouverture, 1972.

Roediger, David R. *The Wages of Whiteness: Race and the Making of the American Working Class.* London: Verso, 2007.

Rogers, Ibram X. *The Black Campus Movement: Black Students and the Racial Reconstitution of Higher Education, 1965–1972.* New York: Palgrave Macmillan, 2012.

Rojas, Fabio. *From Black Power to Black Studies: How a Radical Social Movement Became an Academic Discipline.* Baltimore: Johns Hopkins University Press, 2007.

Rosenfeld, Jessie, and Martin Lukacs. "Six Nations, McGill Clash over Debt." *The Gateway* 97, no. 19 (2006): 5. Reprinted from the *McGill Daily.* http:// peel.library.ualberta.ca/newspapers/GAT/2006/11/16/5/Img/Pg005.pdf.

Ruggles, Clifton, and Olivia Rovinescu. *Outsider Blues: A Voice from the Shadows.* Halifax: Fernwood, 1996.

Ryerson University Aboriginal Education Council. "Egerton Ryerson, the Residential School System and Truth and Reconciliation." August 2010. http://www.ryerson.ca/content/dam/aec/pdfs/egerton%20ryerson _fullstatement.pdf.

Said, Edward W. *Culture and Imperialism.* New York: Vintage, 1994.

Samuel, Edith, and Njoki N. Wane. "'Unsettling Relations': Racism and Sexism Experienced by Faculty of Color in a Predominantly White Canadian University." *Journal of Negro Education* 74, no. 1 (2005): 76–87. https://www.jstor.org/stable/40027232.

Sarvi, Linda. "Create Dangerously 2013: Congress of Black Writers and
    Artists." *Graphite Publications*, 17 October 2013. https://graphitepublications
    .com/create-dangerously-2013-congress-of-black-writers-and-artists/.
Saul, Emily. "Century-Old Federal Debt Not Yet Repaid to Indigenous
    Community." *McGill Daily* 104, no. 5 (29 September 2014), 7. http://
    www.mcgilldaily.com/2014/09/century-old-federal-debt-not-yet
    -repaid-to-indigenous-community/.
Schuetze, Hans G., William Bruneau, and Garnet Grosjean, eds. *University
    Governance and Reform: Policy, Fads and Experience in International Perspective*.
    New York: Palgrave Macmillan, 2012.
Schick, Carol. "Keeping the Ivory Tower White: Discourses of Racial
    Domination." *Canadian Journal of Law and Society* 15, no. 2 (2000): 71–90.
    https://doi.org/10.1017/S0829320100006372.
Scott, Corrie. "How French Canadians Became White Folks, or, Doing Things
    with Race in Québec." *Ethnic and Racial Studies* 39, no. 7 (2016): 1280–97.
    https://doi.org/10.1080/01419870.2015.1103880.
Sears, Alan, and James Cairns. "Austerity U: Preparing Students for
    Precarious Lives." *New Socialist Webzine*, 24 January 2014. http://
    newsocialist.org/736-austerity-u-preparing-students-for-precarious-lives.
–. *A Good Book, In Theory: Making Sense through Inquiry*. Toronto: University of
    Toronto Press, 2010.
–. "Producing 'Intra-preneurs.'" Paper presented at the conference Capitalism
    in the Classroom: Neoliberalism, Education and Progressive Alternatives,
    Ryerson University, Toronto, 4 April 2014. https://www.youtube.com
    /watch?v=1GbayahsOtI.
Seidman, Karen. "The Changing Face of McGill Medical Students." *Montreal
    Gazette*, 10 August 2013, B1.
–. "'Stabbed in the Back' by McGill: Anglophone Community Considers
    Itself Rejects as Med School Seeks Diversity, Francophones – and Is
    Donating Less as a Result." *The Gazette*, 7 May 2014, A3. Republished
    online as "Frustration over Med School Admissions at McGill." http://
    montrealgazette.com/news/local-news/frustration-over-med-school
    -admissions-at-mcgill.
Séminaire de Québec. "Vue d'ensemble: Tel un vieux chêne – Synopsis de
    l'histoire du Séminaire de Québec connu autrefois sous le nom de Séminaire
    des Missions Étrangères établi à Québec sous le vocable de la Sainte
    Famille." n.d. http://www.seminairedequebec.org/vue-d-ensemble/.
"Senate Deliberates over Black Studies." *McGill Daily* 59, no. 94 (4 March
    1970), 3.
Shahjahan, R. "Being 'Lazy' and Slowing Down: Toward Decolonizing Time,
    Our Body and Pedagogy." *Educational Philosophy and Theory* 47, no. 5 (2014):
    488–501. https://doi.org/10.1080/00131857.2014.880645.

Shapiro, Jenessa R. "Types of Threats: From Stereotype Threat to Stereotype Threats." In *Stereotype Threat: Theory, Process, and Application*, edited by Michael Inzlicht and Toni Schmader, 71–88. New York: Oxford University Press, 2012.

Sharp, Hasana, and Will C. Roberts. "The Crisis at McGill: Who Called the Riot Police onto Campus?" *New APPS: Art, Politics, Philosophy, Science* (blog), 14 November 2011. http://www.newappsblog.com/2011/11/the -crisis-at-mcgill-who-called-riot-police-onto-campus.html.

Sharpe, Christina E. *Monstrous Intimacies: Making Post-Slavery Subjects.* Durham: Duke University Press, 2010.

Sheppard, Peggy. "The Relationship between Student Activism and Change in the University: With Particular Reference to McGill University in the 1960s." Master's thesis, McGill University, 1989.

Simpson, Audra. *Mohawk Interruptus: Political Life across the Borders of Settler States.* Durham: Duke University Press, 2014.

Simpson, Leanne. "Anticolonial Strategies for the Recovery and Maintenance of Indigenous Knowledge." *American Indian Quarterly* 28, no. 3/4 (2004): 373–84.

–. *Dancing on Our Turtle's Back: Stories of Nishnaabeg Re-creation, Resurgence and a New Emergence.* Winnipeg: Arp Books, 2011.

–. "Land as Pedagogy: Nishnaabeg Intelligence and Rebellious Transformation." *Decolonization: Indigeneity, Education & Society* 3, no. 3 (2014): 1–25.

–. "Indigenous Resurgence and Co-resistance." *Critical Ethnic Studies* 2, no. 2 (2016): 19–34. DOI: 10.5749/jcritethnstud.2.2.0019.

Singh, Jakeet. "The Ideological Roots of Stephen Harper's Vendetta against Sociology." *Toronto Star*, 26 August 2014. http://www.thestar.com/opinion /commentary/2014/08/26/the_ideological_roots_of_stephen_harpers _vendetta_against_sociology.html.

"Six Nations Claim: Lost Lands." *Windspeaker* 24, no. 3 (2006). http://www .ammsa.com/publications/windspeaker/six-nations-claim-lost-lands.

Smeltzer, Sandra, and Alison Hearn. "Student Rights in an Age of Austerity? 'Security,' Freedom of Expression, and the Neoliberal University." *Social Movement Studies* 14, no. 3 (2015): 352–8. DOI: 10.1080/14742837.2014.945077.

Smith, Andrea. "The Colonialism That Is Settled and the Colonialism That Never Happened." In *Decolonization: Indigeneity, Education and Society,* 20 June 2014. https://decolonization.wordpress.com/2014/06/20/the -colonialism-that-is-settled-and-the-colonialism-that-never-happened/.

–. "Heteropatriarchy and the Three Pillars of White Supremacy: Rethinking Women of Color Organizing." In *Color of Violence: The Incite! Anthology,* edited by Incite! Women of Color Against Violence, 70–6. Cambridge, MA: South End, 2006.

Smith, Dorothy E. *The Everyday World as Problematic: A Feminist Sociology.*
   Boston: Northeastern University Press, 1987.
–. *Institutional Ethnography: A Sociology for People.* Lanham, MD: AltaMira, 2005.
–. *Texts, Facts, and Femininity: Exploring the Relations of Ruling.* London:
   Routledge, 1990.
–. *Writing the Social: Critique, Theory, and Investigations.* Toronto: University of
   Toronto Press, 1999.
Smith, Linda Tuhiwai. *Decolonizing Methodologies: Research and Indigenous
   Peoples.* London: Zed Books, 2012.
Smith, George W. "Political Activist as Ethnographer." *Social Problems* 37, no. 4
   (1990): 629–48.
Smith, Malinda S. "Gender, Whiteness and 'Other Others' in the Academy."
   In *States of Race: Critical Race Feminism for the 21st Century,* edited by
   Sherene Razack, Malinda Smith, and Sunera Thobani, 37–58. Toronto:
   Between the Lines, 2010.
–. "'Race Matters' and 'Race Manners.'" In *Reinventing Canada: Politics of the
   21st Century,* edited by Janine Brodie and Linda Trimble, 108–30. Toronto:
   Prentice Hall, 2003.
Smith, Michael. "CLR James: You Don't Play with Revolution." *McGill
   Reporter* 1, no. 7 (4 November 1968), 6–7.
Solórzano, Daniel G., and Tara J. Yosso. "Critical Race Methodology: Counter-
   Storytelling as an Analytical Framework for Educational Research." In
   Foundations of Critical Race Theory in Education, edited by Edward Taylor, David
   Gillborn, and Gloria Ladson-Billings, 131–47. New York: Routledge, 2009.
Sonnie, Amy, and James Tracy. *Hillbilly Nationalists, Urban Race Rebels, and
   Black Power: Community Organizing in Radical Times.* Brooklyn: Melville
   House, 2011.
Spencer, Elaine A. Brown. "Spiritual Politics: Politicizing the Black Church
   Tradition in Anti-Colonial Politics." In *Anticolonialism and Education: The
   Politics of Resistance,* edited by George J.S. Dei and Arlo Kempf, 107–28.
   Rotterdam: Sense, 2006.
Stanley, Tim. "John A. Macdonald, 'the Chinese' and Racist State Formation
   in Canada." *Journal of Critical Race Inquiry* 3, no. 1 (2016): 6–34. https://doi
   .org/10.24908/jcri.v3i1.5974.
"Stanley Brice Frost (1913–2013)." *McGill Reporter,* 30 July 2013. http://
   publications.mcgill.ca/reporter/2013/07/stanley-b-frost-1913-2013/.
Steele, Claude. *Whistling Vivaldi: And Other Clues to How Stereotypes Affect Us.*
   New York: W.W. Norton, 2010.
Stewart, Anthony. *Visitor: My Life in Canada.* Halifax: Fernwood, 2014.
–. *You Must be a Basketball Player: Rethinking Integration in the University.*
   Halifax: Fernwood, 2009.

Strong-Boag, Veronica. "Independent Women, Problematic Men: First- and Second-Wave Anti-Feminism in Canada from Goldwin Smith to Betty Steele." *Social History* 57 (1996): 1–22.

Sztainbok, Vannina. "Decolonize Together: Indigenous Activists Send Strong Message at Occupy Toronto Talk." *Rabble*, 15 February 2012. http://rabble .ca/news/2012/02/decolonize-together-indigenous-activists-send-strong -message-occupy-toronto-talk.

Tattrie, Jon. "Dalhousie's Black and African Diaspora Studies Adds to 'Grand Canadian Story.'" CBC, 21 June 2016. http://www.cbc.ca/news/canada /nova-scotia/dalhousie-black-and-african-diaspora-studies-starts-fall-2016 -1.3644910.

Taylor-Munro, Sheryl. "Frost Does Nothing Unusual." *McGill Daily*, 58, no. 84 (1969): 1.

Théorêt, Hugues. *The Blue Shirts: Adrien Arcand and Fascist Anti-Semitism in Canada*. Ottawa: University of Ottawa Press, 2017.

Thobani, Sunera. *Exalted Subjects: Studies in the Making of Race and Nation in Canada*. Toronto: University of Toronto Press, 2007.

Thomas, Jeff. *Where Are the Children? Healing the Legacy of the Residential Schools*. Ottawa: National Archives of Canada, 2002. http://wherearethe children.ca.

Thwaites, Reuben Gold. *The Jesuit Relations and Allied Documents: Travels and Explorations of the Jesuit Missionaries in New France, 1610–1791*. Cleveland: Burrows, 1898.

Tierney, William G. "Organizational Socialization in Higher Education." *Journal of Higher Education* 68, no. 1 (1997): 1–16. https://doi.org/10.1080 /00221546.1997.11778975.

TRC (Truth and Reconciliation Commisssion of Canada). "Canada, Aboriginal Peoples, and Residential Schools: They Came for the Children." 2012. http://www.myrobust.com/websites/trcinstitution/File/2039 _T&R_eng_web%5B1%5D.pdf.

Tremblay, Martin. "Bursting the Bubble: Why McGill Students Should Engage with Québec." *McGill Daily*, 22 September 2014. http://www.mcgilldaily .com/2014/09/bursting-the-bubble/.

Trottier, Claude, Jean Bernatchez, Donald Fisher, and Kjell Rubenson. "PSE Policy in Québec: A Case Study." In *The Development of Postsecondary Education Systems in Canada: A Comparison between British Columbia, Ontario, and Quebec, 1980–2010*, edited by Donald Fisher, Kjell Rubenson, Claude R. Trottier, and Theresa Shanahan, 200–90. Montreal/Kingston: McGill-Queen's University Press, 2014.

Trudel, Marcel. *Canada's Forgotten Slaves: Two Hundred Years of Bondage*. Translated by George Tombs. Montréal: Véhicule, 2013.

–. *Mythes et Réalités dans l'histoire du Québec.* Montréal: Hurtubise HMH, 2001.

Tuck, Eve. "Suspending Damage: An Open Letter to Communities." *Harvard Educational Review* 79, no. 3 (2009): 409–27.

Tuck, Eve, and K. Wayne Yang. "Unbecoming Claims: Pedagogies of Refusal in Qualitative Research." *Qualitative Inquiry* 20, no. 6 (2014): 811–18.

Tuck, Eve, and K. Wayne Yang. "R-Words: Refusing Research." In *Humanizing Research: Decolonizing Qualitative Inquiry with Youth and Communities,* edited by Django Paris and Maisha T. Winn, 223–48. Thousand Oaks: Sage.

Tyson, Karolyn, William Darrity Jr., and Domini R. Castellino. "It's Not 'a Black Thing': Understanding the Burden of Acting White and Other Dilemmas of High Achievement." *American Sociological Review* 70, no. 4 (2005): 582–605. https://doi.org/10.1177%2F000312240507000403.

Vallières, Pierre. *White Niggers of America.* Translated by Joan Pinkham. Toronto: McClelland and Stewart, 1971.

Valverde, Mariana. "Racial Purity, Sexual Purity and Immigration Policy." In *The History of Immigration and Racism in Canada: Essential Readings,* edited by Barrington Walker, 175–88. Toronto: Canadian Scholars' Press, 2008.

van Eyken, Eric. "Students Society of McGill University: Celebrating 100 Years." 2010. https://ssmu.ca/wp-content/uploads/2010/01/ssmu_history -final1-opt.pdf.

Von Tunzelmann, Alex. "Rhodes Must Fall? A Question of When Not If." *History Today,* 17 February 2016. https://www.historytoday.com/alex-von -tunzelmann/rhodes-must-fall-question-when-not-if.

Wagner, Anne, Sandra Acker, and Kimine Mayuzumi. "Introduction." In *Whose University Is It, Anyway? Power and Privilege on Gendered Terrain,* edited by Anne Wagner, Sandra Acker, and Kimine Mayuzumi, 11–24. Toronto: Sumach, 2008.

Walcott, Rinaldo. "Into the Ranks of Man: Vicious Modernism and the Politics of Reconciliation." In *Cultivating Canada: Reconciliation through the Lens of Cultural Diversity,* edited by Ashok Mathur, Jonathan Dewar, and Michael DeGagné, 341–9. Ottawa: Aboriginal Healing Foundation, 2011.

–. "Shame: A Polemic." *CLR James Journal* 20, no. 1/2 (2014): 275–9.

–. "'Who Is She and What Is She to You?': Mary Ann Shadd Cary and the (Im)Possibility of Black/Canadian Studies." In *Rude: Contemporary Canadian Black Cultural Criticism,* edited by Rinaldo Walcott, 27–48. Toronto: Insomniac Press, 2000.

–. *Black Like Who?: Writing Black Canada.* Toronto: Insomniac Press, 2003.

Walker, Barrington, ed. *The African Canadian Legal Odyssey: Historical Essays.* Osgoode Society for Canadian Legal History. Toronto: University of Toronto Press, 2012.

Walker, James St. G., and Burnley "Rocky" Jones. *Burnley "Rocky" Jones: Revolutionary.* Halifax: Fernwood, 2017.

Wane, Njoki N., Katerina Deliovsky, and Erica Lawson, eds. *Back to the Drawing Board: African Canadian Feminisms.* Toronto: Sumach, 2002.

Wane, Njoki N., and Erica Neegan. "African Women's Indigenous Spirituality: Bringing It All Home." In *Theorizing Empowerment: Canadian Perspectives on Black Feminist Thought,* edited by Notisha Massaquoi and Njoki N. Wane, 27–46. Toronto: Inanna, 2007.

Warren, Jean-Philippe. "L'Opération McGill français: Une page méconnue de l'histoire de la gauche nationaliste." *Bulletin d'historie politique* 16, no. 2 (n.d.). http://www.bulletinhistoirepolitique.org/le-bulletin/numeros -precedents/volume-16-numero-2/l%E2%80%99operation-mcgill-francais -une-page-meconnue-de-l%E2%80%99histoire-de-la-gauche-nationaliste /#_edn12.

Waters, Mary C. *Black Identities: West Indian Immigrant Dreams and American Realities.* New York/Cambridge, MA: Russell Sage Foundation/Harvard University Press, 1999.

Westley, Margaret W. *Remembrance of Grandeur: The Anglo-Protestant Elite of Montreal, 1900–1950.* Montreal: Libre Expression, 1990.

Weston, Brendan, Collin Tomlins, and Melinda Wittstock. "South Africa: Love It and Leave It. *McGill Daily* 75, no. 4 (12 September 1985), 4.

Whitaker, Reginald, and Gary Marcuse. *Cold War Canada: The Making of a National Insecurity State, 1945–1957.* Toronto: University of Toronto Press, 1994.

"Why Are There So Few Black Professors in South Africa?" *The Guardian,* 6 October 2014. https://www.theguardian.com/world/2014/oct/06/south -africa-race-black-professors.

Wilder, Craig S. *Ebony and Ivy: Race, Slavery and the Troubled History of America's Universities.* New York: Bloomsbury, 2013.

Williams, Dorothy W. *Blacks in Montreal, 1628–1986: An Urban Demography.* Cowansville, QC: Éditions Yvon Blais, 1989.

–. "The Jackie Robinson Myth: Social Mobility and Race in Montreal, 1920–1960." Master's thesis, Concordia University, 1999.

–. *The Road to Now: A History of Blacks in Montreal.* Montreal: Véhicule, 1997.

Wilton, Katherine. "McGill University Releases Details on Budget Cuts." *Global News,* 26 March 2015. http://globalnews.ca/news/430845/mcgill -university-releases-details-on-budget-cuts/.

Winks, Robin. *The Blacks in Canada.* Montreal/Kingston: McGill-Queen's University Press, 1997.

Wittstock, Melinda. "McGill's Apartheid Links Exposed." *McGill Daily* 75, no. 4 (12 September 1985), 10–11.

Woodsworth, J.S. *Strangers within Our Gates, or, Coming Canadians.* Toronto: F.C. Stephenson, 1911.

Wynter, Sylvia. "Unsettling the Coloniality of Being/Power/Truth/Freedom: Towards the Human, after Man, Its Overrepresentation – An Argument." *CR: The New Centennial Review* 3, no. 3 (2003): 257–337.

Yosso, Tara J. "Whose Culture Has Capital? A Critical Race Theory Discussion of Community Cultural Wealth." *Race Ethnicity and Education* 8, no. 1 (2005): 69–91. https://doi.org/10.1080/1361332052000341006.

Yuval-Davis, Nira. *Gender and Nation.* London: Sage, 1997.

Index